Corporate
Governance

Corporate Governance

An Action Plan for Profitability and Business Success

THOMAS SHERIDAN
NIGEL KENDALL

FINANCIAL TIMES

PITMAN PUBLISHING

Pitman Publishing
128 Long Acre, London WC2E 9AN

A division of Longman Group UK Limited

First published in 1992

© Thomas Sheridan and Nigel Kendall 1992

British Library Cataloguing in Publication Data
A CIP catalogue record for this book can be obtained from
the British Library.

ISBN 0 273 03870 2

Phototypeset in Linotron Times Roman
by Northern Phototypesetting Co. Ltd., Bolton
Printed and bound in Great Britain
by Biddles Ltd., Guildford

CONTENTS

PREFACE

Not another book about corporate governance!

Before the reader recoils in horror, we would point out that this is a book on corporate governance, but with a difference. We are not writing just about how to put a strait-jacket on directors, how to control their pay and make sure that they run their companies according to best practice. This is not an establishment book at all. We are starting off from a different point of view to other writers in the corporate governance 'industry', and are concentrating on three aspects that are so often ignored.

First, we look at what a wide range of companies actually do, not just in Britain or even in the Anglophone countries alone, but in Japan and continental Europe as well. We could learn something from the successful economies across the Channel. Secondly, we look at governance in the context of the all-embracing changes that serve as the one constant in the turbulent 1990s; and thirdly, most important of all, we ask how governance can contribute to business success. When you listen to the governance debate in Britain you might be forgiven for thinking that governance exists in a vacuum, and that it lives in a rarified world of its own. Surely that is nonsense! Businesses have to be successful to survive and grow. Governance, as one aspect of business like any other, has to be considered in the context of its contribution to business success. This is a point that is often forgotten.

The book therefore takes a heretical look at the establishment view of corporate governance, and we hope that by attacking some of the current sacred cows we shall be carrying the debate a little further. As convinced Europeans, we have taken a pan-European viewpoint on the subject. Britain is part of a greater Europe, and growing closer to it all the time. We are certain that this decade will see a specific European corporate viewpoint emerging which will increasingly affect us in Britain. It is easy to be negative. We have gone out of our way to be positive and to give our own solutions as well as to suggest a way forward for companies who want to adopt best – and successful – practice.

We are very grateful for the help given to us by the many executive and non-executive directors from a very wide range of companies, who have discussed their ideas and experiences with us. They were very frank and open, but the price for such candour was that we cannot quote them directly or give their names.

Our thanks go to our editors at Pitman for their encouragement and their support; to Arthur Kendall for his help with editing and indexing, and last, but not least, to our wives Sandy Kendall and Ruth Sheridan, for putting up with the best part of a year's disruption to their lives.

Thomas Sheridan
Nigel Kendall

INTRODUCTION

It is probably quite widely understood that multinational corporations nowadays increasingly face the paradox of having to demonstrate more and more national responsibility while being subject to the organisational imperatives of global standardisation. This means fitting in with the local customs of each of their host countries in terms of business philosophy and ethics while seeking to operate efficiently through the use of supranational common rules and procedures. This problem has to be addressed at two levels: top management direction and operational practice. There have been innumerable books written about best practice in executive management and many about the development and implementation of corporate strategy. Too few have focused on the role of the board of directors in its function as agent of the owners and trustee for their interests – what is called governance in Anglophone countries. This is the subject of this book.

In a previous book, *Finanzmeister* (Pitman, 1991) we looked at the requirements for top level financial management in corporations which aspired to do business in the evolving European Community with its many and varied customs, languages and traditions. In particular, we contrasted financial management in Anglo-American companies with that in continental European companies, noting that there were very different conceptions of the purpose of a company and of corporate management. Much of the difference centres around the continental, particularly German (and also Japanese), long-term approach and the Anglophone short-termism. We felt then that these different philosophies of what a company is all about deserved a book to themselves.

In recent years there has been an intense debate in Anglophone countries about corporate governance – who manages the managers and how. Newspapers are full of articles, conferences regularly set top investment managers up to speak against the captains of industry, Members of Parliament rail against the supposed abuses of the present liberal regulatory regime. Ultimately, a committee of inquiry was set up under the eminent and successful industrialist Sir Adrian Cadbury to report on ways in which matters could be improved in the UK. This committee produced its report in the last days of May 1992, to give what was widely regarded as the safe establishment view. Yet across the rest of Europe, mention of the subject produces a yawn or outright incomprehension. Whatever may be thought in the UK and USA, the issue is simply not seen as a problem in those two hugely successful economies, Germany and Japan. Talk in British newspapers about the unfairness of interlocking shareholdings and directorships in German companies and the problems these create for hostile takeovers are not seen by the German owners in the same light; certainly there is no pressure for change to remove a perceived abuse. Similarly in Japan, Western comment about the potential for corruption in the *kairetsu* system and the role of the ministries of trade and finance in fostering industrial development at the expense of foreigners, is seen as little more than the uncomprehending and frustrated complaints of ageing and sclerotic economies.

Certainly, within the UK, at which this book is aimed, there have been enough recent cases of unhappiness between owners and those who manage their businesses for them to justify an examination. There have already been clearly expressed views from all quarters about what the problem really is and how it should be solved. With our experience of European corporations, and following the work we carried out to produce *Finanzmeister*, we were fairly sure that we disagreed with both the general diagnosis and also with the commonly expressed solutions. We therefore determined to back our personal experience of working in almost every country of the EC and Scandinavia with research into over 100 companies, resident in the EC, USA and Japan, to enable us to formulate our own solution, which would genuinely be based on the practices which appear to have produced success for some of the leading global corporations. The results of this research are set out in the following chapters, together with our proposals for a better way of organising corporate governance.

We have worked for many years as line managers and management consultants, and have been used to producing practical and workable solutions for clients – the only way to ensure that our bills were paid! Hence in putting forward our proposals, we have eschewed ideas which would be likely to require major revisions of company law to be implemented. We believe that our proposals will help both large and smaller companies to improve their performance in relation to the interests of all the stakeholders in their success and, of course, to improve thereby their relationship with each of those stakeholders.

1 THE STATE OF GOVERNANCE

When we observe the corporate scene these days we are aware of a vague sense of unease. As business people and industrialists, as professional advisers or senior managers, we are conscious that all is not well in the way many large concerns are run. Or at any rate so it is perceived by many in the media and hence those whom the media address feel that all is not well. Moreover, if all is not well in the large organisations, how many more problems may lurk in the smaller companies, lacking the resources to operate all the protective systems and controls of their larger brothers?

Is this all fair? We in business have long been aware of the bias against industry that appears to exist in the educational system and which has been so devastatingly described by Corelli Barnett in his book *The Audit of War* (1986); a bias reaching back 170 years to Dr Thomas Arnold and Rugby School with its emphasis on the importance of a liberal education and a distaste for getting too closely involved in the sordid affairs of trade. The same bias is seen to extend from academe into the broadcasting media and to demonstrate itself in current affairs and investigative programmes, though interestingly much less so in the printed media.

SYMPTOMS OF DEEPER PROBLEMS

Outside the law

In the last week of August 1991 the beleaguered American securities house Salomon Brothers announced that it was forming a committee to ensure compliance with the law. This followed the illegal activities of some of its employees in the US bond market earlier in the year through which Salomon gained control of more than 90 per cent of an issue of two-year notes, partly through illegal means. This enabled it to bring about a subsequent squeeze using its dominance to extract a high price from the other investors, particularly those who had sold the issue short. It led to claims that some investors had lost millions of dollars and caused a lengthy disruption of market prices. John Gutfreund, the chairman, eventually took responsibility and had to resign.

The knock-on effect was traumatic for this, one of Wall Street's leading firms and a byword for success in its field. It included the appointment of a new chairman, Warren Buffet, untainted by the scandal or indeed by any previous involvement with the company. Mr Buffet was orders of magnitude more wealthy even than the legendary Mr Gutfreund, and had no need to reward himself from Salomon's profits. He was thus able to attack excessive performance-related pay (and perhaps reduce the motivation for the illegal trading). In late October 1991 he wrote to shareholders promising a crackdown on the system of compensating employees which had left shareholders with too small a slice of the cake. He took back $110 million which had been earmarked for bonuses and promised shareholders that the firm would in future conduct 'first class business in a first class way'.

We can only ask what arrogance had persuaded Mr Gutfreund, regarded by many as the most successful trader on Wall Street, that he could for several months ignore his obligation to report to the authorities the illegal activities of his employees once these had been uncovered? The consequence, and rightly so, was the abrupt end of his outstanding career.

Robert Maxwell had been condemned by Sir Ronald Leach and his colleagues on the Department of Trade and Industry (DTI) Inspectorate which examined his performance in the late 1960s takeover bid for Pergamon Press. He was described as 'not in our opinion a person who can be relied upon to exercise proper stewardship of a public company'. Thumbing his nose at the authorities, he rebuilt Pergamon Press, sorted out the problems of British Printing Corporation (saving the investment of a number of influential City figures) and to a considerable extent rehabilitated himself. In going on to make Maxwell Communications Corporation a major global player, he was able to borrow billions of pounds from grateful and apparently trusting banks. This was despite his reputation for a cavalier attitude towards both his investors and the regulatory authorities. After his sudden and unexpected death in the autumn of 1991, his empire began rapidly to crumble as his complex financial dealings emerged from murky secrecy into the bright light of public scrutiny.

No one should have been surprised. So how could the chief executive of a major public company have been allowed by his fellow directors to behave in the way he did? Why did his bankers continue to lend him money? Why was he allowed to manipulate the pension fund of Mirror Group Newspapers in the face of the watching trustees? Everyone knew his bullying ways and his own unique brand of business ethics. His view of accountants was perhaps summed up by the experience of one of our colleagues who was interviewing potential finance directors for one of the Maxwell subsidiaries. The great man conducted the interviews of the final short-listed candidates in his bedroom, sitting up in his four-poster bed while the luckless accountants perched on a footstool at his feet!

How could these two men, highly successful in their different ways, have been allowed by the long-established structure of regulation and the timid compliance of enormously experienced and otherwise forceful and robust colleagues, to behave in the way that they did? How had the system of governance allowed them to operate outside the accepted rules of conduct with such apparent freedom? A cynical view would be that such a system of governance was non-existent.

What happened to the world-wide regulatory regimes which were supposed to prevent an operation such as the Bank of Credit and Commerce International (BCCI) being allowed to operate as an apparently bona fide bank? Clearly, when considering BCCI the regulators and central bankers drew comfort from the fact that the BCCI board contained four experienced Western bankers: Yves Lamarch from Bank of America, Cliff Twitchin who prided himself on being the youngest branch manager of his day at Martins Bank, Dick van Oenen, also from Bank of America, and Alfred Hartman, a Swiss banker who held many positions including vice-president of the Rothschild Bank in Zurich and president of the Swiss arm of the Bank of Scotland. The board minutes indicate an unquestioning and often unanimous approval of many of the bank's largest questionable loans, sometimes it seems after they had been made. There seems to be little evidence from the minutes that they asked tough questions about lending practices. Asked by the *Financial Times* how senior BCCI executives managed to keep their financial manipulations from the board for so long, Dr Hartmann said: 'They were a very close management group who were all together before they started BCCI . . . The figures they produced for the board always looked very good, as they had been audited by a prime company. We always relied on these figures' (*Financial Times* 15 November 1991).

At odds with shareholders

Lonrho has for years been one of the most popular companies with small investors. But Tiny Rowland has never quite managed to gain acceptance by the City despite his outstandingly successful development of the business. A 1 per cent stake in 1961 received a £1,000 dividend; a 1 per cent holder in 1990 received £1 million. Outstanding by most standards, but the City has never really understood Lonrho and therefore has an underlying streak of mistrust. On the morning of Thursday 23 January 1992 the company announced the £118 million sale of its 50 per cent stake in German freight forwarder Kuhne & Nagel, leading the market to infer that the dividend was safe. In the evening, after hours, it announced a collapse in profits and that there would be no interim dividend. The market showed its fury by marking the shares down 43p on Friday to 120p. The Lonrho director Paul Spicer said that dividend cuts and asset sales were part of the 'good housekeeping' initiated eight months previously to bring down the interest bill. A top banker described Rowland's appointment of René Leclezio as chairman as 'silly' and said that 'appointing a mate who has been on the board 15 years but is unknown to the City is hardly the best way to restore confidence' (*Financial Times* 26 Jan. 92). By mid-March 1992 the share price had dropped to under 100p. Lonhro's business problems have been the signal for a shareholder onslaught on the company. Pension Investment Research Consultants, as advisers to institutions with investments in the company, has openly asked for the appointment of four 'high calibre' non-executive directors, as well as the creation of an independent pay committee of the board. It also recommends that shareholders should question management about the group's articles of association which exclude Mr Rowland, the group chairman and chief executive, aged 74 in 1992, from the need for re-election. Shareholders also commented sourly on the chairman's pay increase at a time of falling profits.

So who is right? The board of a hitherto successful enterprise which is addressing difficult trading conditions, or the City analysts and bankers who, by their own admission, do not fully understand the business? Clearly it is unsatisfactory that there should be such a gulf of comprehension and trust between the management and the major shareholders.

In May 1991 Hanson PLC bought a 2.8 per cent stake in ICI, prompting intense speculation that it would mount a bid for the whole company. The ICI board certainly seemed to think so because within days it had engaged three top-line merchant banks to prepare a full package of defence measures. Schroders, Warburgs and Goldman Sachs for ICI were opposed by Rothschilds for Hanson, assisted by three high profile public relations advisers, and the cost to ICI soon ran into millions of pounds. Or, looked at differently, the board's fear of the holder of one smallish shareholding cost that shareholder and all its fellow shareholders a great deal of money. How could this make sense?

The conspiracy theorists suggested that it was all a ruse concocted by the ICI board with the connivance of Hanson to enable it to take firm action over costs and get the blame laid on Hanson rather than itself, while Hanson would benefit by the increase in share price as the company became more efficient and profitable. This became harder to believe over the next few months as the dispute grew increasingly acrimonious. At any rate, the board was seen not to have the confidence of a significant minority of the shareholders. Months later, the board was still intact, if bruised, and had inflicted minor, if temporary, damage on Hanson but ICI still had a threatening 2.8 per cent shareholder. Eventually, perhaps inevitably, Hanson sold out. One could not imagine Sir Denys Henderson inviting either of the Lords Hanson or White to join his board to contribute their entrepreneurial skills to rejuvenate the pedestrian performance of ICI, though Hanson Group's performance has been consistently very much better than that of many of the companies represented on ICI's board, such as Midland Bank, National Westminster Bank and Pilkington. The ICI management also supplied non-executive directors to such commercial non-performers as British Aerospace, Hawker Siddeley and British and Commonwealth. Interestingly, Hanson executives held very few outside directorships by comparison; is there a lesson here?

Sceptics on strategy

Sir Robert ('Black Bob') Scholey, the tough chief executive of British Steel, has been trying to make his company a significant international firm. He talks of a great mistrust among European steel-makers which has led to continuing overcapacity. He believes in co-ordination of investment plans between the major European rivals and has been working to build up British Steel's own presence in Germany and reduce its dependence on the UK economy.

In December 1991, Sir Robert complained bitterly at the failure of his shareholders to support his negotiations with the Treuhand agency to acquire some of the former state-run steel-works in Eastern Germany. They were put off by the very high social and environmental costs apparently involved. Sir Robert was quoted as saying: 'British Steel cannot do what it wants.' Its institutional shareholders were unhappy if profits failed to appear and share prices fell. 'Life would be easier if we had Deutsche Bank behind us', (*Financial Times* 29 December 1991).

In September 1991, BTR made the mega-bid for which its shareholders had long been waiting. It offered £1.5 billion for Hawker Siddeley, a grand old name of British industry which had made the Hurricane fighter and the Harrier jump-jet but which had fallen on hard times. It had appointed a new chief executive two years previously to sort out the problems. Mr Alan Watkins had made his name at Lucas and now had set himself a five-year task of restructuring the whole business.

Unfortunately, just as he was embarking on a programme of divestments and redirecting the company through the worst recessionary conditions for many years, BTR approached his shareholders with an offer to buy them out. The younger brokers in the City were said to regard Hawker as a rather boring hotchpotch of electrical businesses which had gone nowhere through the 1980s. There was probably little question therefore about whether to stay with the chief executive in his five-year programme to refocus the product line, update the engineering skills and develop management skills, or whether to take the immediate increase in value of their holding offered by the bid. Despite the prevailing climate against mega-bids, the bid succeeded. Mr Watkins' shareholders did not stay with his strategy.

Disaffected employees

Ford's operations at Halewood on Merseyside have become almost a byword for disastrous employee relations. They have influenced Ford to direct its investment away from the area, even to direct it outside the UK altogether. The labour relations of the old British Leyland at Longbridge are legendary and the name of 'red Robbo' has gone down in the annals of an age whose memory the anti-union legislation of recent years has done much to expunge. However, though the combination of a reduction in union power and more recently the sobering effect of the recession have given Britain one of the lowest strike records in the world, there is still a strong feeling of 'us and them' between management and staff in many of the larger corporations. Why should this persist after nearly two generations of 'socially aware' educationalists have been trying to root out class-consciousness? This deep-rooted antagonism is one of the reasons, we believe, why British managements are so hostile to employee participation on their boards.

Actually, it does not have to be like this. The new operation of the Japanese car company, Nissan, based in the north-east, appears to represent a completely new departure in UK labour relations and a model of successful management. However, they seem to have decided not only to pick a greenfield site for their factory but also to recruit staff and managers young enough to have little or no experience of traditional British labour relations. In consequence, the workforce seems to be fully in tune with the aims and objectives of management and, for the first time in years, the UK now has a significant car export industry again! In retrospect you could say it was a brilliant *tour de force* for the British government to entice the Japanese into Britain to rebuild the native British motor industry.

In a different sphere, in the National Health Service (NHS), there has been for many years a damaging remoteness between the proprietors (the government on behalf of the taxpayers with its agents the Department of Health and the management of the National Health Service) and the employees (the doctors, nurses and other staff). The rumbling disaffection has occasionally broken out into open war as with the NUPE and COHSE strikes in the so-called 'winter of discontent' in 1979 and with the prolonged guerrilla campaign waged by the doctors during the late 1980s and early 1990s. Over long periods other professional groups such as the nurses have questioned the ethical intentions of their paymasters as well as challenging their basic understanding of what is involved in caring for sick people. It is widely said that morale in the NHS is poor though the staff are valiantly striving to carry out their tasks in a committed and vocational way against the odds and despite the worst efforts of management and the Department to stymie them by crass decisions and starving them of essential funds. Management in turn talks of the need to make high-spending doctors aware of the financial realities of the situation and of the impossibility of coping with a virtually infinite demand out of strictly limited resources.

How do matters reach such a pass? Against a background of record levels of expenditure and every incentive on all sides to make a success of the service, why is there such a gulf of misunderstanding?

Environmental issues

During the night of 3 December 1984, a cloud of poisonous gas escaped from the Union Carbide chemical plant in Bhopal in central India and as dawn broke the toxic chemical methyl-isocyanate was spreading across the poor quarter of the city. The slum-dwellers living around the plant and emerging on the streets to go to their morning's work had no idea what to do as the disaster unfolded. When they realised what was happening they ran towards the plant to seek help from the company ambulances – and ran to their deaths! Over 2,500 people were suffocated and it was estimated that some 100,000 suffered serious injury including blindness and lung damage. The gas causing the catastrophe is so poisonous that it is treated with care even by scientists working under laboratory conditions. This was described as the worst environmental disaster in recorded industrial history and it provoked a world-wide debate that continued for years.

Union Carbide was assailed by a rainbow coalition consisting of 'greens' criticising big, bad, casually-polluting industry, Third World politicians condemning Western imperialists who were careless of the very existence of poor employees while exploiting them for profit, socialists attacking uncaring capitalist, multinational corporations, and industry experts pointing to undoubted failures in management structures and practices which had allowed such an apocalyptic event to threaten the continuing existence of a giant, sound and hitherto respected company. Overall, Union Carbide managed to survive relatively unscathed, though poorer by several billion dollars and much more aware of the need to take care over the running of its more remote activities.

In the early hours, local time, of Saturday 26 April 1986, no. 4 block in the nuclear plant at Chernobyl, 130 km from Kiev in the Ukraine, exploded, completely destroying the reactor building and throwing huge quantities of highly radioactive material into the upper atmosphere. The accident was of a kind which it was thought in the West to be almost impossible, but the impossible had indeed happened. Many people died and many more suffered lasting injuries as a result of the meltdown of the reactor. In the West the repercussions lasted for several years. In the UK, the first few months saw meat from lambs on Welsh and Cumbrian hillsides declared unfit for consumption; in the longer term the whole future of the nuclear power industry was called into question. When the government privatised the electricity industry four years later it found to its consternation that it was obliged to exclude the nuclear plants because nobody wanted anything to do with them and the nuclear sector rapidly became regarded as hopelessly uncommercial. When the planning assumptions changed, as they did in relation to the costs of decommissioning obsolete plant, the costing changed also and none of the reassurances of the scientists could overcome the public's gut feeling that they wanted nothing to do with things nuclear.

The lessons for managers are clear. Environmental issues are an inescapable part of planning business strategy for the foreseeable future and boards of directors who ignore this do so at their peril.

Business and the local community

In 1958 Harold Macmillan's Conservative government was faced with the requirement of the steel industry to make a major investment in steel-making. The correct strategic decision would have been to build a single very large strip mill of a size comparable to those the Japanese competition was building. For political reasons the industry was compelled to build two smaller ones, one at Llanwern in Wales and one at Ravenscraig in Scotland. Neither of these was big enough to enjoy the economies of scale of their foreign competitors and both, in the end, succumbed. The investments were made to assist the local employment situation. In the short term they achieved this but in the longer term they simply put off the day of reckoning.

It could perhaps be argued that the extended period should have enabled the local community to plan for alternative industries to replace the older ones. In practice, the privatised British Steel has not felt financially able, or presumably morally committed, to provide for its local replacement as the major employer.

There are many examples of major employers that personify the town in which they are mainly based. Thus Boeing and Seattle, Philips and Eindhoven, ICI and Middlesbrough, Pilkington and St Helens, Fiat and Turin: the list is lengthy. In all these cases the employer has to take great care to give full weight to its responsibilities to the local community and in most cases this is exactly how these great companies as responsible organisations do actually behave. It is, of course, equally important for less high profile companies to have a similar regard for the local population. For instance, the progressive withdrawal of British Coal from many of the old mining areas of the UK has created vacuums which its best efforts at planning have not proved effective in filling.

Customer and supplier relationships

The relationship between customer and supplier has always been one requiring careful managing. It has been fashionable in recent years to stress the advantages of developing good long-term relationships with customers. This is recognised as leading to profitable business which can stand the test of recessionary pressures. It is also recognised that being unduly reliant on a single customer can leave a company vulnerable, just as single sourcing of supplies is generally less favoured than dual sourcing. In recent years progressively more attention has been devoted to fair trading and preventing the undue dominance of suppliers or customers. Equally, there have been many developments which are calculated to knit together supplier and customer more closely than ever. For instance, just-in-time delivery arrangements require very close co-operation over both production schedules and quality standards.

There is clearly room for bullying of the weaker by the stronger and in the UK one of the more notorious areas is that of delaying payment for goods and services received. This has reached the point where the government is seriously contemplating legislating to provide statutory compensation for creditors who are being penalised in this way by conveying the automatic right to levy interest on the overdue balances.

THE VOICE OF THE INSTITUTIONS IN THE UK

Flexing their muscles

The UK institutions are now estimated to own as much as two-thirds of the London stock market. This puts them in an immensely strong position and one which leaves them clearly a little uncomfortable. They have been increasingly criticised for a 'short-term' approach to their investments, particularly in the later years of the Thatcher era when their support of contentious takeovers was both key to the success of the bidder and apparently disloyal to the existing management. As the capital gains of the takeover years have receded into the past they have been replaced by the worries of collapsing profits, unprecedented cuts in dividends from blue chip companies, and even the unexpected demise of major corporations. Against this background some of the institutions have decided that, even though they have none of the skills to behave as involved owners and certainly would not wish to be counted as 'shadow' directors, nonetheless for the sake of their investment they must exercise some of the duties of owners. Hence we have seen some dramatic muscle-flexing by one or two of the formerly discreet and nameless City investment managers.

Mr Michael Sandland, chief investment manager of the Norwich Union, was quoted as saying that in the past many of the institutions had tended to be 'rather slothful' and that 'if they really disagreed with the way that a company was being run, they would simply sell their stake. But there must be a more responsible approach.' In June 1991 Norwich Union was involved in an acrimonious battle to remove the board of the environmental controls company, Tace, and its chairman, Sir David Nicholson, who was vitriolic in his opposition to this action. 'Sandland wants to be seen as the white knight of corporate governance,' he said.

It is politically motivated and it is vindictive. It is one thing to own shares in a company but they are trying to run the company. These people have no experience of industry and their power should be curtailed. The institutions have become arrogant and they need to be regulated.

Sandland was unrepentant. This was the logical outcome of the failure of a board of directors to pay proper heed to the wishes of its institutional shareholders. 'Companies are getting the message now that it is far better to pay attention to the first quiet phone call or letter and act of their own accord,' he said.

These reported exchanges (*Sunday Times* 16 June 1991) sum up vividly the gulf that has grown between owners who would not pretend to be able to manage the business and managers who are contemptuous of their owners. It is interesting to note, however, that according to an account of the battle, prepared by the accounting firm KPMG Peat Marwick, as quoted in the press, Norwich Union and its ally Framlington were not supported by the other institutional shareholders in Tace.

Other well-publicised examples are: Burton, where the chief executive of the day, Sir Ralph Halpern, appeared to have lost his previously golden touch except as regards his own remuneration, and was forced out by the institutions in November 1990 after unfavourable publicity regarding his brief involvement with a young lady (his successor, Mr Laurence Cooklin, left the company in early 1992, after little more than a year as chief executive, with the princely pay off of £773,000); Budgens, where Schroder Investment Management together with Electra and Gartmore were influential in the removal in May 1991 of the chairman, John Fletcher, on the grounds of poor trading performance; and Granada, where the approval of a £163 million rights issue, also in May 1991, was made dependent on the departure of the chief executive, Derek Lewis, who was held responsible for a diversification programme which had failed. In this last case, Warburgs, as Granada's adviser, appeared to have exercised a pivotal role with the institutions.

Interestingly, Warburgs was also involved as the adviser to Asda when its institutional shareholders brought pressure on the chairman and chief executive, John Hardman, to resign in June 1991. This was followed by the appointment of a non-executive director, Sir Godfrey Messervy, as chairman, who promptly said that his first priority was to strengthen the non-executives and recruit a new chief executive. Why more non-executives should have been a priority action in the very difficult trading situation in which Asda found itself, rather than finding top class executives experienced in the retail food business, was not immediately clear, but it is a very revealing illustration of priorities in British companies.

A final dramatic example of institutional muscle-flexing was the action of the shareholders in September 1991 to remove the legendary Professor Sir Roland Smith from his job as chief executive of British Aerospace. The shares had been tumbling since the company's plan to raise £423 million by way of a rights issue was made public in the *Financial Times*. British Aerospace was financially stretched and the plan was leaked together with a forecast of much reduced profits. This infuriated the big shareholders who felt that they had been misled about the company's prospects during the preceding months. The durable Professor's surprise departure was seen as the culmination of the rumbling discontent felt by the company's non-executive directors, led by Sir James Blyth, the chief executive of Boots, and

Ronnie Hampel of ICI. They had grown increasingly concerned at Smith's management style, with his love of secret deal-making, typified by the deal by which he bought Rover Group in 1988. They felt it was no longer appropriate to British Aerospace and when it emerged that he had been conducting secret negotiations with Trafalgar House to merge the two companies, their patience snapped. He had not kept senior executives in the picture and had entered negotiations without even informing the board. The board turned against him and eventually unanimously asked for his resignation, stimulated by rising press speculation about his position.

Limited objectives

The institutions are clearly starting to believe in their obligation and even their ability to cross swords with managements who they believe are acting in a way detrimental to the profitable conduct of the business. But is this the full extent of their obligations as owners? What about some of the very important issues that we discussed earlier in this chapter?

Did the institutional shareholders of Union Carbide suggest to the board after Bhopal that the company should establish a project to improve the quality of life in the devastated region around the Bhopal plant?

Have the institutional shareholders of British Aerospace, after getting rid of Professor Smith, required the board to study the management of Nissan and tasked them with learning the appropriate lessons to enable the Rover Group to become a major exporter, like Nissan (UK)?

Did the institutional shareholders of British Steel listen to Bob Scholey's plea for German-style long-term support and respond with a meeting of all the major shareholders to discuss with management the formulation and financing of a mutually agreed long-term strategy that would take the company successfully into the next century?

Has the National Association of Pension Funds been listening to the political discussions about the relative lack of training provided by British industry compared with its German competitors and formed a collective pressure group to change the practices of the companies in which they all invest, for the sakes of both their own shareholdings and for the British economy as a whole?

The answer to all these questions is – unless they have been very secretive about the discussions – no. Certainly there is no evidence generally available that such actions have been taken by the institutional investors concerned. But why not? Are they not all very important issues for the long-term future of the companies concerned? The answer must surely be a resounding *yes*. So why are the major shareholders concerned simply and solely with the short-term trading performance of their investments and not, apparently, with the broader issues of management of a modern corporation?

INFLUENCE OF THE USA

Corporate governance and directors' pay

When George Bush made a state visit to Japan in January 1992, part of his purpose was to increase the opportunities for US manufacturers, particularly car-makers, to export to the Japanese domestic market. Unfortunately, the move rather backfired, drawing criticisms from Japanese industrialists about the size of US bosses' pay packets in relation to their performance which seemed rather out of line with Japanese bosses' pay packets in relation to their performance. Chief executives' pay rose rapidly through the 1980s. According to Towers Perrin, a consultancy which specialises in pay and benefits, when the recession hit in 1989, pay went on rising by a median 6.7 per cent in the USA's top 350 companies even though shareholder value actually fell by 9 per cent. There is a growing argument about pay in the USA as part of the wider debate about corporate governance. A highly vocal group of critics is now questioning whether very high pay does in fact motivate managers to run their companies better Certainly, though hard information is difficult to obtain, it does appear as if US bosses are paid much more highly than their equivalents in Japan or Germany, whose economic performance in recent years has undoubtedly surpassed that of the USA.

One of the most active of the public pension funds, Calpers (the California Public Employees' Retirement System) is one of the leading members of the fast growing corporate governance movement, which consists mainly of institutional investors and wants to make companies more responsive to shareholders' wishes. At the end of 1990 it had some $56 billion in assets under its control. At the 1991 annual general meeting of ITT, Calpers voted against the re-election of the directors in protest at the large pay and benefits package enjoyed in 1991 by chairman Rand Araskog, who received between $10 and $11.5 million (scourge of US management, Professor Graef Crystal at the University of California who has made extensive studies of US bosses' pay, says the latter) and this was up from $7 million in 1990. Calpers said that he did not deserve this because of the company's mediocre results. In the past two to three years Calpers has started challenging poorly performing companies, not only on directors' pay but also over such devices as poison pills.

There has been a growing chorus of disapproval among the institutions as attention has been focused on some of the enormous remuneration packages received in the larger corporations, particularly as the performance of these companies has faltered during the prolonged recession. In 1990, for example, according to *Business Week*, Stephen S. Ross, joint chief executive of Time Warner, made between $39 and $78 million depending on how a special one-time gain is calculated. Stephen Wolf, Chairman of United Airlines, made over $18 million and John Sculley of Apple, $16.7 million. These are not really representative and consist mostly of one-time gains on share options, but a Towers Perrin study showed that the average pay of chief executives in the top 350 US companies was $1.4 million in 1990 – still a substantial figure against a background of workforce redundancies and mediocre results. The question has been asked with increasing vehemence – is the compensation system structured to get the best performance out of managers? With such devices as 'golden parachutes' to protect managers against being at the wrong end of hostile takeovers (possibly resulting from their own poor performance) and even 'golden coffins' to compensate their families against their death in office (on top of normal death benefits), there is a general feeling that the businesses are in too many cases run for the benefit of top management rather than for the shareholders.

Michael Jensen of Harvard Business School in a *Harvard Business Review* paper in 1990, argued that the focus should not be on how much executives are paid but on how they are paid. In most publicly quoted companies the compensation of top executives is virtually independent of performance. Boardroom compensation committees are usually composed of outside directors and seek advice from independent consultants on comparable rates at similar companies. A ratchet effect exists as companies always try to outbid their competitors. Cynics say that chief executives can influence this by ensuring that the board is full of outside directors who are even more highly paid than themselves. As has been said, 'If you are running a company and want a raise, you wouldn't ask Mother Theresa to join your board.' Professor Crystal says in his book *In Search of Excess* (1991), as an apologia for his time as a compensation consultant with Towers Perrin, advising companies on executive pay: 'I never focused very well on the fact that unless other companies were willing to pay their executives below market levels, the market would simply explode, and explode it did.' He dubs Stephen S. Ross of Time Warner as 'the Prince of Pay' who received $111 million in 1990 through a mixture of cash and the present value of history's largest stock option grant. Crystal also reveals that the late Armand Hammer of Occidental Petroleum had set up a compensation package which will pay his estate $2 million a year until 1998.

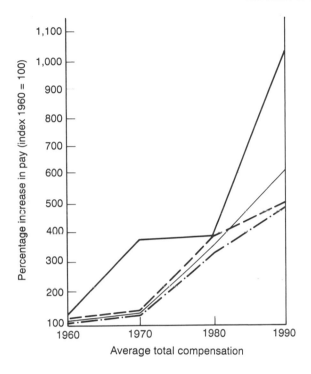

	1960	1990	
Chief executive	$190, 383	$1, 952, 806	———
Engineer	$9, 828	$49, 365	— — —
% of chief executive	5.2%	2.5%	
School teacher	$4, 995	$31, 166	———
% of chief executive	2.6%	1.6%	
Factory worker	$4, 665	$22, 998	— · — · ·
% of chief executive	2.5%	1.2%	

Figure 1.1 The pay gap in the USA
Source: US Bureau of Labor Statistics

Among the disturbing assertions made by Crystal is that in the last 20 years (to 1990) the pay of US workers has stagnated while that of US chief executives has increased by over 400 per cent. United States chief executives earn 85 times more than the average worker while their German counterparts earn 21 times more and in Japan just 16 times the average. Figure 1.1 shows the growing discrepancy in the last 30 years between the average total compensation of a US chief executive and other workers.

Takeovers and greenmail

In the USA, pension funds own 40 per cent of the equity and debt of the largest companies. It is interesting to observe how the view of the responsibilities of management to its shareholders has changed over recent years. In a 1950s publication, management guru Peter Drucker argued that senior executives were responsible for managing companies 'in the best interests of shareholders, customers, employees, suppliers and plant community cities'. In this stakeholder theory the manager was a trustee. In the 1980s, a more recent theory describes management's responsibility to shareholders in terms of its ability to create and indeed maximise shareholder value. The respected leading UK companies like Hanson and ICI subscribe strongly to this idea. Companies thus move from stakeholders to shareholders through takeovers, which become the vehicle for addressing management's failure to perform in relation to building shareholder value. In an article in the *Harvard Business Review* in March–April 1991 Drucker argues that the concentration of power in the hands of the funds has made takeovers easier because the bidder does not have to woo a myriad of private shareholders.

Takeovers have kept alive for the institutions the illusion that they could sell what they owned. But what have they exchanged their shares for? More shares and possibly junk bonds, convertible warrants or unsecured loans. At the present time index tracking is becoming more and more widespread, as is programme trading. It has been said that, carried to its logical conclusion, this will result in all fund managers owning the same portfolio! Meanwhile, in the case of a takeover a fund manager is increasingly likely to be faced with the prospect of involuntarily increasing his or her stake in a corporation in which he or she is already a shareholder.

One significant factor driving the corporate governance movement is revulsion against the excesses of the late 1980s when managements paid 'greenmail' to get rid of corporate raiders, and put in place elaborate 'poison pills' to protect themselves against unwanted attentions. A whole industry grew up to promote buyouts, which encouraged less ethical managements to take over the companies that employed them. It gave them the opportunity to make vast personal gains often for relatively small personal effort, and raised the question as to why they had not been able to improve performance earlier when working as employees. The final, biggest and most notorious of these was the unsuccessful bid for RJR Nabisco by its high-living chief executive, Ross Johnson, at a price which later frenzied bidding was to prove extremely cheap. The story of the battle, *Barbarians at the Gate*, by Burroughs and Helyar 1990, has apparently been distributed to all members of the Calpers corporate board and the chief executive has described it as having done 'more for corporate governance than anything we or any of the other activists will ever accomplish'.

Lockheed was another case in point. The poorly performing aerospace group was forced to talk to its institutional investors after the Dallas-based investor Harold Simmonds built up a stake of almost 20 per cent and tried to get seats on the board through a proxy battle. The institutions made it clear to the chairman, Dan Tellep, that if he wanted their backing for his candidates he must begin to start making changes to the way the business was run. So in 1990 the company watered down its anti-takeover poison pill on lines similar to those suggested by Calpers. Calpers devised a compromise which it called a 'chewable pill' and which allowed the poison pill to be suspended while the shareholders considered any offer for the company. If the shareholders agreed, the poison pill could then be reinstated. Dan Tellep was obliged to undertake a programme of regular briefings to the institutional shareholders, to introduce a newsletter on important issues affecting the company, and to conduct regular surveys of shareholder opinion on important policy matters. He described this as producing heightened awareness by management of the needs and views of shareholders. Arguably he should not have needed to be threatened by a proxy battle to make him take regular account of the wishes of his owners.

But how relevant is all this confrontational activity in the USA between the investing institutions and the ranks of top managers to the governance of companies in the European Community?

FORTRESS BRITAIN AND FORTRESS GERMANY

Continental and Pirelli *et al.*

By autumn 1991 the Continental–Pirelli differences had apparently narrowed to the point where it seemed that the two would co-operate together. But it would be far from the full-blown takeover/merger that was first mooted. Pirelli fell foul of the German establishment (and shareholder indemnities). It had to indemnify its allies in the abortive takeover to get round Continental's rule that no individual shareholder may hold more than 5 per cent. Pirelli had to divest and restructure. It had resorted to pacts and accords between allies, which are the hallmark of the Milan stock exchange. The bid was eventually called off on 1 December 1991 when Pirelli, which had agreed to compensate its allies if no merger was agreed by the end of November, said its pledge could cost it L350 billion or $287 million. In the meantime, Continental's share price had fallen about a third during the period of negotiations. The cultural problems clearly baffled Pirelli: Leopoldo Pirelli thought he had the backing of Ulrich Weiss, board member of Deutsche Bank and Chairman of the supervisory council of Continental. In fact he remained neutral. Pirelli misread the situation, trying to make a takeover seem like a friendly merger.

During the same period, Krupp was successful in gaining establishment backing for a far from friendly bid for its rival steel-maker Hoesch. The opening shot was the disclosure that Krupp had secretly bought a 24.9 per cent stake for DM500 million. This was an unusually aggressive move by a member of the German industrial establishment and raised suspicions that the whole process had some kind of official blessing. The acquiring company needed to achieve its majority holding by acquiring a number of widely dispersed holdings. The key as always was a bank, in this case the WestDeutsche Landesbank, which owned 12 per cent of the shares, and several Swiss banks also owned stakes. Furthermore a member of Deutsche Bank's board, Herbert Zapp, was President of Hoesch's supervisory council. The Chairman of Hoesch, though a reluctant bride, probably remembered that the last chief executive who failed to do the bidding of Deutsche Bank was Horst Urban of Continental, who then lost his job. This all-German takeover was completed successfully and the interest of UK British Steel in buying its way into Germany received short shrift. This was widely seen as an attempt to protect the relatively inefficient German steel industry and give it time to restructure itself while in the process defeating the attempt of the relatively efficient British company to broaden its interests away from the domestic market into the emerging single European market.

Clearly, the building of pan-European companies will not be a straightforward affair and there are major issues of governance and board structures to be addressed if cross-border (and cross-cultural) alliances are to be successfully established.

ICI and Hanson

The purchase of a small stake in ICI by Hanson referred to earlier in this chapter caused incredible ripples and was a good opportunity to view British attitudes. *The Economist*, commenting on 22 June 1991, said:

Whether Britain's largest manufacturer should pass into Hanson's hands has become central to all kinds of questions: about government intervention versus the free market, about corporate governance, about the role of research in industrial growth, about the motivation of workers and managers, about the status of corporate pension funds, and much else. All these arguments have shared a curious premise: that ICI is a national asset, to be argued about on the national stage. Yet it is not – it is a company owned by shareholders. Its fate will rest on their decision. So far, the big institutional shareholders have been silent.

But why is the argument curious? Surely ICI is indeed a national asset. That is how it would be regarded in Japan and in continental Europe, and perhaps even increasingly in the USA.

By autumn 1991, a curious development in the ICI/Hanson imbroglio was that the ICI-inspired revelation of the Lord White interest in horseflesh and later the affair of his threatened prosecution by the US police for an alleged assault on his young girlfriend, were beginning to turn the spotlight on Hanson itself and its corporate governance. There were increasing rumours that the institutional shareholders were unhappy about Hanson's style and wanted the company to change it. There was pressure for the appointment of more non-executives, coupled with a succession plan for replacing the two near-septuagenarians who were running the company. The major shareholders, who included Prudential portfolio managers, Norwich Union, Standard Life, and most of the institutional establishment, wanted a meeting to discuss strategy. In the end Hanson did appoint three new non-executives but they were not regarded as heavyweight industrialists by the City. Hanson appointed Jonathan Scott-Barrett, senior executive of Centaur Communications, a small publishing firm established in 1982, Simon Keswick, a director of Jardine Matheson Holdings and David Hardy, chief executive of London Docklands Development Corporation. These new directors were widely seen as placemen who would be unlikely to exercise any real restraining influence on the two noble lords.

It is interesting to consider the fuss created by Hanson's acquisition of a small stake in ICI, not even followed by a bid, in comparison with the comments made in connection with both the unsuccessful Continental–Pirelli courtship and the successful Krupp–Hoesch marriage. In the British case all the talk was of the break-up of the target company and squeezing the assets to improve profitability and shareholder value. In the case of both the German companies it was about industry restructuring and the production of a merged operation which would be more powerful than either of the constituent elements and better able to compete on the world scene.

THE STIRRING MINORITIES

It seems as if the position of continental minority shareholders, long dependent on 'friends at court' rather than legal rules for their protection, may be improving.

In June 1991 shareholders of Nedlloyd, spurred on by the Norwegian 'shipping doctor' Torstein Hagen, who was seeking a seat on the supervisory council, withheld their approval of the 1990 accounts by a 55 per cent majority. This was the first major Dutch company to have its report and accounts thrown out by the shareholders, not because they contained errors but because the board refused to admit Mr Hagen, who held around one quarter of the equity. He clearly persuaded a significant number of the shareholders that he could do a better job than the incumbent management and subsequently gained a seat on the supervisory council.

In France the bank-industry culture makes life very difficult for small shareholders. When in the autumn of 1991 the Agnellis made a bid for EXOR, which owned Source Perrier, they extended their two-thirds bid to the remaining shareholders even though not required to by French law. This was in sharp contrast to the bid by the Pinault timber to furniture retailing group for Au Printemps when they made a two-thirds offer in December 1991 rather than go to the expense of making a full bid. Though heavily criticised, they stuck to their guns. The Conseil des Bourses de Valeur (the stock market regulator) disappointed minority shareholders by not putting pressure on the company to make a full offer. Clearly the conduct of takeover bids in France is likely to be the subject of intense debate and corporate governance may soon enter into the French vocabulary.

DEVELOPMENTS IN BRITAIN

The continuing debate

In a discussion paper issued in March 1991, the Association of British Insurers (ABI) suggested that institutional shareholders should take a more active role in companies in which they hold shares. It expressed itself as opposed to the creation of equity shares with varying rights as being likely to leave some classes of shareholder at a disadvantage in relation to others. It called for the appointment of genuinely independent directors who were not simply former employees and who did not act as professional advisers, nor were significant suppliers to the company or buyers of its goods or services. These directors should not benefit from share option schemes or other incentive schemes and not have compensation for loss of office. They also should be sufficiently numerous for their number to carry weight. The ABI enunciated nine principles of good practice for institutions and said: 'Institutional investors should encourage regular, systematic contact at senior executive level to exchange views and information on strategy, perform-ance, board membership and quality of management.' They should not, however, receive price sensitive information. They should give positive support to the executive members of boards and take a positive interest in the composition of boards, particularly regarding the calibre of non-executives. They should also support the idea of audit and remuneration committees.

The Confederation of British Industry (CBI) welcomed the recom-mendations but pointed out that adherence to good practice does not necessarily make for success and that many good companies do not adhere to the guidelines of the Institutional Shareholders' Committee (ISC).

The continental approach of two-tier boards with one group having a supervisory or monitoring role over the other is rejected. However, this is surely the principle behind an audit committee.

In 'The role and duties of directors', an Institute of Directors (IOD) booklet, issued in April 1991, the ISC recommends the separation of the roles of chief executive and chairman. It also recommends the appointment of strongly non-executive directors and the complete separation of the executive directors from any control over the way their remuneration is calculated. It rejects the idea of supervisory boards, saying that all directors, whether executive or non-executive 'have an equal responsibility in helping to provide their company with effective guidance and leadership'. However, non-executives are expected to take on many supervisory functions. For instance, compensation committees would be staffed entirely with non-executives and the same group would also decide service contracts. During a management buyout, non-executives should form a separate committee and retain separate outside advisers. Non-executives should monitor the per-formance of the board as a whole and report direct to shareholders if they are unable to resolve dissatisfaction.

Unfortunately for best solutions, Britain tends to leave problems until politicians, stirred into action by some actual or perceived scandal, launch new legislation, often hastily conceived and badly drafted, to cure the ill. The currently fashionable belief is that non-executive directors are the solution to the perceived problems with corporate governance. Sadly, a recent survey of the major companies showed that two-thirds appoint non-executives without defining what they should do. Many do not contribute at all or receive enough information to play any real part. Yet all are equally liable in the eyes of the law. Half the companies in the survey said they would support training for non-executives – but training in what?

Non-executives generally have a significant role in assisting the formulation of strategy, particularly in relation to acquisitions and mergers. Generally the larger the company, the more non-executives it has. The great majority (two-thirds in public companies and over three-quarters in investment companies) are appointed because they are known to the chairman or other board members. It may reasonably be asked whether appointing people whose names are well known is really more useful than appointing people for their knowledge of the particular industry concerned.

Overall, the owners of the major companies in Britain, the institutions, have not been properly discharging their duties as owners. The issue of corporate governance in Britain seems to be really about short-termism. Too many British managers act as if they own the company. The owners have to get the managers to behave as proper managers – which is what the German system is all about.

2 WHAT IS CORPORATE GOVERNANCE?

This book is all about corporate governance. However, this much-used term means different things to different people and we need now to define it. In attempting to do so, we shall propose our own definition which is rather different from the conventional Anglophone understanding. In making the case for this, we shall consider: the objectives and needs of the modern, global corporation, the apparent requirements for governance of such a business, and the current views on responsibilities of owners and managers. Finally we shall draw conclusions about the way in which this whole issue of corporate governance should be approached. This is the logic behind the structure of this book.

CURRENT DEFINITIONS OF CORPORATE GOVERNANCE

Most of the discussion on corporate governance in the past few years has appeared in the British and US press. The continental Europeans barely know the expression. In consequence, most of the written commentary emanates from Anglo-American corporate experience. Thus we have the chairman of Lockheed Corporation, Dan Tellep, at a 1991 London conference listing some of the chief issues of corporate governance as executive remuneration, proxy reform and cumulative voting. During the course of a fraught three years, Mr Tellep was engaged in fierce proxy battles with groups of shareholders intent on wresting away control from the current board. His view of corporate governance was apparently that it was an accommodation (or even a state of armed truce) between the management board and the institutional shareholders. To safeguard his and the board's position, therefore, he embarked upon an intensive schedule of visits to major shareholders to explain his viewpoint on the board's strategy for Lockheed. He visited 15 cities and 70 institutions in the space of six weeks and reckoned to have interviewed 90 per cent of his shareholders. Speaking in all humility, he said he believed he had taken to heart the shareholders' message that they wanted to be kept informed about strategic policy and he had accepted their resolutions and agreed to appoint up to three new directors. In fact they appointed four, not one of whom was known to the chief executive. He described as a 'renaissance' the resulting improvement in relations with his shareholders which he safeguarded by meetings and personal contact, newsletters on issues, surveys of shareholder views, and heightened awareness by management of the shareholder position.

These actions would probably not be regarded with any great surprise by US observers of the corporate scene when considering a major company which had been performing poorly and had probably neglected its shareholder relations.

Indeed, the view of the US institutions is probably summed up by the remarks of George Cones, chairman of the executive committee of the Council of Institutional Investors made at a 1991 London conference. For him, corporate governance was actively running the portfolio of assets, and for him both institutional investors and management had to benefit. Investors used to 'take the Wall Street walk' and sell stock on bad perform-ance but they were now taking a broader view. For him, there was a clear difference between the duties of management, which had to add value to the shareholders of the company, and portfolio managers, who had to add value to their whole portfolio.

These two opinions probably sum up the relative positions of the manage-ments and the investing institutions in the Anglophone world.

Colin Short, finance director of ICI, has expressed the view that the principle of corporate governance is to achieve shareholder value for share-holders: no mention here of other interested parties. He does say that the concentration of investment into fewer and fewer hands will probably result in calls for a change in approach from both companies and investing institu-tions. He notes that at present some institutions prefer not to get involved in meetings with ICI.

On the other hand, James Fisher, associate director of Scottish Amicable, a company with an £8.5 billion investment in smaller businesses of under £200 million value, regards the corporate governance debate as all about the separation of control from ownership. Since Scottish Amicable is in small companies, it cannot simply 'take the Wall Street walk' and sell; it has to regard itself as being in a partnership with management. For Mr Fisher, the potential problem areas are: non-separation of roles of chairman and chief executive, balancing the interests of the long term and short term, non-performing management teams and devices to protect managements such as excessive executive compensation packages, golden parachutes, poison pills and the like.

Effective governance for Mr Fisher involves him in improving communications between himself, the investor, and the managers, so as to gain a better understanding of management's strategy and business aims. This entails building up a long-term relationship so that he can successfully invest long-term. For him, though, the decision as to whether to back management in a takeover situation will turn on his view as to whether the management is likely to make a better fist of building long-term shareholder value than the bidding company.

Jon Aisbitt, managing director of Goldman Sachs International, at the 1991 conference referred to above, described his view that corporate governance consists of two elements:

(i) The long-term relationship, which has to deal with checks and balances, incentives for managers and communications between management and investors.

(ii) The transactional relationship, which involves matters relating to disclosure and authority.

It has to be said that this seems to apply primarily to publicly quoted companies rather than to private businesses. Of course, in continental Europe there are relatively few of these and the vast majority of companies might therefore not understand the importance of this issue in the Anglophone world. Most non-Anglophone countries' systems place more emphasis on changing non-performing management than on changing ownership.

A development in the USA which may cross the Atlantic but which may be resisted as a result of the re-election of the Conservatives in the UK, is the growing split between bottom line-driven investors and politically motivated investors. There is already some evidence for this in the UK in the existence of funds which are described as 'conscience' funds. In a way, regardless of whether this is commercially sensible, it does represent a broadening of the relationship between owner and manager, because most of the above discussion has stayed within the bounds described by an arms-length investor and an independent management. This has possibly reached its limit in the increasingly fashionable practices of 'programme trading' and 'buying the index'. These must represent the most uninvolved form of ownership yet devised.

There is still widespread ignorance about practices of governance across borders, though this does not prevent confident opinions being expressed. For instance, it is believed in Anglophone circles that ideas of US shareholder activism could soon spread globally because of increasing world-wide investment by US corporations influenced by 'politically correct' advisers, a growth in world-wide investor relations which will lead to more discussion between investors, and a push to uniformity in trading procedures which will tend to result in increasing adoption of US standards. Though there is recognition that German and Japanese models for ownership can contribute to a more stable corporate environment, these are dismissed as being susceptible to corruption and therefore likely to be superseded by the US model. This rather underrates the success of these two economies and therefore pays little attention to some of the factors in their form of governance which may have contributed to their success.

For instance, in the Japanese system the interests of shareholders matter, but they are not regarded as superior to those of the employees, management, customers or suppliers. The domestic market is fiercely competitive and success has in the past depended on anticipating the market and keeping ahead of, or at least up with, the competition rather than on the short-term profits generated. In this market-driven environment, a company will start with a target market share, estimate what pricing policy is likely to be needed to achieve that share, then work back towards a product and production process that will enable it to meet those price criteria. In the Western world, producers still very much have a cost-plus approach that causes them to work out the cost of producing a new product, add their profit margin and then determine how they can persuade buyers to pay the resulting price. Clearly, the two very different commercial environments are bound to have their impact on what is likely to constitute successful governance of companies operating in the two environments. Equally clearly, the two cultures are likely to have different ideas as to what constitutes corporate governance itself.

In Germany, at the time of writing, the German cartel office has moved to try to reduce the power of the insurance giant Allianz, Europe's largest insurance company by requiring it to reduce its stake in Dresdner Bank, Germany's second largest bank. It has concluded that the Dresdner–Allianz partnership holds very powerful minority stakes in several large German companies, including Thyssen steel, Metallgesellschaft, Lufthansa, MAN engineering and Bayer and Hoechst chemicals groups. German anti-trust law requires that cartel office approval is needed for the purchase of any stake over 25 per cent in another company. This is seen to be the level at which the acquirer is able to exercise a significant influence over the policies of the company in which it has invested. By the summer of 1991, Allianz had increased its stake in Dresdner from a disclosed 10 per cent to over 22 per cent and Dresdner, in turn, had a 10 per cent stake in Allianz. This was in connection with an arrangement to market each other's services. Though Allianz was careful to keep its shareholdings below the key 25 per cent level, the cartel office appears to have concluded that the *de facto* control it exercised was very much higher. Indeed, it was suggested that Allianz effectively controlled as much as 47 per cent of Dresdner as a result of a complex web of indirect shareholdings. This is termed *vorauseilend-gehorsam*, indicating the taking of direction or instruction from Allianz, even though there is no formal and overt control mechanism in place. By way of example, some people quote the fact that Deutsche Bank has set up its own life assurance company, whereas Dresdner has still been prevented by the wishes of Allianz from following suit.

Allianz's view of corporate governance would clearly not be familiar, or probably acceptable, to the US Council of Institutional Shareholders or the British Institutional Shareholders' Committee. However, it appears to have been successful as a means of building one of the most powerful insurance groups in the world, and the Allianz shareholders are presumably reasonably content with it.

WE GIVE A BETTER DEFINITION

The preceding discussion illustrates two things:

(i) Different countries have different ideas as to what constitutes good corporate governance.

(ii) Nowhere does anyone appear to have defined corporate governance *per se*.

At this stage, we should like to suggest that any satisfactory definition, to be applicable to a modern, global company, must synthesise best practice from the biggest economic powers into something which can be applied across all major countries. We shall devote the remainder of this book to making the case for our definition. In essence, we believe that good corporate governance consists of a system of structuring, operating and controlling a company such as to achieve the following:

(i) Fulfil the long-term strategic goal of the owners, which , after survival may consist of building shareholder value or establishing a dominant market share or maintaining a technical lead in a chosen sphere, or something else, but will certainly not be the same for all organisations.

(ii) Consider and care for the interests of employees, past, present and future, which we take to comprise the whole life-cycle including planning future needs, recruitment, training, working environment, severance and retirement procedures, through to looking after pensioners.

(iii) Take account of the needs of the environment and the local community, both in terms of the physical effects of the company's operations on the surroundings and the economic and cultural interaction with the local population.

(iv) Work to maintain excellent relations with both customers and suppliers, in terms of such matters as quality of service provided, considerate ordering and account settlement procedures, etc.

 (v) Maintain proper compliance with all the applicable legal and regulatory requirements under which the company is carrying out its activities.

We believe that a well-run organisation must be structured in such a way that all the above requirements are catered for and can be seen to be operating effectively by all the interest groups concerned. There must be sufficient transparency for this to be readily observable by them without their having to rely on extensive and expensive independent monitoring procedures. A company achieving its owners' goals under such an organisational structure will, we believe, have a good and effective form of corporate governance.

3 CORPORATE PRACTICE

SURVEY OF BUSINESS PRACTICES

The objective of the survey

This chapter sets out the results of our survey into corporate practices of major companies as described in their latest financial statements. We looked at 100 major international corporations, situated in Europe, the USA and Japan. The European ones were all in the European top 500, the US and Japanese ones were all in the top 100 for each country. The references are to the latest accounts available as at end 1991. We were therefore basically looking at the statements for financial periods ending up to September 1991 with the majority, however, being the reports for the calendar year 1990.

Our comments are based on the information contained in these annual reports, but also supplemented by our personal knowledge of the companies concerned. Readers should not, however, think that we were so naïve as to accept what we read uncritically. We have approached the analysis with a more than usual dose of cynicism. We know that companies are adept at showing their financial figures in the best light possible, and that they will certainly not shrink from extracting the last ounce of public relations benefit from the way they present their company and its corporate image to the outside world in the annual report. We read what the writers who put the words together are paid by the chairman and his or her colleagues to want us to read.

We therefore realise that if there are comments in the reports on the employment of minorities, a care for the environment or social programmes in the local community, it is partly because such statements are required by law, and partly because it pays the company to demonstrate concern. As part of its environmental programme one retail chain is encouraging its customers to recycle the plastic carrier bags. This could be a neat way of combining environmental concern with cost cutting. Sometimes there is a certain selectivity with facts. Shell was fined £1 million in February 1990 after 156 tonnes of crude oil spilled into the River Mersey from a fractured pipeline. No mention of the incident appears in Shell Transport and Trading's annual report and accounts. We realise too, that the emphasis on training and development is understandable given companies' development needs, and if the staff are complimented by the directors on the way they have supported a company in its reorganisation or retrenchment programmes, one might well ask if they had any other option.

The reports set out a position at a point in time. Situations change; for instance since the production of the 1990 annual report, ICI's chairman has changed his role, the chairman of British Aerospace (BAe) has lost his job, as has the chief executive of CMB, among others, and companies have not ceased to remove their directors and appoint new ones. Moreover, lists of directors do not convey the subtle gradations of power and the interaction of personalities that are central to any organisation. Does this chairman listen to his or her non-executives? Who has the real power, the chairman, the chief executive, or the representative of a leading shareholder sitting quietly in a corner at the board meeting? The annual reports do not tell us.

And yet the format of the different companies' annual reports is very significant, for what they choose to emphasise, what they say, how they say it, and, particularly, what they omit to say. There are companies whose annual reports are works of art, with exquisite pictures of flowers, but with only minimum comment about the business. Others go into great detail about staff welfare and communication. Many companies set out their corporate goals: do they concentrate on shareholder value, or international growth, or good citizenship? Some describe their business alliances in detail. Such pointers, coupled with what we know of the companies concerned, are very revealing, and have enabled us to put together a representative picture. We need to emphasise above all that the survey focuses on corporate governance and not business success. Some companies have been criticised for their attitude to governance, but like Hanson PLC they may well nonetheless be undoubtedly successful businesses. Others, such as Philips, cannot be faulted on their organisation for governance, but have performed poorly. The British clearing banks have a glittering array of non-executives on their boards, but that has not prevented their heavy losses from non-performing loans in the last year or so.

The business background

For major quoted corporations the production of the annual report is a public relations as much as a financial reporting exercise. They unashamedly use the annual report to demonstrate their good citizenship: Hoechst talks of its 'Responsibility towards the Environment'; Nissan speaks grandly of 'Nissan and the environment. Working for nature . . . a symbiosis of people, automobiles and the environment'; ICI recognises its responsibilities in a section headed, 'Towards a better World'. Many of them combine this social awareness with some hard-hitting advertising of their products and services. The banks are particularly good at this, but none do it as elegantly as the US J. P. Morgan bank, whose annual report virtually doubles up as a sales brochure. In the last decade, however, we have noticed a new trend. It is now commonplace for companies to list not only their directorate but also the names of their top managers. Many go further and, like the German banks, give a company address list which also features telephone numbers and the names of those in charge of the different units. There is a logic to this. Large, multinational organisations are run not just by their main board directors but by a wider group of top executives. Companies like to emphasise their strength in depth. Péchiney, the French engineering and canning company, makes the point by listing the 37 top officers as well as the 18 members of the board. For good measure it shows the photograph of the eight members of the executive committee, only one of whom, the chairman Jean Gandois, is on the main board. He is also a director of Lyonnaise des Eaux-Dumez, which also shows a photograph of its directors and top officers. Others, such as the Belgian chemical company Solvay, show the photographs of all the top two dozen senior executives.

In many companies, most particularly British ones, it is common to personalise the divisional, regional and functional reports that are standard in any annual statement, against the name of the senior executive in charge. In BP's case this takes well over half the non-financial part of the document. Hanson PLC goes one better: whereas BP merely has a bland picture of the director in charge of the area he is reporting against, Hanson shows its executives in an action pose: against heavy earth-moving machinery or carefully scrutinising some of their company's products. It seems to take a particular delight in showing its senior executives in hard hats.

THE DIRECTORATE

The business establishment

While the phrase 'corporate governance' seems particular to the Anglo-Saxon world alone, and different companies have different ways of organising their top management structures, there is one thing all major companies have in common. In every country the directorate of major companies is a veritable roll-call of the business establishment. BAT has four non-executive directors, two lords and two knights. Nor is it unusual in this. The directorates of the British clearing banks and the top British corporates such as Shell are studded with titles.

The same corporate names appear in innumerable company boards of directors particularly the bank boards: in the four British clearers, the three top German banks, SEB and Svenska Handelsbanken in Sweden, and so on. The same individual names kept appearing (and not only in their own countries), e.g. Umberto Agnelli, director of the French BSN and of Fiat; Sir Peter Walters, chairman of Midland Bank and of Blue Circle Cement, and deputy chairman of Thorn EMI amongst others; Baron Janssen in Belgium; and Karl Otto Pohl, the former president of the Deutsche Bundesbank in Germany, who has continued to add to his directorships since retiring from the bank. His blue chip jobs include membership of J. P. Morgan's international council and an advisory directorship at Unilever. He is also partner in one of Germany's biggest private banks, Sal Oppenheim, and has directorships in Bertelsmann and the Dutch investment group Robeco. The Swedish tycoon Peter Wallenberg does even better: he is chairman of Atlas Copco, Providentia, Investor, and Stora, and deputy chairman of ASEA, Telefon, Ericsson, Electrolux and SE Banken as well as of the Swiss Bank Corporation.

Just to take one of those companies Peter Wallenberg is deputy chairman of: Electrolux. The board contains representatives of the Swedish industrial élite: the chairman of Saab-Scania, the deputy chairmen of Axel Johnson and Nordbanken; directors of Atlas Copco, Stora, Ericsson, ASEA, Astra, Svenska Handelsbanken, Trelleborg, and Gota Bank. This is not an isolated example. On the other side of the Atlantic the board of IBM contains, *inter alia*, the chairmen and chief executive officers (CEOs) of Pepsico, J. C. Penney, Boeing, and du Pont, and the CEOs of Eastman Kodak and Chevron, quite apart from 'mere' directors of other companies.

There are interesting cross-border links: Dirk de Bruyne, chairman of the supervisory councils of Royal Dutch Shell and ABN–AMRO, was formerly also a director of the British company, Ocean Group. At the end of 1991 Ocean Group hired another Dutchman as a non-executive director, John Loudon, who also has a connection with Shell, both his father and grandfather having been managing directors of the international oil group. He also sits on Heineken's board and his cousins are the chief executives of Akzo and Pierson, Heldring and Pierson.

You have only to look at the court of governors (July 1991) of Henley Management College to appreciate the British establishment at work. The chairman is Sir Denys Henderson, chairman of ICI; then there is the chairman of Barclays Bank, Sir John Quinton, and two other directors of the bank, Lord Camoys and Sir Michael Franklin; the chairmen of Dalgety, Bechtel, and Total Oil Holdings UK; the chief executives of Smiths Industries and of Thorn EMI; and the permanent secretary of the Department of Employment, and Bill Jordan, the President of the AEU, among others. Non-British members include Ellen Schneider-Lenné, director of Deutsche Bank, Serge Tchuruk, chairman and CEO of Total, and Mr N. Kobayashi, chairman and CEO of Mitsubishi (UK). 'When they get together', an awed insider said to us, 'they know everyone who counts.'

Classes of directors

Directors can be grouped into three main classes:

(i) Directors who also have executive functions in the company. Sometimes, as with Colin Southgate, chairman of Thorn EMI, or Hilmar Kopper, chairman of the management board of Deutsche Bank, they will also have other directorships, but there can be no doubt as to where their primary allegiance lies.

(ii) Directors who have no executive responsibility. In Britain and the USA they will be called non-executive directors; in Germany and the Netherlands they will be members of the supervisory council. That is not to say, of course, that there are no other companies in which they have executive power and responsibility. Thus Edgar S. Woolard Jr is a non-executive director of IBM. He is, however, also chairman and chief executive officer of E.I. du Pont de Nemours & Co.. Giovanni Agnelli is director of Credito Italiano, but, as is well known, he is also chairman of Fiat.

(iii) At a second level – but still very important in a multinational – there will be directors of the major subsidiaries, and one should not underestimate the honour and prestige of being a director of such major companies in their own right as Hanson Industries Inc. or Deutsche Shell. It goes without saying, of course, that Deutsche Shell, like all major German companies, will have to have its own supervisory council.

Directors' roles

Another way of looking at directors is to see them as having six main functions:

(i) To run the operations of the company as the executive management.

This is, after all, the purpose of the directorate, and remains its job in all but the larger corporations: multinationals are more complicated.

(ii) In multinationals, boards more often operate at a strategic level and regard their job as one of monitoring management rather than managing the operations.

(iii) The work of monitoring management referred to above may, in fact, consist of monitoring the management board (from a supervisory level), or monitoring the executive directors from a non-executive level.

(iv) To give their advice and experience, whether from a business point of view as Sir John Harvey-Jones does at Grand Metropolitan, or at a political level as Mr P. D. Sutherland, former EC Commissioner, does at BP.

(v) To represent outside interests, whether of shareholders, as do the Volvo directors on the board of Renault, of the state, as do state directors on the boards of the Italian and Spanish state companies ENI and INI, or of the employees, as do the employee directors appointed by law on the boards of German and Swedish companies.

(vi) International networking. This is such an interesting aspect that we comment on it separately and in greater length later on in this chapter.

NATIONAL ATTITUDES

The three main categories

Despite the similarities there are also many differences between national attitudes. We have discerned three main strands:

(i) The Anglo-Saxon world: there is a growing concern for governance which is frequently mentioned in the company reports, though there are significant differences between the US and British approaches.

(ii) The north European attitude: there is little mention of the subject of governance, and we have not seen the actual word referred to at all, but there is an institutionalisation of boardroom monitoring in several countries, and a marked concern to highlight the importance of employee participation. German law has just changed, and as a result employees of German companies have held elections for managerial employee committees and spokespersons' committees. Deutsche Bank has engaged in discussions with these committees on personnel and business policy.

(iii) The south European (and Japanese) approach, with little sign of a recognition of the need either to cater for governance or to discuss formal employee involvement. This does not mean that these companies do not care for their employees. The strength of the employer-employee relationship in Japanese companies is well-known.

Corporate governance: Anglophone attitudes

US corporations: the formalisation of governance

Major US corporations are at great pains to spell out the care they take to ensure compliance with best practice in corporate governance. They do this by a formal statement in their annual reports, couched in almost identical terms. Du Pont is typical. It has 18 directors, of whom four are full-time and two are ex-employees. There are three committees of the board: the finance, the audit and the compensation committees. The audit committee of six persons has the oversight of the company's accounting controls and accounting principles. Subject to shareholder approval, this committee also has the responsibility for employing the external auditors. Both the internal and the external auditors have the right of direct access to this committee, whom they meet from time to time, with and without management present, to discuss accounting, auditing and financial reporting matters. In du Pont as in other companies, no member of this committee is an officer or full-time employee of the company, nor a member of the finance committee. There are other committees, of course, such as the compensation committee, which is entirely composed of outside directors, and the finance committee, which has a majority of outside directors.

Some companies go so far as to spell out the fact that it is the audit committee's job to follow up on reports by both the internal and the external auditors as well as to have regular meetings with the various government agencies the company is concerned with.

The existence of an audit committee is absolutely standard practice, but some companies go further and have a whole structure of board committees. Citibank has sixty-seven committee places for its twenty-three board members, who are spread over the following committees:

(i) Audit: all non-executives; meets four times a year; this committee meets not only the auditors, both internal and external, but also the principal regulatory agencies.

(ii) Committee on directors, which deals with directors' compensation and recommends qualified persons for election to the board.

(iii) Committee on subsidiaries and capital.

(iv) Consulting committee: Citicorp directors, on a consultative basis.

   (v) Executive committee.
  (vi) Fiduciary and investment review committee.
 (vii) Financial institutions acquisitions committee.
(viii) Personnel committee.
  (ix) Public issues committee.

British corporations: a wide diversity

British boards show a much greater diversity of approach. There is, of course, no *legal* obligation to have non-executive directors on the board. The late Robert Maxwell had definite ideas on the subject: 'Someone has got to be in charge,' he was reported to have said in a radio interview, 'and all this nonsense about independent directors is a complete waste of time.' Yet he too had to bow to the prevailing business climate and had to demonstrate the presence, at least, of non-executive directors on the boards of his companies. In practice, few major British public companies would dare risk public criticism by not having outside independent directors. Even companies such as Sainsbury, where the family shareholding stake has been estimated at about 40 per cent, make sure they have outside directors: six of Sainsbury's board members are non-executive directors. We could find only one company in the FT-100 list of companies that did not have any non-executive directors, and that was Lonrho PLC. At the time of writing, in Spring 1992, it was already under considerable attack for this attitude, particularly after its unsatisfactory 1991 results, and by April 1992 it had dropped out of the FT-100 index. Ms Anne Simpson, the joint managing director of Pension Investment Research Consultants, a consultancy for private pension funds in the UK and USA, criticised Lonrho for its attitude to the appointment of non-executives, saying that: 'we recommend that shareholders set Lonrho a timetable for producing a team of independent directors with first class track records to bring the board up to strength' (*Financial Times*, 6 February 1992). The phrase 'up to strength' is very revealing of the attitude of the pension fund industry.

    While it is common practice to refer to directors as executives and non-executives, there are wide differences in practice. At one extreme, Hanson PLC shows only three non-executives out of 14 directors in its 1990 accounts (though it has since appointed some more), and BAT has four non-executives out of 13 directors. In its annual report, BTR does not even distinguish between executive and non-executive, though this can be deduced from the description of their roles. The company has every legal right to take this approach. As the chairman, Sir Owen Green, pointed out (in a letter to the *Financial Times*, 16 December 1991), there is no such thing in law as a non-executive director – BTR regards every director as having a job to do. In fact the BTR board relies heavily on former executive directors. There is no mention of any board committees, though we should point out that this does not necessarily mean that they do not exist, merely that BTR has not seen fit to mention them in its annual report.

In the middle there are companies such as British Gas, where the number of non-executives equals the number of executive directors. At the other extreme there are large numbers of companies where the non-executives are in the majority: BP has a majority of non-executives, as have the clearing banks and major companies such as ICI and Guinness. Audit and Emoluments Committees are commonplace, and it is clearly regarded as best practice for these to consist only of the non-executive directors, even in companies such as Cable & Wireless that have a majority of executive directors on the board.

Grand Metropolitan follows US practice in having a number of committees which are listed in the 1991 report and accounts by Richard Giordano in his corporate governance report:

(i) Appraisal and remuneration committee: consists of the four non-executive directors only, chaired by the (non-executive) deputy chairman, Richard Giordano. It meets to appraise the performance of the executive directors (including the chairman and group chief executive) and certain other key executives, to determine their remuneration and to consider succession issues.

(ii) Audit committee.This committee consists of non-executive directors only, but with the internal and external auditors, chairman and group chief executive, group finance director and group financial controller normally present. It meets to consider audit, accountancy and financial control matters and to ensure that appropriate procedures are in place. It is the forum for ensuring that internal and external auditing procedures are properly co-ordinated and work effectively, and that it is reasonable for full reliance to be placed on the integrity and consistency of the figures in the annual report.

(iii) Chairman's committee: consists of the five executive directors and the executives responsible for group strategy and corporate affairs. It meets monthly under the CEO's direction to consider all policy matters not delegated to another committee.

(iv) Community affairs committee: this committee comprises the members of the chairman's committee and meets twice a year to discuss strategic plans and operating budgets for charitable and community activities.

(v) Group operations committee meets four times a year under Sir Allen Sheppard, the chairman and CEO, to discuss policy and operational issues that affect the group as a whole. Its membership consists of the members of the chairman's committee plus the legal director, company secretary and five senior general managers.

(vi) Management development committee, chaired by the chief operating officer. It meets twice a year to consider overall development and succession issues and to review development plans for the top 250 group executives. The membership consists of the chairman's committee and the deputy chairman.

(vii) Nomination committee: this consists of the chairman and CEO, Sir Allen Sheppard, and the two longest-serving non-executive directors. It meets, as appropriate, to consider possible changes to board or board committee membership, for recommendation to the full board.

Readers will note how the company's very top management echelon extends beyond the board, in that senior officers of Grand Metropolitan who are not main board directors are usually in attendance at many of these committee meetings.

It is invidious to select a company as an example of best practice, but perhaps Glaxo is a case in point. The latest accounts show that it has 15 directors, of whom seven are non-executive. The post of chairman (held by Sir Paul Girolami) is separated from that of chief executive (held by Dr E. Mario). There are four key board committees: the group executive committee, chaired by the chairman with a non-board executive, the group director corporate affairs, also present; the group appeals committee, two out of three of its members being non-executive, and the group audit and senior emoluments committees, all of whose members are non-executive. The non-executives are extremely distinguished, consisting of persons such as Sir Geoffrey Howe and Sir Ralf Dahrendorff. Three of the seven non-executive directors are not British.

British companies talk a lot about their approach to corporate governance, and both Grand Metropolitan and Thorn EMI have gone so far as to set out a statement on corporate governance in their annual reports. In 1990 these were written by Sir John Harvey-Jones and Sir Peter Walters respectively. Both make the point that the responsibilities of the non-executive directors are no different from those of the executive directors and that they are fully involved in strategic discussions. Sir John underlines their independence, saying they are a 'fiercely independent bunch', and that 'meetings are lively and robust events'. Grand Metropolitan's 1991 statement of corporate governance was written by Mr Richard Giordano, the deputy chairman as from 1 November 1991. We have already referred to his description of the different board committees but it is perhaps relevant to mention his comment, echoing Sir John Harvey-Jones' point from the previous year, that board discussions are 'lively and uninhibited' and that the experience and advice of the non-executives are sought, and are welcome even when that advice is not palatable.

A statement by the supervisory council on its role is standard in the annual reports of Dutch and German companies, while US companies will set out a statement on the financial controls and how the board committees of independent directors oversee these, deal with the internal and external auditors and monitor the financial reporting.

It will be interesting to see if such reports on governance become more common in Britain. We would welcome such a development, and also the fact that in this way we are seeing the beginnings of a move to a business climate where the non-executives too have to account publicly for their stewardship. We should also emphasise that this reflects a growing trend towards an even further separation of the roles of the two types of director, executive and non-executive.

Another interesting reflection is that while British informed opinion appears hostile to the idea of a supervisory two-tier system, many British companies have *de facto* accepted that there is a fundamental difference between executive and non-executive directors: they openly call them non-executives in their published statements and announcements of board appointments, and they emphasise the essentially supervisory nature of their role in overseeing audit and remuneration as Sir Peter Walters admits in the Thorn EMI report. Indeed BP, Thorn EMI and ICI are three companies out of many which have practically institutionalised the division of the boardroom's two groups by picturing the executive and non-executive directors on separate pages of their annual reports. The power of the BP non-executives was shown in June 1992 when they spearheaded the action to oust the respected chairman and CEO, Bob Horton, who had been too vigorous in his shake-up and modernisation of BP. Speaking at a conference on governance in summer 1991, Colin Short, ICI's finance director, said that though the ICI board was officially a unitary one, it was felt that with the weight of the non-executives that they had, the non-executives in fact worked at a supervisory level.

You might say that here we already have supervisory councils in all but name! This point was, in fact, stressed in the correspondence started by Sir Owen Green's letter to the *Financial Times*. Other correspondents agreed that there was no legal difference between the two types of director: a director was a director. They also argued, on the other hand, that actual practice had developed to the point where there was now a clear difference in their roles.

The supervisory concept: Dutch and German companies

As is well known, both Dutch and German major public companies have to have supervisory councils with a well-defined split of responsibilities between them and the management boards, as well as an obligation to have directors representing the employees on the supervisory councils. At the last count, no fewer than 30 of the 61 supervisory council members of the big three German banks were representatives of the employees or trade unions.

In northern European countries this concept of employee rights and entitlement to board seats is a well-established one. In Germany, as we have seen, this is institutionalised around the membership of the supervisory council. The deputy chairmen are usually employees. Thus the deputy chairman of Siemens' supervisory council, which contains at least four company chairmen, is a mechanic employed by the company, while that of Hoechst is an electrician, who is also the chairman of the works council. Indeed, Hoechst's supervisory council of 21 members contains seven members of the works council and only one member of the senior executives' committee. In Dutch companies this emphasis on the employee focuses on discussions with the management, particularly at such crucial times as mergers or major structural changes in the organisation.

The monitoring and controlling nature of the supervisory councils is made quite clear in their reports in the accounts of German and Dutch companies: they 'approve' the accounts presented by the management boards and 'concur' with their decision as to the dividend payment. The word 'governance', however, is not once mentioned in any of the financial statements we have seen, nor is there any comment on the need to check directors' remuneration nor any insistence on the independence of the audit. It may be that these things are taken for granted as being so naturally within the sphere of the supervisory council as not being worth mentioning.

Thus while British and US companies go out of their way to demonstrate the control non-executives are exercising on executives' pay and the financial controls on the company, perhaps taking their input into strategic matters for granted, with German and Dutch companies it is the other way round: they talk of strategic matters, perhaps taking the overview of matters such as executive remuneration for granted. Hoechst, for example, spells out how its supervisory council interests itself in research, in developments in the fine chemicals field, in technical matters and in social welfare in the united Germany. It is interesting to compare its committees with those of British and US companies. Hoechst has the following committees:

(i) Financial committee.
(ii) Technical and scientific committee.

(iii) Social welfare policy committee.

German companies make the point that the supervisory councils not only meet with management on various occasions but also receive verbal and written reports from the management boards.

The supervisory council of the Dutch bank ABN-AMRO concerned itself in the year 1990 specifically with the social plan that was implemented as a result of the merger of the two banks. Its latest report commented that during the year the permanent items on its agenda were:

(i) Balance sheet development.
(ii) Financial results.
(iii) Business development.
(iv) Major items of lending.
(v) Appointment of the auditors.

Akzo's supervisory council concerned itself with strategic matters such as planning, investments and divestments, but it also met regularly with the management board to discuss such matters as the financial statements and internal control.

Major Dutch and German companies have the inevitable array of prominent persons on their supervisory councils. The banks are well represented. Deutsche Bank, the largest German bank, has its own representatives on the boards of well over 100 German public companies. In its latest annual report it has had to list its shareholdings of over 10 per cent in German companies, and very interesting reading this makes too. The list of the bank's shares in blue chip German companies includes 28 per cent of Daimler-Benz (where it has three members on the supervisory council as noted below), and many others, which we have listed in Chapter 4 (page 64). Given the size of its holdings above 10 per cent one can only wonder at the extent of its stakes in companies below that level, which it was not forced to disclose.

Hoechst includes representatives from the boards of Commerzbank, Dresdner and ABN-AMRO on its supervisory council. This link with the banks is in line with British and US practice, but with a difference. Whereas the Anglo-Saxon emphasis is on the person, for his or her own qualities, the German emphasis is just as much on the bank the person represents. The link between Deutsche Bank and Daimler-Benz is extremely close. The chairman of the management board of Deutsche Bank is also the chairman of the supervisory council of Daimler-Benz. Currently (Spring 1992) it is Hilmar Kopper. Indeed, Daimler-Benz also has the honorary chairman of Deutsche Bank, Hermann Abs, as the honorary chairman of its supervisory council, as well the speaker for the board of Dresdner Bank, the chairman of the board of management of Commerzbank, and yet another member of the board of management of Deutsche Bank. Alfred Herrhausen sat on the supervisory council of Veba. After his assassination, his place was taken by his successor as chairman of Deutsche Bank's management board, Hilmar Kopper. The replacement was a matter of routine. The replacements went down the line: thus Hilmar Kopper's place on the supervisory council of Siemens AG was, in turn taken by his Deutsche Bank colleague Ulrich Cartellieri. Contrast this with British attitudes. Grand Metropolitan appointed Sir John Harvey-Jones as a non-executive director while he was still chairman of ICI. On his departure from the ICI chairmanship there was no question of his giving up his Grand Met chairmanship: he was valued by the latter because of his personal qualities, and so he remained a director.

The Royal Dutch Shell Group, as an Anglo-Dutch organisation, has an interesting compromise between the two business cultures. Royal Dutch has a supervisory council, Shell Transport has non-executive directors. The group's audit committee is made up of three members of the supervisory council plus three non-executive directors of Shell. That other Anglo-Dutch multinational, Unilever, follows much the same pattern. It has an advisory board of distinguished non-executive directors whose job it is to advise the board on a variety of business, social and economic issues. They are invited to serve on at least one of three committees which consist entirely of advisory board members: audit, external affairs and remuneration.

We are only concerned here with public companies. Family firms in both countries, like everywhere else, are a special world of their own. The German *Mittelstand* companies combine paternalism with autocracy and a reluctance to divulge more figures than they have to, to the outside world, as does the Dutch C & A group which is particularly well known for its secrecy.

A concern for the workforce

Swedish companies have a unitary board and, as already noted, these glitter with the jewels of the Swedish business establishment. As you go through the Swedish company boards, the outside directors always seem to come from the same companies, and the company names reappear again and again. Often the same directors' names reappear again and again. They also have worker directors, however. Electrolux is not untypical: out of 16 directors there are three employee representatives as well as their three deputies. The employee directors represent the trade unions, including the Foremen's and Supervisors' Union and the Swedish Federation of Salaried Employees.

In Denmark, too, there is a similar approach. Under the Danish Companies Act, No. 370, 13 June 1973, the employees may elect representatives to sit on company boards. Baltica Holding, the large Danish insurance group, with nearly 12,000 employees, is only one of many companies to take advantage of the provisions of the law. It has four employee directors (an insurance salesman and three senior clerks) out of a board of 13, and they are elected for a four-year term of office.

Directors rule, OK?

In most other European countries we could find little sign of any concern with either the need to comment on governance or to control the management, nor of any sign of employee representatives on the board, with the significant exception of such state companies as the French Crédit Agricole and Aerospatiale (see below).

There are differences between nationalities, however. Italian and Spanish state companies are very politicised, and their top directorates (as distinct from their executive managements) are chosen by government and therefore often reflect political allegiances and pressure groups. Even their managements are often politicised in practice and it is very common for senior managers to have links with political parties, or groups within them, and to use such linkages for their personal advancement. These links are well known by company insiders. This politicisation is a matter of considerable criticism, especially in Italy, where the *lottizazzione* or apportionment of spoils system is regarded as one of the most scandalous features of Italian public life. It is coming increasingly under attack but we doubt if it will change very quickly because of the enormous power of patronage it gives to politicians to reward their adherents – at no cost to themselves – with well-paid posts in the large number of companies in the public sector.

France is different because of the close inter-relationship at the *cadre* level between government, public administration and business. The directorate of Aerospatiale illustrates this perfectly. Of the 18 directors (not counting the Chairman), five represent the French state and include such persons as the controller-general of the armed forces; six persons are appointed by decree, and these include prominent personalities such as Bernard Attali, chairman of Air France; six represent the employees and one, the relatively small number of outside shareholders.

FOREIGNERS ON THE BOARD

Different national attitudes

An interesting aspect of the world of boardroom relationships is the atttitude of different companies, and most particularly, different national cultures, to the appointment of foreigners to the top boards. We define foreigners as persons of different nationality from the nationality of the company in question, and we have excluded persons appointed because of a shareholding relationship as, for example, Mr de Benedetti, who is chairman of the French domiciled company Cerus, or Mr Terumichi Tsuchida who represents the interests of Meiji Life on the board of Société Générale de France.The analysis makes interesting reading.

Japanese, Swedish, Italian, French and Spanish companies appear extremely nationalistic in their attitudes, though Nissan, like many other Japanese companies, emphasises its overseas 'good citizenship' in its 1990 financial statements, adding that four out of five of its major overseas manufacturing plants are managed by local CEOs, and also taking pains to show how much research and development is now carried out outside Japan. Honda takes the same approach as Nissan, but like Nissan it has no foreign directors on its main board.

Italian and French companies, too, tend to be very nationalistic in their choice of main board directors. The exceptions, such as Mr Felix Rohatyn on the board of Péchiney, and Mr Michel François-Poncet on the board of Banca Commerciale Italiana, are few in number, and are worthy of comment simply because of their rarity. Fiat, of course, has to be an inevitable exception, given its size and status as an international company and as the second biggest automobile manufacturing company in Europe. Its board contains several foreigners including Etienne Davignon and Antoine Amedé Riboud. Lyonnaise des Eaux-Dumez by contrast has only a couple of foreigners on its board and none, apparently, in its top management echelon. This is despite the fact that only 42 per cent of its turnover comes from France. Ciments Français too, even with 42 per cent of its business derived from international activities, still has a virtually total French board and executive. It is, however, worthy of comment that companies from even the most nationalistic of countries find that they have to use US citizens to run their US operations, an arrangement US companies do not universally reciprocate in Europe.

Germany

German companies used to be among the most nationalistic in the world, but this is now changing with their drive to become major players in global business. Their annual reports underline their emphasis on creating international staff groups and the training they are carrying out, not only of Germans in Germany. When Hoechst bought Celanese Corporation in the USA it took the opportunity to change its US operations from being dominated by Germans from Frankfurt, to becoming a US business, run by US citizens. Hoechst itself has three foreigners on its 21-member supervisory council: the ex-president of Switzerland, the chairman of the management board of ABN-AMRO and Mr Abdul Baqi Al-Nouri of the Kuwait Petrochemical Industries. Kaufhof has a Swiss banker on its supervisory council (which also contains representatives of the big three German banks). Deutsche Bank has a Briton, John Craven, on its management board. Admittedly, he is the British chief executive of its subsidiary Morgan Grenfell, but it is nonetheless worthy of comment that a foreigner has been admitted to that holy of holies, the management board of Deutsche Bank. He had to learn German though! The bank also has a Belgian, Mr André Leysen, on its supervisory council. He is also on the boards of Treuhand, BMW, Bayer and Viag, and is chairman of Hapag-Lloyd. It is a surprise, however, to note that Daimler-Benz has no foreigners on its boards and that Siemens only has one, the chairman of the board of administration of UBS.

Benelux and Switzerland

Even without considering the Anglo-Dutch Unilever and Shell, Dutch companies, like their Belgian cousins, are no stranger to foreigners on their boards of directors. Until his death, Alfred Herrhausen was the deputy chairman of Akzo's supervisory council, which also contained Mr J. G. A. Gandois, chairman of Péchiney, and Solvay numbers two foreigners among its 15 directors: Mr Hilmar Kopper and Sir John Milne (who replaced Lord Ezra on his retirement). With the appointment of Mr Eustace as vice-president for finance in March 1992, Philips could boast of two non-Dutch members of its board, the second being Dr Carruba, an American, the executive vice-president of technology. Cynical outsiders are uncertain as to whether this calling-in of foreign nationals represents a new open-mindedness on the part of the Philips Company, or whether it is a sign of its need for managerial rejuvenation.

Swiss companies too, even such establishment ones as Nestlé and Swiss Bank Corporation, have opened their boards to foreigners. Nestlé's non-Swiss directors include Paul Volcker. Ciba-Geigy goes further: one quarter of its board is non-Swiss (shown as non-Swiss domiciled in the annual report).

Britain and the USA

But it is the British and US companies that win the prize for internationalism in the composition of their boards. BP boasts four foreigners out of 10 non-executives, including Dr Hahn, the chairman of Volkswagen's management board. Commercial Union has a reputation for being one of the most international of British insurers, and has two foreigners on its board: Roger Faroux, president d'honneur of St Gobain (and also a former industry minister), and Professor Henk Melj, who is also a director of Unilever.

BAT has a German executive director, and ICI, the heart of the British establishment, goes even further. Its ten non-executive directors in 1990 included five non-Britons: Paul Volcker, who is also a director of Nestlé, Mr W. G. L. Kiep, the managing partner of a German insurance group, Mr S. Saba, adviser to the board of Toshiba Corporation, Mr T. H. Wyman, a director of several companies including General Motors, and Miss Ellen R. Schneider-Lenné, a member of the board of managing directors of Deutsche Bank, and as we have already noted, a governor of Henley. We have noticed in our researches how widespread the Deutsche Bank network is becoming, with directors on the boards of non-German companies in addition to its network of directorships on German company boards. There are exceptions, of course, to the internationalism of British company boards: BTR is an international company but its directorate is firmly British, as is that of Cable & Wireless, even though the bulk of its business is international. British clearing banks traditionally have restricted their directorships largely to British nationals, though this began to change with Barclays' appointment to its board in May 1991 of the deputy governor of the Japan Development Bank, and a Dutch national, who is also a Unilever main board director.

United States international companies, too, have appointed prestigious foreigners to their boards. IBM has the chairmen of Hoffman-La Roche and Henkel; Citibank has two foreigners out of 16 outsiders, a Dutchman and a Brazilian, while Philip Morris has the president of Tabacalera (perhaps not surprisingly), and Rupert Murdoch, an Australian.

NATIONAL AND INTERNATIONAL NETWORKING THROUGH THE BOARD

It is inevitable that companies regard the composition of their boards as a means of rallying their allies and promoting their business as well as representing their shareholders and obtaining best advice. There is a limit, however, to the number of people who can be appointed to the board without making it totally unwieldy and useless even as a talking shop. German and Dutch companies can make use of the mechanism of the supervisory council, but though companies in other countries are denied this possibility, the really smart company can gain the same objective by the device of having regional or advisory boards.

Lloyds Bank has done away with its regional boards, saying they serve no purpose any more, but other banks, such as NatWest in Britain and the Svenska Handelsbanken in Sweden, find they are still a useful way of networking. The German banks make considerable use of the advisory management board concept. Dresdner has 36 on its advisory council, most of whom are the chairmen of either the management boards or the supervisory councils of such companies as Allianz, Krupp, Deutsche Bundesbahn, Hoechst, Kaufhof, Preussag, Veba, Lufthansa, Bayer, and so on, a veritable roll-call of top German companies. Surprisingly there is only one foreigner, the president of SKF. Deutsche Bank's advisory board of 17 persons follows the same lines: the chairmen of top German companies, and, again disappointingly, only one foreigner, the chairman of the supervisory council of the Agfa-Gevaert Group. The prize must go to Commerzbank, however. It not only has an advisory board of 19 members (top chairmen, one non-German), it also lists the members of its regional advisory committees in its annual report for all the world to see. These contain the great and the good of the *Länder*. A small *Land* like Schleswig-Holstein might only have an advisory committee of nine members, North Rhine-Westphalia, on the other hand, has 96 members! You wonder, cynically, what they all do, and if they all ever meet together.

ABN-AMRO also has an advisory council, which appears to contain no foreign nationals, but Swiss Bank Corporation applies this concept on an international scale and its international advisers are very international indeed, including such persons as the president of Litton Industries, the Rt Hon. David Howell MP, Cesare Romiti of Fiat, the chairman of the management board of Thyssen, and Peter Wallenberg, to name just a few. Having advisers of such eminence is really networking on a mega-scale. United States companies, too, make use of this concept. The much admired J. P. Morgan Bank has the following:

(i) A board of 17 directors which includes the cream of the US business establishment, such as the president of Exxon.
(ii) An international council under the presidency of the Hon. G. P. Shultz, with 13 non-Americans out of 22, such as the presidents of Stora, Bunge & Born, Peugeot, Fuji-Xerox, Société Générale de Belgique,

and Nestlé, the chairmen of Akzo and Courtaulds, and Carlo de Benedetti.
(iii) There is also a directors' advisory council of ex-chairmen of major corporations.

IBM goes one further. In addition to its main board it has an advisory board of 22 members: 12 of these are retired senior IBM officers. The others include William McChesney Martin, retired chairman of the Federal Reserve Board, and William Scranton, former governor of Pennsylvania and US ambassador to the United Nations. As if that were not enough, it rallies its regional support through regional boards: Asia Pacific; Europe, Middle East and Africa; and Latin America. Usually around half of the membership of these boards is non-executive, with persons of the calibre of Kenichi Ohmae, the managing director of the National Australia Bank, Romano Prodi, the chairman of Svenska Cellulosa and the vice-chairman of Unibanco Brazil. It will be interesting to see how these regional boards will fit into the new, more devolved, structure of IBM that was announced in late 1991.

INFLATION IN TITLES

Reviewing organisation charts is a bewildering business. It is common knowledge that the vice-presidents of AGIP, for instance, have a very different role and position from the innumerable vice-presidents of the typical American bank, and that there are whole hierarchies of directors in service companies, such as consultancies, who are given the title to make them sound more important though they may have nothing to direct. The inflation in titles, however, is now threatening to get completely out of hand.

Once upon a time it was very simple. The person who chaired the meetings of the board of directors and was the company's public face to the outside world was the chairman, and the person who ran the company was the managing director. But who is in charge now, and what do all those people whose names are listed in the annual reports really do?

IBM has a chairman, a president and a chairman of its executive committee, as well as 11 senior vice presidents and 52 vice presidents. The Midland Bank has a chairman, vice chairman, two deputy chairmen and a CEO. Who takes the chair if the chairman is absent, the vice or one of the deputy chairmen? Barclays Bank lists them the other way round, but it too has two deputy chairmen and one vice-chairman.

J. P. Morgan has three vice-chairmen but no deputies. Banco Bilbao

Viscaya has resolved the problem: it has a first and a second deputy chairman. Nissan has a chairman, a president, three executive vice-presidents, five executive managing directors, 12 managing directors and 22 directors. Marks & Spencer has a chairman and chief executive, a deputy chairman and managing director, and a simple managing director. Sainsbury has two joint managing directors who are clearly junior to the chairman and chief executive. Dai-Ichi Kangyo Bank, as befits the world's biggest bank, has a chairman, a president, two deputy presidents, 12 senior managing directors, 12 managing directors and 19 directors, all Japanese despite being an international bank.

It is well known that Lords Hanson and White run the Hanson Group, yet, to add to the confusion, Lord White is not even a main board director of Hanson PLC, the top company in the group.

We have no doubt that inside the well-ordered companies that we surveyed everyone is perfectly well aware of how important the senior executives are, and the relative order of their importance, but pity the poor outsider trying to make sense of it all!

Then we have some quite extraordinary titles: du Pont and Bechtel have a president emeritus, while Philip Morris has both a chairman and a director emeritus. Goldman Sachs Group has a senior chairman, Solvay has an honorary chairman, the Société Générale de Belgique, an honorary president, Société Générale de France, on the other hand, has two honorary chairmen, and the Belgian Delhaize company has a whole group of honorary members of the board, including no less than four honorary chairmen and two honorary directors. There is also one honorary member of the management committee.

Petrofina's list of executives sums up the inflation in titles. It has the following:

(i) On its board: a chairman, a deputy chairman, a managing director, three executive directors, a director and honorary chairman, 12 directors, a director and honorary deputy chairman, a president of honour, five honorary directors and the secretary-general.

(ii) Its management consists of: the chief executive officer and managing director (who is the single managing director on the board), the three executive directors on the board, five general managers, a senior adviser, and 11 vice-presidents.

And who is the boss? Perhaps one clue is provided by the list shown in the financial statements: this usually puts the chairman before the president, though Electrolux lists the chairman, then the two deputy chairmen, and only then the president and CEO. Nobel of Sweden, however, lists the chairman first and the president and chief executive officer last. Sainsbury heads its list with the joint presidents, followed by the chairman and chief executive. SKB shows its chief executive as third in the list, but he is clearly the most senior as he is ahead of the chairman and in the centre of the group photograph! When the directors and officers are listed in alphabetical order there is no way of telling who is the most senior.

GOVERNANCE AND SUCCESS

We would emphasise that governance and the appointment of outside directors are no substitutes for entrepreneurship and business success. The Hanson and BTR Groups have been criticised for the way they use (or rather, do not use) outside directors, but there can be few complaints about their business performance. At the other end of the scale no amount of non-executive directors were proof against Midland Bank's Crocker Bank disaster, nor did the existence of the supervisory councils in Philips or in Continental, the German tyre company, guard against business downturns. Even the most prestigious outside directors did not save BP from adverse criticism over its dividend policy early in 1992 when its profits declined. Similarly, non-executive directors can be in place but be regarded as ineffective as the various legal actions from the collapse of the Maxwell business empire in 1991 revealed.

But structure is important and significant. It may only be a straw in the wind, but it is interesting that CMB, the Anglo-French canning manufacturer, which has just undergone a dramatic organisational shake-up, has reorganised its command structure, changing from a unitary board – on Anglo-French lines – to a two-tier board system in all but name: a management board of executive directors, and a supervisory or partners' council, on which are represented the shareholders and such interested and committed outsiders as Lazard Frères, advisers to the group. Another group, the British Reuters company, manages very well with what is effectively a two-tier system: it has executive directors, coupled with trustees in a supervisory role. The trustees are charged with safeguarding the company's independence, integrity and freedom from bias in the gathering and dissemination of news and information. Its share structure is designed to prevent any one group from owning more than 30 per cent of the votes in Reuters Holdings. The trustees, who contain such illustrious names as Mrs Katherine Graham, the owner of the *Washington Post*, have enough shares to carry the day at AGMs in cases where they believe any other group is seeking control of the business.

The final word, however, goes to the French state aircraft company Snecma, where the directors are divided into the following categories in the 1990 financial report: directors appointed for their specific expertise; directors representing the government; directors representing the shareholders; directors representing the employees; the government auditor; the government commissioner; and the representative of the company's central employee committee. No one could describe a company's success to the interested parties more clearly than that.

4 THE LEGAL AND CULTURAL BACKGROUND

OWNERSHIP AND CONTROL OF CORPORATIONS

The different approaches

So far we have discussed the events of the late 1980s and early 1990s as well as the way companies have actually reported their situations. It is now appropriate to stand back and take a look at the legal and regulatory regimes in the main European countries, and examine these against the background of their business cultures. That is the subject of this chapter.

One way of characterising different countries' business climates is to divide them into bank-based and market-based financial systems. The former are characterised by banks that are closely involved in ownership in the corporate sector, the latter by corporate sectors that rely more heavily on the securities markets for their financial requirements. Germany and Japan are examples of the former, the UK and USA (and Anglophone countries in general) of the latter. In Germany banks hold shares either in their own right or as custodians for others, and are heavily represented on company boards. In Japan, while no bank may hold more than 5 per cent of an individual firm, already in 1985 the banks held in aggregate 18 per cent of corporate equity. Figures are not easy to come by, but research has shown that Japanese companies tend to borrow from the banks who are also their own shareholders.

In the UK and the USA it is not the custom for banks to hold company equity – except by default when a company crashes – and their representatives do not sit *as bank representatives* on company boards, though bank directors as individuals are well represented. Therefore, in the Anglophone countries banks can only exercise control through the normal lending process, and while the impact of this should not be underestimated, it is nonetheless true that in Germany and Japan this influence can be exercised more directly. In Germany and Japan it is not only the banks' holding of the equity that distinguishes them – often it is quite modest – it is the cross-holding of that equity. Their power is still used sparingly – typically in Germany action is taken only when there is transparently poor performance, and in Japan when a rescue operation is necessary. This is true not only of Germany and Japan but of other countries as well. Banks hold corporate equity and their directors sit on company boards also in France and Spain, and they are often instrumental in restructuring firms.

The Anglophone countries are the exceptions

What is important to understand is that it is the Anglophone countries that are the exceptions, and that Britain is very much the exception in Europe.

There is another significant difference, and that is the number of public companies in existence. Table 4.1 sets out the number of listed domestic companies on the various international stock exchanges in 1991. It will be obvious that the fewer listed companies there are, the fewer the public takeovers that can take place.

Stock exchange	Number of listed domestic companies
Amsterdam	232
Copenhagen	290
Germany	609
London	1,804
Luxembourg	422
Madrid	369
Milan	228
Paris	459
Australia	1,393
Hong Kong	282
NASDAQ	4,179
New York	1,604
Tokyo	1,571
Toronto	1,147

Table 4.1   Stock exchanges with over 200 listed domestic companies

Source: Christoper Nobes, Coopers Deloitte Professor of Accounting at the University of Reading, taken from the article 'Financial reporting in France and Spain', *Management Accounting*, October 1991.

The difference is essentially between outsider and insider systems, and that, in a sense, is what this book is all about. Outsider systems, as in the Anglophone countries, are identified in the Centre for Economic Policy

Research (CEPR) discussion paper no. 603 (1991) as having the following characteristics:

(i) Dispersed ownership and control.
(ii) Separation of ownership and control.
(iii) Little incentive for outside investors to participate in corporate control.
(iv) A climate where hostile takeovers are not unusual, and they can be costly and antagonistic.
(v) The interests of other stakeholders are not represented.
(vi) Low commitment of outside investors (whatever they may say in public!) to the long-term financial strategies of the company.
(vii) Takeovers may create monopolies.

Insider systems, on the other hand, are much more common in Japan and continental Europe, and they are characterised by the following:

(i) Concentrated ownership.
(ii) The association of ownership with control.
(iii) Control by related parties such as banks, partners and employees.
(iv) Absence of hostile takeovers: in fact, an aversion to them.
(v) The interests of other stakeholders are represented.
(vi) The intervention of the outside investors is limited to periods of clear financial failure.
(vii) Insider systems may create collusion and cartels.

One of the features of insider systems is that in practice, shareholding is concentrated in a group of key insider investors such as banks, business partners and related companies. Even where there are outside investors the existence of dual classes of shares allows insiders to retain control by restricting the outside shareholders' voting rights. This is now being eroded, but only slowly. Takeovers are decided within the family as it were, and outsiders have the cards stacked against them, as Leopoldo Pirelli (an insider in Italy, of course) found to his cost when trying to take over Continental, the German tyre company, in 1991. In Germany he was an outsider.

Indeed, there have been only four reported cases of hostile takeovers of German public companies in the post Second World War period (if one includes Krupp–Hoesch). In Japan, hostile takeovers are virtually unknown. The incentive to monitor and control company managements is not through disposals of ownership but is provided by the substantial stakes other companies have in the company in question: cross-holdings representing allies, suppliers and purchasers, as well as the banks as providers of finance. It may be control through co-operation but it is none the less effective for all that. When the stakeholder-shareholders want to intervene, they have the means to do so. All this makes short-termism less likely because shareholdings are stable over long periods of time. Major share-holders are implicitly in for the long term.

In the Anglophone countries, competition for the control of firms through takeovers (at least in the roaring eighties) kept inefficient firms on their toes by the constant threat of being taken over by those willing to pay. It is widely felt that this fear makes managements look to the short term at the expense of investment, R & D and training. A further drawback is that the process of auction is often accompanied by hostility and antagonism. Look at the way Lonrho fought off Bond by, rightly, detailing his indebtedness. But even in lesser cases it is expensive in resources used up and in the public insults traded between the two parties. Nor does this process consider the interests of any of the stakeholders besides the shareholders. This has already resulted in many US states moving to impose stringent limitations on the operations of the takeover process.

Impediments to takeovers

The general complaint in Britain is that the playing field is not level, and in many ways this is true. The continentals play by different rules when it comes to governance. As we have already pointed out, their view of the company is different from that in the UK. As a consequence, takeovers are much more difficult, if not nearly impossible, in most continental countries as the comparison with the UK in Figure 4.1 shows.

Continental countries have erected barriers to takeovers that would not for a moment be tolerated in most Anglophone countries, though these are now being slowly weakened. We have already referred to some of them in this book. In Sweden for instance, even though it is under attack, the Wallenberg family holds enormous power through a corporate structure that would rightly be regarded as completely unfair in Britain. It is reputed to hold about one-third in value of the Stockholm bourse through a network of often minority holdings. In Switzerland too, the same situation obtains, where companies can restrict the voting rights of holders of their equity, as Nestlé still does, though to a lesser extent than previously. When Mr Klaus Jacobs sold Jacobs Suchard to Philip Morris in 1990 he owned only 34 per cent of the share capital, but he had 60 per cent of the company's voting rights. In Germany too, companies such as Deutsche Bank, Veba, Bayer and many others all have clauses in their articles limiting the voting rights of a single shareholder to 5 per cent or 10 per cent, irrespective of the actual

	Belgium	France	Germany	Italy	Netherlands	Spain	UK
Supervisory boards			●●		●●		
Shareholders voting powers	●●	●●	●●	●	●●		
Availability of information							
– list of shareholders	●●	●●	●●	●●	●●	●●	
– financial	●●	●	●	●		●●	
Monopolies/cartel commissions	●	●●	●	●		●	●●
Management barriers/powers		●●	●●	●	●●		*
Quality of financial information	●●	●		●		●●	
Availability of companies on Stock Exchange	●●		●	●●		●●	
Ability to obtain 'inside' advisers	●	●	●●	●●	●		
Lack of emphasis on shareholder value	●●	●	●●	●●	●●	●●	
Attitude to unfriendly takeover bids	●●	●	●●	●●	●	●	

*Possible, but heavily criticised where used.

Key
No impediments   Left blank
Some impediments   ●
Substantial impediments   ●●

Figure 4.1   Continental barriers to takeovers

Source: Nigel Kendall and Thomas Sheridan, *Finanzmeister*, 1991

number of shares held. A further device in Germany, France and Italy in particular, is to protect companies from hostile bids by a series of cross-shareholdings, and in the Latin countries, the power of the 'families' can be clearly seen: the Agnellis and de Benedettis in Italy, the Mellos in Portugal, the banking families in Spain, the networks of the Banque Worms and Banque Indo-Suez in France. In those countries alliances are often very personal and can be very dynastic indeed. The takeover battle for Perrier that surfaced in the first half of 1992 was a dramatic example of how personal and dynastic company management can be even in France.

THE UK

The legal framework: companies

There are about a million registered companies in the UK, of which some 7,000 are plcs. The law implicitly assumes growth and survival, but the key aim of companies is to make a profit, both for the providers of capital and as a source of investment for future growth.

The shareholders have the main interest in the company. Their interest is a property right which is limited by the extent of their shareholding, hence the term 'limited liability'. The other stakeholders, such as creditors and providers of finance, have a contract with the company which defines their interest. The company is managed by shareholders in general meeting who may (and usually do) delegate their powers to the directors. The directors are appointed by the shareholders, though, in practice, the shareholders usually confirm the appointments made by the board between public share-holders' meetings. The function of the board, which is a collective function and responsibility, is determining:

  (i) The company's purpose and 'ethics'.
 (ii) Deciding the direction, that is, the strategy.
(iii) Planning.
 (iv) Delegating to managers or committees of the board and controlling them.
  (v) Reporting and recommending to shareholders.

Directors

The directors are elected by shareholders in general meeting, and while the law in the UK provides for them to have regard to the interests of employees and to those who have legal contracts with the company, there is no legal requirement for any specific party or interest group to be represented on the board. It is up to the annual general meeting of the shareholders. No employee consents are required for company actions such as takeovers or mergers.

The directors' duty is to the company and to those to whom the company has a legal liability. Directors have a duty to ensure compliance with the Companies Acts 1985 and 1989 in relation to the preparation of company accounts, and though one director may actually sign them, there is implied approval by all the directors unless they have taken steps to show otherwise. Directors – all directors – have personal liability if the company can be shown to have been trading 'wrongfully', that is, continuing to trade when there was no reasonable prospect of its being able to pay its debts.

The law does not recognise any separate class of director, such as executive and non-executive. All directors are equally responsible, and furthermore the decisions that are taken are of the whole board, even if a director has voted against it. Authorities are increasingly taking action for breaches of statutory or other duties by directors.

Under the provisions of the 1985 Insolvency Act, a director who fails to take every step he or she ought to have taken to prevent the company going into insolvent liquidation if he or she knew or ought to have concluded that there was no reasonable prospect of avoiding the outcome, may be required by the court to contribute personally to the company's assets for the benefit of the creditors. The main purpose of the recent legislation is to protect company creditors and shareholders, and this is being achieved by making directors personally liable. Resignation will not relieve a director of this liability.

The law has widened the number of persons who may be considered directors. Directors are recognised by their functions and authority as well as the power that they exercise, rather than by the title alone. In some companies the title of director is handed out liberally – often as an excuse for paying less than adequate salaries. However there is also another side to the coin. All persons in accordance with whose directions or instructions the directors are accustomed to act (that is, the shadow directors so-called) may be treated as if they were directors for the purposes of the Companies Acts and for associated legislation such as the Insolvency Acts.

Some of the statutes that can affect British business people are set out in Appendix 4.1.

GERMANY

The legal framework

There are basically two types of company in Germany: the *Gesellschaft mit beschranker Haftung* (GmbH) or limited liability company, and the *Aktiengesellschaft* (AG) or stock corporation. The former is the most popular type of business organisation for private companies, and there is no legal responsibility to have a supervisory council unless the company employs more than 500 persons. However, in this book, we are concerned with the second, the public company, of which there are some 2,500–3,000, and, as we have already noted, only about 600 of these are quoted on the stock exchange. The total capital of the AGs is smaller than that of the 360,000 GmbHs.

The AG can issue bearer or registered shares and it is common for the articles to provide (as in many UK private companies) that any transfer of shares must be subject to the approval of the company ('vinculation'). It is estimated that about one-third of all AGs have made use of this provision. Cross-holdings between companies are permitted up to certain levels. Allianz Insurance announced in July 1991 that it owned 23 per cent of the Dresdner Bank, while Dresdner, in its turn, owned 10 per cent of Allianz (*Financial Times*, 30 July 1991). Mr Wolfgang Roller, CEO of Dresdner Bank, revealed to shareholders that the bank had 10 per cent of Allianz at the AGM held in May 1991). As this book was going to press, this relationship was under sustained attack by the federal cartel office, which claimed that the real figures were higher than that because of indirect holdings. We have already pointed out that a number of AGs have also introduced limitations on the voting rights of shareholders, such as limiting voting powers to 5 per cent or 10 per cent of capital no matter how many shares are actually owned. Mannesmann, Bayer and Deutsche Bank limit any one shareholder to 5 per cent of the votes, regardless of the actual stake. At Volkswagen the figure is 20 per cent, and at Hoesch, 15 per cent. It is worthy of comment that Hoesch's restriction did not stop Krupp effectively taking it over once the banks had decided that control by Krupp was necessary for commercial reasons. It was, of course, a German solution, and the minority shareholders were virtually ignored.

It often requires a 75 per cent board majority to change these restrictive shareholding rules. This was one of the areas where Pirelli so badly stubbed its toes in its abortive 'takeover' of Continental (see p. 17). A Pirelli takeover, by definition, would not have been a German solution!

German companies have to have a two-tier structure: a management board and a supervisory council. We must emphasise that the correct translation of the German term *Aufsichsrat* is supervisory council, not supervisory board, and that the law which governs companies makes it quite plain that the body that runs companies is the *Vorstand*, which is composed of professional managers. It is not that one is superior to the other, as is commonly believed in Britain: they function side by side with different but very specific duties. The phrase 'two-tier' therefore gives the wrong impression. The management board has total responsibility for managing the company, both its day-to-day operations as well as questions of policy. It must be emphasised that the supervisory council plays no part in management, which is why we are careful to use the word 'council' in this book. Its role is to appoint and control the members of the management board. In practice, a company's articles frequently provide that major matters require the approval of the supervisory council. The members of the management board, however, are in a strong position with their five-year tenure of office. Basically, therefore, the supervisory council can be likened in many ways to a British board of directors, and the management board to its executive committee.

It is an interesting comment that it is extremely likely that Czechoslovak companies will adopt the two-tier system on their privatisation. The privatisation plan of the Czech Power Company (one of the largest companies in the country) provides for a supervisory council and a management board. The plan states that the membership of the supervisory council will be equally divided between the representatives of the shareholders and of the employees.

The labour laws

The labour law is based on employee representation and co-determination, both at shop floor and supervisory council level. The *Betriebs-verfassungsgesetz* – BetrVG ('Works Constitution Act') states that one-third of the members of the supervisory council of any AG or of a GmbH with over 500 employees must be elected by the employees. As a result of the *Mitbestimmungsgesetz* – MitbestG ('Co-determination Act'), 1976, half of the supervisory councils of AGs and GmbHs which have over 2,000 employees must be employee representatives. In practice, the chairman of the supervisory council, who has a casting vote, is invariably a representative of the shareholders. The employees, however, are strongly protected by the provision that a 75 per cent vote is required for changes to the articles, including any changes in share capital, mergers and liquidations – though it could be argued that in the latter case the situation could be such that there would not be much protection for anyone any more!

Employee representation at shop floor level is based on the Works Constitution Act, which provides for the formation of a works council or *Betriebsrat* at all plants with over five employees. It has the following responsibilities:

   (i) To ensure compliance with all statutes and collective bargaining agreements protecting the employee.
  (ii) To recommend actions for the benefit of the plant and the employee.
 (iii) To serve as an intermediary between employees and employer to take care of such special groups as the handicapped, the young and old, foreigners, etc.

A works council has a wide range of measures available, from access to information to real co-determination in social matters such as the fixing of general working conditions. Where there are substantial changes in the operation of the business the works councils of plants with more than 20 employees have to be consulted about such changes in advance. These substantial changes include:

(i) The closing down or reduction of plant facilities or a substantial part of these facilities.
(ii) The relocation of the facilities or a substantial part of them.
(iii) The merger of facilities.
(iv) Substantial changes in the purpose of the organisation or the organisation of facilities.
(v) Introduction of new working or manufacturing methods.

Where there are such changes the employer is under an obligation to agree with the works council on a compensation plan which should harmonise the potentially conflicting interests of the employer and the workforce in a reorganisation. The employer and the works council must agree on a scheme to compensate the employee for the social disadvantage caused by the reorganisation (*Sozialplan*). Mass dismissals always require such a compensation scheme.

The law on employee representation has been further tightened in the early 1990s and German companies are adapting themselves to this.

Business attitudes

An industrial not a financial culture

The German business culture is like the Japanese in that it does not regard the company as a piece of property, owned by its shareholders to do with what they will, but as a community, with obligations to its employees, customers and the surrounding communities, as well as to those who have provided it with finance. Profit is of course necessary and essential if the company is to survive and grow, but it is not an end in itself. Both investors and employees can take a long view because in their different ways they are locked in, and they have a structure of governance that separates the long from the short term. The stakeholders therefore understand why dividends should be kept low in less than good times (let alone bad times) and money retained in the business. It has been reckoned that the UK's top 100 companies pay at least twice as much and sometimes three times as much out of their profits as their German counterparts. Corporate Germany takes a long term view, epitomised by the ambition of the *Mittelstand* companies, to provide for 'life beyond the grave'.

A notable feature of both German and Japanese companies is the quietness of the dialogue between the interested parties in a takeover situation. Effective dialogue is almost impossible through megaphones as in a British or US takeover battle. In a German company the bloodbath takes place much more tidily (but no less bloodily!) in private, and a communiqué at the end will announce the names of the victors. British business people often console themselves with the thought that the German supervisory system is bureaucratic and over-rigid. When you look at the two countries' economic performance, you can only wish that the UK had some of this rigidity!

Germany: an example for Britain?

What the two-tier system in Germany does is to create a structure that makes accountability easier, and that, after all, is what governance is all about. It has been said that German companies are really dominated by a couple of key managers and the banks. That is about as true as saying that British companies are dominated by one or two strong personalities and no one else. Of course it happens. It is never possible to generalise. All that can be said with regard to Germany is that the system is there with its built-in safeguards. The chairman of the supervisory council always comes from the management side, and always has the casting vote. Even so, in practice, management has ceased to regard itself as exclusively answerable to the shareholders. This attitude extends to reporting as well, and one of the complaints German companies have about the US and UK financial regulatory regimes is against what they regard as the over-frequent profit reporting that these entail.

Article 14 of the German constitution declares that 'ownership involves obligations', and that 'its use should at the same time serve the common good'. The mission statement of a company like Continental places commitment to profit a poor fourth after commitment to quality, customers and employees. Compare this with the attitude of a British company such as Hawker Siddeley, which thought it a reasonable defence against BTR in 1991 to propose the sale of some 60 per cent of its businesses, presumably as a prelude to acquiring other businesses. You wonder what the bankers (and employees) on a typical German supervisory council would have made of that.

The two-tier system may be a recipe for stability, but German managements had better not be complacent. Julian Franks and Colin Mayer of City University have studied the restructuring of three firms in the 1980s: AEG, MAN and Bayer. The firms all hit trouble, and there were dividend cuts, closures and redundancies, though, significantly, spending on R & D and on capital projects was maintained. Managerial turnover was high in these three companies over the decade: AEG had eight departures from the two boards and 11 new arrivals on its management board alone, MAN had two departures and seven arrivals, and Bayer 11 departures and seven arrivals.

The power of the banks

When discussing governance with German business people, we have to admit that they tend to play down the influence of banks in the corporate scene. Even a cursory glance, however, shows that this is not true. As countless mergers, such as Preussag–Salzgitter, and proposed mergers such as Continental–Pirelli, have shown, the German banks are enormously powerful as power brokers. They sit on the supervisory councils, from where they can analyse and scrutinise management performance. The power of Deutsche Bank was sufficient to unseat Mr Horst Urban of Continental during its battle with Pirelli, even though his robust defence of Continental was arguably vindicated by subsequent events. However, Mr Ulrich Weiss of Deutsche Bank, the chairman of Continental's supervisory council, carried more guns than Mr Urban did. Mr Weiss, it should be mentioned, is a powerful force in industry, being a director of Fiat and Volkswagen as well as of Deutsche Bank. It cannot be denied, however, that there are serious dangers in allowing the banks such powers.

The German banks have a mechanism for evaluating companies which is virtually unknown in the Anglophone world's banks, the Sekretariat, invented in 1870 by Deutsche Bank, which consciously modelled it on the Prussian general staff. In Japan, incidentally, the same function is handled by the big and powerful planning departments of the *kairetsu's* main bank and trading company. Perhaps consultancies should try and interest British and US banks in the idea of setting up such a business audit function to look into their client companies and their management.

We have already mentioned the power of the German banks in Chapter 3. A 1984 Monopolkommission report showed that the banks were heavily represented on the supervisory councils of the top 100 companies. The three major banks alone had 76 representatives on those boards. In return, the directors of industrial and manufacturing companies sit on the boards of the banks, thus further cementing the close relationships. As the 1990s began, a survey for the magazine *International Management*, March 1990, reckoned that the top managers and directors of Deutsche Bank held seats on over 400 boards in Germany (not to mention boards of non-German companies), and in addition, the directors also held positions on over 150 advisory councils and educational/research foundations, one of which, incidentally, is Henley Management College in Britain.

Deutsche Bank's 1990 report sets out its holdings of over 10 per cent. These are listed in Table 4.2. We also give the companies' main line of business to show the wide extent of the bank's sectorial holdings.

Company	Holding (%)
Daimler-Benz (automotive)	28.37
Philipp Holzmann (building)	30.00
Hutschenreuther (porcelain)	25.09
Karstadt (retailing)	25.26
Klockner-Humboldt-Deutz (engineering)	41.14
NINO (textiles)	23.93
Allianz (insurance)	10.00
Fuchs Petrolub (oil, chemicals)	10.00
Hapag-Lloyd (transport, tourism)	12.50
Heidelberger Zement (cement)	10.00
Leifheit (household electricals)	10.00
Linde (engineering)	10.00
Munchner Ruchversicherung (reinsurance)	10.00
Phoenix (rubber)	10.00
Salamander (shoes)	10.00
Sudsucker (sugar)	10.00
Vereinigte Seidenwebereien (silk)	10.00
Josef Vogele (construction machinery)	10.00

Table 4.2 Deutsche Bank's holdings of over 10%

NORTHERN EUROPE: CARE FOR THE WIDER COMMUNITY

The Netherlands

Legal aspects

In the Netherlands, a public company is likely to be a *Naamloze Venootschap* (NV), which is comparable to a British PLC or German AG. It is empowered to issue priority shares, that is of a restricted class with special powers (such as to appoint and dismiss management). Companies can also, effectively, issue non-voting shares.

The directors are appointed and dismissed by shareholders at general meetings of the company; however, a two-tier system may be adopted, and the law provides for works councils.

A supervisory council may be adopted by any NV of whatever size, but it is mandatory for large corporations. These latter are defined as 'structure companies', i.e. with a capital of over DFl22.5 million (some £6.5 million), which, together with dependent companies, have over 200 employees in the Netherlands, and which have set up a works council. If they meet these criteria for three consecutive years they must set up a two-tier system.

In such a structure company the supervisory council elects its own members subject to certain procedures which are designed to give the AGM and the employees (through the works council) influence on the composition of the supervisory council. The management board is appointed and dismissed by the supervisory council and it is the supervisory council that adopts the accounts. The supervisory council members are not seen as representing interest groups, they represent everyone. The supervisory council also elects new members to fill its ranks.

There is some exemption for companies that have more employees outside The Netherlands than in the country, but they must still have the structure regime in The Netherlands. Here, however, the shareholders will appoint and dismiss the management board and adopt the accounts. The powers of the supervisory council are more extensive in a large corporation than in a normal company, to the detriment of the AGM and the management board. In particular, the management board needs supervisory council approval for:

(i) Issuing and acquiring shares in large corporations, and debt securities.
(ii) Entering into, or terminating a lasting co-operation with another entity, if such co-operation or termination is of substantial importance to the company.
(iii) Participating in another corporation, if such investment would amount to at least one quarter of the issued capital and reserves of the company.

Works councils

A works council may be instituted by any company, under the Works Council Act 19..... . However, any enterprise with more than 35 employees must set up a works council to be elected by the employees. Works councils in enterprises with over 100 employees have more power than those in smaller companies.

The law provides for prior advice from the works councils on a number of business decisions, such as a proposal to take over or merge with another enterprise, as with the ABN and AMRO banks, for instance. If the advice is hostile, the company must wait for a month before implementation, and within this period the works council may lodge an appeal with the Ondernemingskamer (the business enterprise chamber of the Amsterdam appellate court). The court has powers to order the company to revoke the decision.

If the company has at least 100 employees, or if there are 35 or more and as a result of a merger the employment agreement or conditions of at least one-quarter are significantly changed (or they lose their jobs), then the prior advice of the works council must be sought not only regarding decisions on the transfer of control of the company, but also of any part of it.

Takeovers

Though Dutch companies do not have the same structural barriers against takeovers as German companies because they are rarely owned by banks or institutional investors, protected companies, nevertheless, have a long list of defences against hostile takeovers. What Dutch corporations usually do is to incorporate a structure company which means that a self-perpetuating supervisory council has the final say in appointing the management board, thus making it very difficult for shareholders to unseat the incumbent management. Other defensive measures are the issue of preferred shares, the obligation to consult the employees and measures to restrict share-holders to 1 per cent of the voting rights regardless of their shareholding. There is a limit, however, as was shown by Mr Torstein Hagen's eventual victory in securing a place on Nedlloyd's supervisory council, based on his control of around one quarter of the company (see p. 20).

Belgium

The most widely used organisation in Belgium is the limited company, *Société Anonyme* (SA)/*Naamloze Vennootschap* (NV), and though as a general rule shares may be transferred freely, the articles of association often provide for limitations on this.

The most important provisions from the corporate governance point of view are those providing for a works council. This is a representative committee of the employees, which any company may have, but which is mandatory for companies with over 100 employees. The works council must be informed of any merger or acquisition which the company is negotiating, before any external announcement is made. It must also be consulted on the effects of a merger or acquisition on the employment situation within the enterprise concerned. This does not mean, however, that a prior authorisation must be obtained from the works council. It may only pass on certain suggestions or objections from the employees, but it has no powers in law to enforce its opposition.

Sweden

Legal aspects

An *Aktiebolag,* that is a company limited by shares, is the most common form of legal entity in Sweden, and is used for businesses of all sizes.

Shares can be free (to be held by anyone) or restricted, in which case they can only be held by Swedish nationals. Companies in the past have been able to, and certainly did, incorporate a restriction clause into their articles to the effect that all or certain numbers of their shares could not be held by foreign nationals or by companies that did not have a similar clause in their articles. These provisions are now under pressure as Sweden applies to join the European Community (EC), and there will certainly have to be a considerable easing of the hitherto tight restrictions on foreigners holding commanding stakes in Swedish companies. This is described in the next section.

Companies may issue shares of different classes which carry different voting rights (which is the way the Wallenberg family keeps its hold on its empire), but according to the Companies Acts 1944 and 1975, companies may not confer a vote which gives more than 10 times the value of another share.

The Board Representation for Employees Act 1976, provides for the local trade unions to have the right to appoint two directors to the boards of companies employing 25 or more people. The Co-determination Act 1975 put employers under an obligation to enter into negotiations with local unions before taking any action that might substantially change the company's operations and therefore affect the employees. The unions' right does not amount to a veto, however.

Impediments to takeovers

Sweden is yet another country whose restrictiveness in shareholder control is under pressure to change from its desire to join the EC. This will result in amendments to the law so as to allow foreigners to acquire over 40 per cent of the equity and 20 per cent of the voting rights of a Swedish company.

We have several times referred to the way the Wallenberg family has geared up its control of about one-third of the capitalisation of Swedish companies on the basis of what is proportionally a much smaller investment. The most blatant examples, when comparing voting percentage with equity ownership, are Electrolux and Ericsson: on the basis of a 6 per cent stake the family has 59 per cent of the voting rights of Electrolux. The figures for Ericsson are 4 per cent and 42 per cent. Analysts estimated that in 1991 the Wallenberg family had control over some SKr200 billion (£18 billion) worth of companies on the basis of SKr37 billion of capital employed.

It will be interesting to watch how this situation will develop under the impact of both the centre-right government elected in 1991 and dedicated to lift restrictions on company ownership, as well as of Sweden's entrance into the EC.

ITALY AND SWITZERLAND

Italy

Legal aspects
The emphasis on employees' rights is very much confined to the laws of northern Europe, and there is little evidence of it in the southern European countries. In Italy the form of governance even for the top-tier companies, the *Societa per Azioni* (SPA), is solely determined by the shareholders in annual general meeting, as it is in Spain with the *Sociedad Anonima* (SA). There has, however, been a considerable change starting as a result of the Maastricht Agreement at the end of 1991, as all EC countries, apart from the UK (and Denmark?), will work towards the implementation of the EC social policies.

Governance and business culture
It is difficult to compare Italian governance with that of the Anglophone countries, or indeed, with that of any other country. Italian big business is dominated by the state-controlled giants and the 'families' as we have already shown. An examination of the Fortune 500 shows that Italy – though one of the world's economic majors – has far fewer entries than France or Britain, or even Sweden, and about the same number as Finland, though it has many excellent small firms which are the real backbone of a very rich country. Almost invariably these firms are privately owned and therefore not really within the scope of this book. The state companies, IRI, ENI and EFIM, receive more competition-distorting subsidies than any other sector in Europe. These companies account for about 18 per cent of Italy's gross domestic product (GDP). Directorships are politicised, as we have already pointed out. The fewer state companies, the less will be the politicians' power of patronage. Hardly a recipe for successful privatisation.

Only some 200 companies are quoted ones – barely more than at the turn of the century – and only a handful of these are truly public in the sense of having a widespread shareholding base: in most of them control is effectively in the hands of the families and their allies, or the Italian government. The usual practice is to have a cascade of companies which can exert control through a complicated shareholding structure at minimum cost. Pirelli is a good example, where the founding family owns just a small percentage but can exert control through a pact with other shareholders. It required a big disaster such as the misplaced 'bid' for Continental to shake this up and secure the departure of Leopoldo Pirelli from control. Even so his place will be taken by another member of the family. It has been reckoned that the number of companies where there is an open shareholding is less than half a dozen. What counts in Italy are the informal networks of families and allies. Decision-making is very secretive indeed. It is not the official meetings that count, but what goes on before and afterwards. In our consulting careers we have always cautioned our clients who wanted to operate in Italy to steep themselves in Machiavelli as an essential preliminary to working successfully in that country! It is not surprising that in their annual reports Italian companies do not refer to issues of corporate governance at all.

Spain, too, exhibits many of the same characteristics as Italy. The issue for Spain is the move out of the protected cronyism of the Franco era into the late twentieth century. The problem at this point is one of business infrastructure rather than governance.

Switzerland

In Switzerland the limited company (AG or SA) is the most common form of public company, the majority of whose directors have to be Swiss citizens residing in Switzerland. The board of directors runs the company, but in practice many companies have chosen a two-tier system with an executive management managing the day-to-day business and a supervisory council. Each share carries only one vote, but companies still have the possibility of issuing shares of different nominal values, but with only one vote each.

The defences that Swiss companies have against foreigners are well known. These are basically enshrined in the *Lex Friedrich* which serves as the pretext for *Vinkulierung*, the word used to denote the restrictions imposed historically by Swiss companies on the transferability of their registered shares. This is changing – albeit slowly – under the impact of Switzerland's alignment with the European Community. The law will probably have to be abolished under the recent agreement to establish a European Economic Area consisting of the EC and European Free Trade Association (EFTA). Very many companies, however, have said that they would not be prepared to alter their (restrictive) practices.

These restrictions have been in place for over a century, but were given greater scope in the 1936 revision of company law to protect Swiss companies against Nazi participation. Research into Swiss companies by an analyst, Mr Beat Kunz, published by Bank Julius Baer in 1991, found that of 112 major companies examined by the bank 64, just over half, restricted the transferability of their shares. Thirty-five per cent of these did not even accept as shareholders private foreign investors domiciled in Switzerland, and 63 per cent refused to have foreign institutions as shareholders.

Prior to 1989, for instance, Nestlé provided in its articles that the board may refuse to register a shareholder without giving any reasons. Foreigners in any case were not accepted until November 1988. In May 1989, however, in a sensational move, the articles were amended, though the board still retained the right to refuse shareholders more than 3 per cent of the voting rights even though they might own over 3 per cent of the registered share capital. Therefore no shareholder may represent more than 3 per cent of the entire share capital (including bearer shares) at the shareholders' meeting. Nestlé has now begun publishing interim financial statements as well as information about its budgets and strategies. Perhaps Nestlé had no option; its world-wide turnover is equivalent to one-seventh of Swiss gross national product (GNP). Several companies, such as Ciba-Geigy and Brown-Boveri, have followed Nestlé's lead in opening their share registers to foreigners, though still with some restriction. Ciba-Geigy's new openness has coincided with the restructuring of the group, started in July 1990 by its chairman Alex Krauer in his 'Vision 2000' programme.

Roche too, has improved the standard of its financial reporting to attract outside, foreign, investors. Sandoz, another major international corporation, finally gave way in April 1991, when it announced a rights issue to raise SFr400 million and said that it would open all its shares to foreign investors. Previously only Swiss citizens were able to buy Sandoz-registered shares, which accounted for 70 per cent of the issued capital and 87 per cent of the voting rights, with foreigners restricted to bearer shares and non-voting participation certificates. Anyone was able freely to buy any of the three classes of equity as from 16 May 1991, but there was nonetheless a restriction that no one shareholder could own more than 2 per cent of the capital. The Swiss banking and insurance world, on the other hand, has still to liberalise its share structure in the same way, though the big three Swiss banks, UBS, Swiss Bank Corporation and Crédit Suisse, have at last begun to reveal details of their hidden reserves.

The inability of the Swiss capital markets fully to service the international financial needs of the Swiss multinationals is forcing these latter to open their shareholdings to foreigners and to accept the more rigorous reporting and disclosure requirements of the international capital markets.

FRANCE

Legal aspects

Even before Maastricht, there was some evidence in France of a move towards employee involvement in governance. In France there is already a legal obligation to consult workers' committees in any company with 50 or more employees where ownership is being transferred. French companies with overseas interests are already hitting problems. Rhône-Poulenc, the French chemical multinational, established a European works council in 1990 and very quickly found itself in a dispute with the British unions who insisted that the British culture was that employee representatives should be appointed by the trade unions.

Employees do not have board representation in French companies, however. In addition, shareholders' rights can be restricted. Though the so-called *auto-contrôle* was abolished in 1989, the articles of a French *Société Anonyme* (SA) may still limit the number of votes each shareholder has at general meetings, and may go so far as to grant two votes per share for those shares which have been held by the same shareholder in registered form for anything from two to four years.

A unique business culture

France is run by its star pupils. Business is led by the best in French society. It is the dominance of the most numerate. What Japan achieves by consensus and groupism, France achieves through élite convergence. Because the French establishment is run by a core of like-minded people (due to the fact that they have been trained in the same way in the same places) it can take concerted action. The accepted career path runs through the state and private sectors: par for the course would be to enter public service, and then use one's privileged knowledge of its workings to attain a second career in industry. If in the USA one could say that what is good for General Motors is good for the USA, then in France what is good for France is good for Renault. To be a French public sector company is to bask in the glory of the French state.

Leslie Mitchell de Quillacq, in his book *Powerbrokers: An insider's guide to the French financial élite* (1992), is quite definite as to how to get to the top in France:

The path to influence and status in the French financial sector is clear. It is best to be born into an upper-class family and go to a top Parisian lycée, then to the Institut d'Etudes Politiques de Paris (Science Po), and then to ENA, where it is necessary to graduate in the top 10 in order to become a member of the Inspection des Finances (part of the inner circle of the finance ministry). This should be followed by a stint in the French Treasury and time in a ministerial cabinet to get the requisite political patronage.

This close circle of key people moves between the state sector, public administration and the private sector. It should be noted, however, that though it is a marvellous training ground, the civil service does not pay well in France. It is a good launching pad, but it does not make your fortune. Governance is very special in France, and very much dominated by the state. Many French companies, such as Michelin, L'Oréal, L'Air Liquide, Alcatel, Carrefour and Peugeot are world leaders, but management in France is considered a state of mind rather than a set of techniques and the French managerial class has a sense of belonging to an élite. In fact, France has come closer than any other country to turning management into a separate profession with its own entry requirements and regulations. The word for managers, *cadres*, is borrowed from the armed forces, and *cadre* status is attained through educational qualifications or loyalty to a particular organisation. A graduate of a *grande école* has immediate *cadre* status: others have to work up to it over time if they can. French industry, like German industry, is dominated by engineers. But in France to be an engineer does not mean that one can fix a machine, rather it implies something about your social standing, your outlook, professional esteem and national pride.

The design of the organisation structure reflects the cerebral manager. France's long tradition of centralisation, hierarchical rigidity, and respect for authority is reflected in its attitude to governance, with the *président directeur general* (PDG) at the helm of companies, and virtually not answerable to anyone. If matters are put to the vote it is tantamount to a vote of no confidence in the PDG. Top executives believe that they owe their positions to their intelligence (or, perhaps, their cunning). It therefore follows that they should make all the critical decisions. It can be very compartmentalised, and we have noted very many French companies with the chief executives and their personal assistants on the top floor, and the typing pools in the basement.

Corporate governance in France

French companies have an array of protective devices against unwelcome bidders, such as restrictions on voting rights, shares with double voting rights and stock warrants that can be converted into shares in the case of a bid. Legal structures can frustrate unwelcome bids. For instance, Bernard

Arnault, the boss of LVMH, France's luxury goods company, has created a barrier of holding companies to protect his business. The most potent weapon of all is the power of the institutions, the so-called *zinzins*, which can well be under the thumb of the state, and more often are under its influence. Some French companies have been selling big chunks of their equity to the banks, eager to emulate their German cousins. Who owns the banks? The state of course. Thus by the end of 1990 Banque Nationale de Paris had built up a portfolio of FFr16 billion of investments in French firms, while the state-owned Crédit Lyonnais had built up a total holding of FFr24 billion, including investments in such private sector firms as Bouygues and BSN. Its policy is to buy minority stakes, around 10 per cent, and it stresses that it will not usually sell out to a hostile bidder. The Caisse des Depots has substantial holdings as well, mostly concentrated in the tourism and media industries. The insurers are following the same policy. The state-owned UAP and AGF, plus the privately owned AXA-Midi have about a fifth of the capitalisation of the French bourse. It was the French banks that enabled French companies to go on their corporate buying spree in the late 1980s, allowing Saint-Gobain, for instance, to outbid BTR to buy the US maker of abrasives, Norton, for some $2 billion, just before the onset of the US recession.

The Agnellis' abortive bid for Source Perrier in early 1992 showed the power of the French establishment to resist an interest even as powerful as the Agnelli family, even though they were already well established in France. In its way this episode mirrors Carlo de Benedetti's failure to win Société Générale de Belgique against the Belgian establishment four years earlier. However, the fact that another 'outsider', Nestlé, won the Perrier battle shows that French business is becoming less closed to outsiders than is sometimes supposed. However, in a move, as astutely political as it was commercial, Nestlé has announced that it will move the headquarters of its minerals water business over from Switzerland to France. As the book was going to press, it still remained to be seen whether the EC would allow this acquisition.

How to get to the top: France compared to Britain

In France it is important to be attuned to the ways of government if one wants to get to the top. A survey by *Director* magazine in June 1991 reported that 15 of the chairmen of France's top 25 companies were ex-civil servants, with eight of the remaining 10 being either the founders or the inheritors of large firms. Typical would be Renault, PSA Peugeot, Elf Aquitaine, Alcatel Alsthom, Total CFP, Péchiney, Rhône Poulenc, Saint-Gobain and Air

France, all headed not only by ex-civil servants, but by ex-civil servants from the most prestigious part of the public administration, such as the Ponts et Chaussées, the Mines or the Finances. At the other extreme, Carrefour is run by its founder, Denis Defforey, BSN and Bouygues by inheritors. It is worthy of note that those at the helm of international majors in France such as Shell Française or IBM, are long-standing company men, in the well-trodden international multinational tradition.

It is very different in Britain. Unlike in France, the chairmen of British companies should not be renaissance men. Indeed, they would be regarded with very great suspicion if they were to try to be this. They have to have different skills from their French equivalents, such as being adept at investor relations (particularly when their shares are falling). In France the principal shareholder is so often the state, therefore it is important to know how to handle the bureaucracy. In Britain if the dividend is cut, even if the profits are down, this is read as a commentary on the long-term health of the business, and such a situation needs careful handling.

Unlike the French, British chairmen have, more often than not, worked their way up through the organisation. The last five chairmen of that most typical British company of all, ICI, took an average of 33 years apiece to climb up to the top, though Sir John Harvey-Jones, an exception, did it in a mere 24 years. Oxbridge still predominates, though its influence is gradually waning. BP, Shell, ICI, BAT, Unilever, Grand Metropolitan, Ford, Esso, BTR, Marks & Spencer, Tesco and RTZ are all led by company men; a small number of companies such as GEC, Dalgety, and Cable & Wireless have chairmen from the public sector, and inevitably some, like Sainsbury, Trust House Forte, Lonrho and Hanson are led by either the founder or inheritors. It should be mentioned, however, that being a permanent secretary of a government department leads not only to an inevitable knighthood but also to a whole series of equally inevitable lucrative non-executive directorships.

THE USA

Legal aspects

Governance is a matter of serious concern in the USA and it is already a stock exchange requirement that companies should have audit committees as a condition of quotation. This also means that company boards must have a proportion of outside directors.

In the USA companies incorporate under the laws of various different states which differ from each other and, indeed, compete in a sense with each other. The USA has no national corporate law, and therefore every state has developed its own. In particular states have developed anti-takeover laws to entice companies to their state. In 1990 there was a rash of anti-takeover legislation at state level, most notably in Pennsylvania and Massachusctts. In Pennsylvania, and in several other states, for instance, a company has to take account of other parties' interests, such as the suppliers, when making takeovers. The state of Delaware is, in fact, the market leader in such legislation and the rulings of its courts are therefore carefully watched. In 1989 there was a landmark decision by a Delaware court over the proposed Time–Warner merger which upheld the right of management to reject one takeover bid in favour of a lower-priced deal which the board considered was better in view of its long-term strategy.

There is a growing tendency in the US courts to look at the process of decision-making to see whether it is reasonable, coupled with a rise in shareholder activism and lawsuits.

Audit committees, in particular, are seen as being central to corporate governance and already in October 1987 the regulations were recommended to be tightened by the National Commission on Fraudulent Financial Reporting (known as the Treadway Commission). The US accountancy bodies too, have moved to tighten their collaboration with the audit committees.

A revolution at General Motors

Readers will have appreciated from Chapter 3 that the boards of major US corporations are heavily dominated by non-executive directors, but despite the committee structure we have also noted that the power of the ruling management is usually extremely strong. There are two main reasons for this:

(i) A tendency to combine the positions of chairman and chief executive which puts the person concerned in a position of enormous strength.
(ii) The fact that the majority of these non-executives are usually executive officers (often chairmen and CEOs) of other companies.

Though boards of directors contain a sprinkling of academics and political worthies, there is a feeling that the system is too comfortable for the executive management, and that it smacks of cronyism. Graef Crystal, a noted critic of US directors' pay levels, has described the composition of a typical US board as '10 friends of management, a woman and a black' (*Financial Times*, 13 April 1992).

This has, of course, been under attack for some time, spurred by the excesses of the 1980s takeover wave with its examples of corporate greed. There have been growing signs of shareholder restiveness. Institutions are pressing for key 'governance' board committees to be controlled by the non-executive directors (which, to be fair, is the policy of the blue chip corporations already) and shareholders are increasingly putting down hostile resolutions on directors' pay at AGMs. Non-executives, too, are beginning to flex their muscles. A notable example is at Chrysler, where the directors resisted efforts by Lee Iacocca to stay on as Chairman after his due retirement date. And at least five other major companies have provoked investor anger: IBM, Digital, Kodak, American Express and Sears, Roebuck.

Nonetheless, what happened at General Motors early in April 1992 was nothing less than sensational. The corporation had been under attack for its ailing performance and its apparent reluctance to change for some time. The outside directors lost patience and, led by John Smale, former chairman of Procter & Gamble, finally took action. They demoted two of the Company's most senior managers, including Lloyd Reuss, the president, and strengthened the function of the corporation's executive committee which had been inactive in the past, but which now was to be headed up by Smale. If what is good for GM is good for the USA, who knows what the repercussions are likely to be! If it can happen at GM, it can happen anywhere. Indeed, in June 1992 it happened at BP, in Britain, as Bob Horton's reform programme became too uncomfortable for his board.

JAPAN

Businesses in Japan which seek the benefit of limited liability with public subscription for their shares, have to register as *kabushiki kaisha*. These must have a minimum of three directors, elected by the shareholders, but most major company boards have many more: Toshiba, for instance, has over 30. There is little place for non-executive directors in the British or US sense of the word, though there are directors appointed to the board through the links the company has with its business partners. In some cases too, retired executives could be appointed to the board. The commercial code also calls for 'representative directors' (*daihyo torishimariyaku*) to be elected to the board. Their role is to represent the company in its dealings with third parties such as government, the authorities, banks and other companies in the industry. The chairman and president will usually be among the most senior of the representative directors.

The symbolic role of the board is crucial in providing the focus for reflecting the vision and values of the leadership to the members of the organisation, but a key part in the management of the corporation is also played by the meetings of the top management group (*jomukai*) and the meetings of the general managers (*keiei kaigi*).

It is well known that Japan has a business culture that is all of its own. Corporate governance takes place behind the scenes between the senior corporate officials and the major institutional shareholders in whose hands ownership is concentrated. The background to the company will be the *kairetsu*, or grouping of cross-shareholdings, into which the company fits. Many of the shareholding institutions will be banks, which will also be substantial lenders to the company. The company itself is very much regarded as a social unit with a unity between management and labour, and the managers (who will have risen through the ranks) will see themselves as representatives of the employees as much as of the shareholders.

There is a virtual separation of operation from supervision, and the management changes that take place tend to occur as a result of discussions behind the scenes between the financial interests and senior management. There is usually no publicity. It is all done very quietly. It is a world of insiders, of consensus, with much less reliance on lawyers (and lawsuits) than in the USA, and where governance appears to be far less of a problem because the different parties follow the unwritten rules, which are none the less powerful for being unwritten. The 1990s will see how far this can continue to operate for international Japanese companies as they have to come to terms with other people's cultures.

THE EC PROPOSALS

European Economic Interest Grouping

Slowly but inevitably the EC is moving into centre stage in company law provisions. The European Economic Interest Grouping (EEIG) is governed by Regulation number 2137/85 dated 25 July 1985, which has been applicable from 1 July 1989. This derives from the French *groupement d'intérêt économique*, which is the collaborative regime under which the Ariane space project and Airbus Industrie operate. This regime allows the partners to work together while retaining their legal and economic independence.

There are certain provisions that must be followed:

(i) The EEIG shall be governed by the law of the state in which the official address is maintained.

(ii) It may not invite investment by the public.
(iii) The grouping is not a holding company and its members continue to be economically, legally and financially independent.
(iv) The grouping may not have a share capital.
(v) The activities of the EEIG must relate to and be ancillary to those of its members.
(vi) It may not employ more than 500 persons.

The contract between the parties will contain the substructure, and must contain objectives, the identity of the members and the duration of the agreement, if it is not indefinite.

The purpose could be, *inter alia*, R & D, the carriage of goods, joint buying and selling, the provision of services or manufacturing.

The grouping has two organs, the members acting collectively, that is the partners (at a supervisory level?), and the managers (at an executive management level). The first two EEIGs were a grouping of lawyers from three countries registered at Eindhoven in July 1989, and five TV stations from France, Italy, Luxembourg, the UK and Germany, also in July 1989.

The European Community statute

This statute is currently being negotiated, and we quote it at some length because we believe it is a sign of the trends that will dominate EC company organisation thinking in the 1990s.

It is controversial, we admit. It provides a uniform but optional regime for the formation and operation of a *Societas Europea* (SE) with available employee participation. It excludes certain areas, such as social security and employment law, taxation, competition, intellectual property and insolvency law. It can be formed by two plcs (or equivalent) registered in two different member countries, or by the merger of such companies. There are provisions regarding the accounts, and these follow the respective accounting Directives rather than being an implementation of national accounting legislation.

A further connected Directive requires member states to enable employees to participate in the supervision and strategic development of an SE.

Member states are required to adopt at least one of three models of the administration or supervisory council. The question of workers' representatives is determined by the law and procedures of the country where the SE is registered. The different models are:

(i) The board (whether administrative alone or supervisory) must contain at least one-third, and no more than half, of persons who are appointed by the SE's employees, or are their representatives.

(ii) Under the co-option model (which is basically the Dutch system) such persons may be co-opted, but the shareholders may object and take their objections to an independent tribunal. Pending the determination of their objection the appointment does not take effect.

(iii) A separate body representing the SE's employees (that is, basically the French system), set up in consultation with the law and practices of the relevant country. Such a body is entitled to be consulted every three months on progress and prospects, and to receive the necessary reports from management as well as being consulted on matters which require the full authority of the supervisory council and administrative board.

There are two board structures: a two tier one, that is, a managing board and a supervisory council, or a one-tier structure with a single, administrative board only. The supervisory council, which is appointed at the annual general meeting does not engage in management activities. The management board is required to report to the supervisory council every three months. The administrative board must meet at least quarterly. Management is delegated to one or more of its number, and they must comprise a minority on the board. Subject to the employee participation Directive, members are appointed at general meetings. Important decisions such as closure, change of activities, establishing subsidiaries, etc., will require the authorisation of the supervisory council or the full administrative board, as the case may be.

APPENDIX 4.1

Some of the statutes that can affect British business people

Companies Acts 1985 and 1989
Competition Act 1986
Company Directors Disqualification Act 1986
Company Securities (Insider Dealing) Act 1985
Contract of Employment Act 1972
Data Protection Act 1984
Employment Act 1980–82
Employment Protection Act 1975
Employment Protection (Consolidation) Act 1978

Environmental Protection Act 1990
Equal Pay Act 1970
Fair Trading Act 1973
Financial Services Act 1976
Health and Safety at Work Act 1974
Insolvency Act 1986
Misrepresentation Act 1967
Race Relations Act 1976
Sex Discrimination Act 1975–86

5 IS THE BRITISH POSITION TENABLE?

MYTH AND REALITY

The never-never land of corporate governance

The debate on corporate governance in Britain starts from a simple and attractive premise. A company is a piece of property owned by its shareholders, and they get together once a year at least, to exercise their proprietorial rights in annual general meetings when, *inter alia*, they approve the accounts, appoint the auditors and elect the directors. If they disapprove of what the company is doing they can vote the directors out of office, or if they cannot do that, they always have the option of selling their shares. At the extreme, if enough people with enough shares do so, this can result in the sale of the company itself and such sales, or the threat of them, the theory goes, act to promote efficiency in a market economy by facing inefficient and badly performing managements with the prospect of being taken over.

Only shareholding gives such rights. Bankers and other lenders of money are not seen as playing any significant part in the governance of companies. Their role is regarded as strictly limited to lending money on the basis of commercial criteria. Their relationship with the company is a contractual one.

The company itself is run by a board of directors, some of whom will be executive managers and others, non-executive directors, that is, directors without portfolios. These outside, or independent directors are elected for their wisdom, experience and contacts. They are independent of the detailed operations of the company and therefore they can bring a disinterested but expert viewpoint to bear on its affairs. In particular in the last few years their role has come to be seen as participating in (and often running) two key committees, the audit committee, which oversees the financial probity of the company, and the emoluments (or remuneration) committee, which fixes the chairman's and the executive directors' remuneration. Above all, their job is to ensure that the chairman does not overstep the mark. On occasion they have to be instrumental in getting rid of him or her.

The outside or non-executive director is therefore regarded as quite essential in maintaining a balance in a company. If the problem is one of balance, or so goes the theory, then it can be solved by recruiting the right non-executive director. Mr (or Ms) Right will solve everything.

The world has changed

The basis of British company law, which grew up in the nineteenth century, was to offer businesses the protection of limited liability by separating personal liability from that of corporate organisations. Personal liability could therefore be limited to the amount of the shareholding in an incorporated company, limited by shares. This worked well when the shareholders were truly proprietors, and it still obtains today, of course, in medium and small businesses. Major companies, on the other hand, the 7,000 or so plcs that are the subject of our book, do not usually function like that any more. Big companies began to change a century ago when shareholders ceased to manage them directly and hired professional managers – below board level – to run them instead. As time went on the managers began to graduate to board level, and gradually came to form the majority of board members.The process of completely separating ownership and control was accelerated after the Second World War when the financial institutions started to build up their industrial investment portfolios. The fund managers who handled these investments had no interest in individual shares as such. By definition their job was to balance their portfolios which they did by diversifying them. They were content to leave the management of the companies to the professional managers. The formal division between boards of directors and the business management lasted longest in the financial services sector where it was for a long time customary to separate the board, the gentlemen, from the executive management, the players. The chief general manager was often the only member of management to sit on the board. Banks began to change their structures in the 1970s and building societies and insurance/assurance companies followed suit in the 1980s, though there are still many examples left of this former structure, especially in the smaller organisations.

The reality of ownership

Today's reality is very different from the myth, and also from the business structures envisaged by company law. Though the government talks of a share-owning democracy, the vast majority of private investors (other than those who have shares in their own firm through share schemes) appear to behave as punters not as owners. In its report for 1990, in fact, the Central Statistical Office's Social Trends affirmed that the percentage of shares in private rather than institutional hands had declined, even though a larger proportion of the British population were shareholders in 1990 than in 1981. The private shareholders tend to look to short-term capital gains, as evidenced in the various privatisation issues where the newspapers have openly pandered to them, pointing out when profits could be made on quick in and out trading.

The legal position is that ultimate control and profit belong to the shareholders by means of a majority show of hands or of proxy votes at annual general meetings. Practice is very different. Anyone who has ever attended an annual general meeting of a major corporation will realise that it is almost a ritual that appears far removed from the reality of corporate governance. The meeting usually lasts a very short time, very few shareholders attend it, even fewer ask questions, and most boards of directors have little difficulty in normal times in using the proxy voting device as a rubber stamp for their decisions. Occasionally shareholders are offered a glass of sherry as an inducement to turn up, and the only excitement comes if some pressure group decides to make a public attack on the company to publicise its message to a wider world. The connection between annual general meetings and policy-making is remote. Commenting on AGMs, it has been remarked that never have so many given so little information to so few. The shareholders simply do not attend what is, in theory, a key company meeting. As an effective policy-making arena, the AGM is a joke. The real owners of the company – the institutions – do not use the AGM to promote their interests, preferring to put their points in private. Even when there are the upheavals described in Chapter 1 – still the exception rather than the rule, incidentally – they are agreed on by the institutions in private meetings outside the AGM. The AGM merely ratifies these decisions formally.

Who runs the company?

Any discussion of governance must take note of the fact that it cannot just be limited to the members of a company's main board of directors. The reality of major corporations is that they are run by a group of key managers that is larger in size than just the executive board. It is not unusual for annual reports to name them. Thus ICI lists its 19 directors (of whom 10 are non-executive) and also a further 19 senior executives. Marks &

Spencer, similarly, has 20 directors (five of whom are non-executive), but it also lists a further 28 senior managers. In our experience the inner management group in companies such as these would probably be larger still, say around 50 persons: such a group would include the controller and treasurer and other key individuals, the head of research in ICI's case, the top buyers in Marks & Spencer's. In a company such as BP the group would be bigger still, perhaps numbering as many as 100 persons.

The strength of a company is derived from the coherence of such a group. Not for nothing is the term 'management team' used. Its members will have grown up in the company together, they will have worked together and shared experiences together. In a very real sense they feel that they, and not the shareholders, are the company, hence the traumas of takeovers and the culture clashes in mergers. You have only to go to a meeting of, say, Shell old-timers, to appreciate the strength of such a culture. We discuss the employees as business stakeholders in the next chapter, pp. 134–137.

But however close-knit the group, major companies have to rely on systems, and on people lower down the line. These are not infallible. Even with blue-chip companies, top managements have found themselves powerless as with the Midland Bank's Crocker Bank disaster in the early 1980s, when the entire board appeared to have been at the mercy of events and unaware of the details of the disaster as it was unfolding.

Just recently, in May 1991, we had another example which has caused tremors to run through industry, when the UK drinks and food group Allied-Lyons announced that it had lost £147 million in the year 1990, on the group's foreign exchange trading. The losses were incurred by a treasury department that, in the words of the chairman, was 'dealing in foreign currency instruments that were inappropriate, and in which it lacked the requisite trading skills'. Nonetheless, the responsibility stops at the top, and the chairman and chief executive had to pay the price for this failure of controls. If this can happen to the two most senior people in a company, what chance would a part-time non-executive have had in trying to keep abreast of events?

This question again came to the fore in Spring 1992, when it transpired that Polly Peck International had contributed over £400,000 to Conservative party funds in previous years without the amount of the payment being reported in the accounts as required by law. The auditors side-stepped the issue and the newspapers pointed squarely at the company's directors (all of them, without exception), quoting company law, which puts the onus for disclosure on the directorate: 'In respect of any failure to comply . . . every person who was a director of the company before the end of the relevant period is guilty of an offence.'

Company managements as self-perpetuating oligarchies

The continental and Japanese financial worlds have a much more industrial tradition than in Britain. They view their relationship with industry much more in partnership terms. The City world of institutions and banks, on the other hand, has always sought to keep at a distance from commerce and industry. Historically the relationship between the financial and industrial worlds in Britain has been a much more passive one, with contact mainly at the financial reporting level. Provided that things went reasonably well, that the shares performed adequately, and that dividends and interest payments were made, there was little reason for the financial world to interfere with business, and each of the three parties was content to be left to get on with what they were best at: the banks at lending, the institutions at investing, and the companies at managing. A very successful company such as BTR has no problem with this, and can confidently comment in its annual report:

Apart from the individual expectations of the smaller shareholders, the large institutional investors have to serve a variety of requirements. Some require high income growth, others high capital appreciation. Recovery funds are characteristically short term. Life funds take the longer view . . . Perhaps the common factor is that they all want growth.

And BTR remains confident that it can continue to provide this growth to satisfy the institutional investors.

The relative passivity on the part of the investors has given great scope to the boards of the major British companies, which are able to act virtually as self-chosen and self-perpetuating oligarchies. Armed with the proxy votes, it is not usually difficult for a board to get its own way at general meetings and to ensure that those that have already been nominated come to be elected as directors. Inevitably they have often begun to feel that they, and no one else, are the company and that the company has a life of its own and has to be preserved at all costs. The power of an entrenched company management must not be underestimated and City fund managers have to be very sure of themselves and also very sure of their support before they take it on. A report by Pensions Investment Research Consultants in May 1992 ('Mid-Season Corporate Governance Report') highlighted the powers of company boards. The report found that:

- more than half of Britain's largest corporations allow shareholders no say in the appointment of top executives;
- 27 of Britain's top 52 companies have adopted provisions by which all or some of their executive directors need never seek re-election by shareholders, and;

- companies such as Coats Viyella, Comercial Union, Guardian Royal Exchange, Inchcape, P & O and TSB all insulate their executive directors from shareholder votes.

Non-executives have to be viewed in this context. They are in theory elected at the AGMs; in reality they are selected by the chairman and the board, going through the same type of self-selection as with the choice of one of their executives. The system is voluntary in any case. Of course blue-chip companies go to great lengths with their non-executives. That is not the point. It is in the large but less than blue-chip companies, with a more cavalier attitude to the use of non-executive directors, where the problems arise, and there have been too many scandals in the last few years to be ignored.

You might well ask, who has the real power: a 20 days a year part-timer, however distinguished, or a divisional director running a business with several thousand employees and a capital expenditure budget of many tens of millions of pounds?

It is true that managements talk of shareholder value. This phrase figures prominently in the accounts of companies from Lloyds Bank to Hanson. The latter states unequivocally in its company profile: 'We aim to enhance shareholder value by increased earnings per share and dividends, generated through profitable internal growth, selective acquisitions and control of the positive cash flow from our companies.' Shareholder value is to the 1980s and 1990s what synergy was to the 1970s. Yet what does it mean? Hanson plc in its 'profile' does not mention the shareholders as such, and we suspect that for many companies the emphasis is on the word value rather than on the shareholders, and that the measure is popular because it is a useful way of gauging a company's performance and comparing it with its rivals. Shareholders benefit from dividends and make capital gains on selling out if the price rises. They could also benefit, hugely, by cash distributions when a company divests itself of assets or sells its non-core businesses, for instance. But practically without exception the money goes back into the business. No management would ever dream of handing cash back to the real owners – its shareholders. Perhaps they are right. Do the shareholders really think of themselves as owners of the company, or only as possessing negotiable pieces of paper to which rights of financial consequence are attached?

The confusion of roles in a British board is neatly illustrated in the 1990 annual accounts of the Midland Bank. There are 19 directors: five executive and 14 non-executive. All, of course, are elected by the shareholders (i.e. the proxies in the chairman's hands) at the AGM; but only one of the directors actually represented a specific interest. He was Mr Wrangham, director of the Hong Kong & Shanghai Banking Group, as a representative of its interest in Midland Bank at that time. This was before the HK & S Bank announced its bid for the Midland Bank. Such confusion should be no surprise given the growing divergence between the legal position and actual reality.

THE LEGAL QUAGMIRE

What is a director?

We have already commented on the fact that in English law all members of the board have equal responsibility. In cases of negligence a director's responsibility is unlimited, though we accept that there has to be a difference in what is construed as negligence in the case of a director who is a full time executive, and one who is a part-time non-executive. However, the law does not recognise the title non-executive. It is therefore legally perfectly in order for companies to have as directors only those with executive responsibility, however much this may be frowned on by the media. All directors are entitled, by law, to all the information they require to perform their functions, and so long as they have no grounds for suspecting that the information they have received is misleading or wrong, they are entitled to rely on it. Interestingly enough though, there is also no legal requirement for a director to be competent, as is the case in Germany.

Shareholders, for their part, are deemed to have property rights in a company, and their liability is limited to their shareholding. The general meetings of shareholders, along with the meetings of the directors and of management, are seen in law as the three bodies with responsibility for shaping a company's future.

But what is a director? The title is almost impenetrable in Britain, applying equally to a director of the main board of Barclays Bank and the owner of a corner grocery shop. The title has suffered from inflation: commercial companies have directors who run no more than small units or departments, advertising agencies are full of directors so-called: the title is seen as important in impressing clients. On the other hand, many of these divisional managers or vice-presidents, or whatever they are called in major companies, have more real power than the non-executive directors on the main board. Is it any wonder therefore that so many companies are unclear about what they expect from their non-executive directors? There is a conflict of roles.

The duties of directors

Directors by law have to act in the best interests of the company and they can be sued for failing in their duty to do this. Based on the notion of ownership this means that directors have to act in the best interests of the shareholders, and this excludes other parties' interests unless they coincide with those of the shareholders. Pity the poor non-executive who has to interpret this in a typical situation where the management may not have a very significant stake in the company, and where the shareholders do not regard themselves as owners. Indeed, the laws with regard to shadow directors have made the institutions very wary of being seen to stand behind any directors (executive or non-executive) and give them instructions.

Boards are normally permitted by their articles to delegate their functions down the line, either to committees of the board or to the management of the company. It must be clearly understood, however, that the purpose of a committee is to go into greater depth into certain issues than is possible at a full board meeting, such as at an audit or an emoluments committee. The board – and that means all the directors without exception – retains full responsibility however. The existence of a committee does not mean that some board members' responsibilities are enhanced and those of others are diminished.

The purpose of granting limited liability to an organisation in the first place was precisely that: to protect the shareholders, lenders and creditors, but leave management free to run the company. The world has moved on from such certainties: companies have grown to a size and complexity where they span the globe and have turnovers exceeding many countries' GNPs. They operate in a world of regulation, labour laws, laws on equal opportunities, accounting requirements, EC Directives, stock exchange regulations, regulatory regimes, administrative decrees, and, increasingly, environmental legislation. Part-timers cannot run such complex organisations whatever the law might say. A reconsideration of their role is long overdue. It is easy in Germany and The Netherlands to allocate different legal responsibilities because there are two quite distinct boards: it is much more difficult under a unitary board system as in Britain where the legal understanding (or is it the legal fiction?) is that the board runs the company.

The weight of legal pressures

Legal pressures are becoming increasingly onerous. Directors' liability has assumed growing importance in the wake of lawsuits and the result is a soaring rise in the cost of liability insurance. The USA is witnessing an ever-increasing trend for litigation against directors and company officers personally, as opposed to their companies. Shareholders' lawsuits against board members have been increasing by approximately 20 per cent annually with claims averaging $3 million by 1991. The trend is crossing the Atlantic.

The regulatory framework is becoming more burdensome as well, as we showed in the previous chapter. The Environmental Protection Act 1990 has raised the potential for personal litigation against directors. These are risks of a criminal nature and therefore cannot be insured against. Civil insurance policies themselves often have clauses excluding pollution risks. As the insurance companies have learnt to their cost, the courts are awarding heavy penalties against companies found guilty of polluting the environment. Insurance companies are being forced by US courts to pay even if the pollution in question took place some generations ago when the actions were not illegal. The slogan for the 1990s is: 'the polluter always pays – and pays heavily'.

Industrial accidents and occupational health are yet another area where the regulatory climate is becoming more severe. In late 1991 the union-backed think-tank, the Institute of Employment Rights, published a report on improving safety at work. In this it advocated a general audit across industry to analyse the common causes of accidents and recommended that directors and managers found guilty of causing harm to workers should face criminal penalties. Many prominent companies, such as ICI, are publicising in their annual reports their record in reducing accidents. Many more are collecting the statistics 'just in case'. It may only be a matter of time before there will be a requirement to publish them. Companies could eventually also face an increase in claims for damages after the launch, in January 1992, of the Environmental Law Foundation, which aims to help people protect their environment and will provide lawyers to take up cases on their behalf. Companies are becoming increasingly concerned that they may be liable to prosecution on environmental grounds by the growing number of private bodies.

The recession of the early 1990s has also become a spur to litigation. Former directors of failed companies have, for some time, faced the risk of being accused by liquidators of, in effect, aiding their companies' collapse by failing to halt 'wrongful trading' in good time. But when is a good time? Increasingly that date is being left to the courts to determine. It can start surprisingly early. A Glasgow accounting firm, F. L. Walker, carried out a survey early in 1991, and came to the conclusion that company directors of small and medium-sized companies were giving up the fight for survival much earlier than ever before. The reason was identified as a reaction to the 1986 Insolvency and Directors' Disqualification Acts. These Acts were intended to curb abuses in the limited liability protection afforded by company law. Instead they appear to be frightening directors off from fighting for their companies' survival in difficult trading conditions. We have already, on page 58, pointed out the extent of directors' personal liabilities in the event of their companies becoming insolvent. The penalties are severe, and the threat is very real: sufficient to frighten potential directors from situations that are even remotely risky. Nor can we blame them in the circumstances.

Our advice to even the most experienced non-executive director would be not to risk being involved in such a situation, and yet, arguably, that is exactly the sort of situation where an experienced non-executive would be most valuable. Non-executives will watch with interest what legal actions will be taken against the former non-executives of the Maxwell and Polly Peck companies.

THE CITY AND GOVERNANCE

The banks

Banking attitudes

The difference between continental and British attitudes to business relationships is highlighted by the historical difference in their focus on public company reporting, though this is beginning to change under the impact of the EC. The basis of continental company accounts has, historically, always been to show lenders and other creditors what the assets of the individual companies amounted to. Anglophone accounts on the other hand, emphasise the total value for the shareholder, hence the focus not on individual companies but on consolidated group accounts.

The German house-bank has as close a relationship with its company client as has the company's shareholder and sees its role as supporting its clients with long-term, low interest lending. More than that, the bank often is both a shareholder in the company and a nominee for individual shareholders. German banks, like Japanese banks, see themselves as companies' business partners, and are therefore intimately involved in the companies' governance. They are most often the key decision-makers when it comes to corporate restructuring or mergers: there is a whole line of recent examples: Preussag–Salzgitter, Siemens–Nixdorf, Continental–Pirelli. In all those cases the banks played a decisive, if not *the* decisive role. British banks, on the other hand, are used to a much more hands-off relationship as between lender, with specific rights, and borrower. They think in terms of commission and fee income rather than a long-term business partnership. They are most comfortable with such a purely financial relationship. Unlike the German and Japanese banks, the British banks do not have the skills to protect their investments in an industrial way. Nor do they have the inside knowledge that comes from participating in company affairs from the vantage point of the supervisory council. So British banks have to move more cautiously, lend on stricter terms, ensure that the loans are short term, heavily collateralised, and roll them over frequently to give the lender a chance of an out. This is exactly the type of lending that British industry feels puts it at such a disadvantage.

Deutsche Bank stands behind Daimler-Benz with its £10 billion of capital spend in the next five years as well as its £12 billion of R & D. The relationship is very close: the chairman of the management board of Deutsche Bank has for the last 60 years also been chairman of Daimler-Benz's supervisory council. A member of Daimler-Benz's supervisory council is also on Deutsche Bank's advisory board. The relationship is not just one of governance, it is a powerful alliance. How can BAe counter this, living as it does in a culture of an ever-changing share register of institutional shareholdings, and relying on clearing banks who act as if a three-year loan is long term?

The banks are having responsibility thrust on to them
The onset of the recession at the end of the 1980s forced the British banks to move from their traditional hands-off attitude, and to take a much more interventionist role. They competed hard – perhaps too hard – in the boom years of the 1980s to expand their loan books and build up their lending to corporate businesses. The bad debts at the end of the decade hit them badly, and all of a sudden the sharp traditional dividing line of the lender–borrower relationship between the banks and the corporates became blurred as companies went to the wall in increasing numbers. The banks had already moved to relationship-banking and they began to discover, to their cost, that relationships can become too close for comfort. Like the Midland Bank, they had set up 'Intensive Care Units'. These departments concentrated in the main on the financial aspects of management, that is, the area of business the banks were expert at. Sometimes they could nurse companies out of trouble; often not, and when a company goes into administration or receivership, it is very often at the behest of a bank. So we have seen the banks' involvement in a string of failed companies: Brent Walker, Polly Peck, the Maxwell companies, Olympia & York, to name only a few of the more prominent ones. The banks have had to become almost owners: they have had to become involved in business policies, sales of assets,

recruitment of management. They became the virtual proprietors of the Mirror Group of newspapers for a time, for instance. Who knows, but it is extremely likely that the commercial property débâcle of the early 1990s will leave the banks in virtual control of groups such as Olympia & York and Heron under the guise of rescheduling debts. It is an interesting sign of the times that when in early 1992 the question of Lonrho's corporate governance became newsworthy, it was not only the institutions that put pressure on the company to appoint non-executive directors. The banks also did so, led by Standard Chartered, Barclays and National Westminster, and strongly supported by Crédit Suisse and the Swiss Banking Corporation.

In a curious way the banks have come back full circle to an earlier age when the local bank manager knew his customers' business inside out, and acted as their guide, adviser and friend. Brian Pearse, on being appointed chief executive of the Midland Bank, and newly into his job, talked wistfully of returning to this operating style, and publicly lamented the lack of 'old style' 50-year-old bank managers to put such a policy into effect. What a pity the banks were so enthusiastically early retiring just such managers all through the 1980s!

In many cases the situation is not clear cut. The alternative is not between a continuing, successful business and failure and bankruptcy. The banks know how to deal with such situations. What they have difficulty in handling is a situation where companies are in trouble, where perhaps they have breached their banking covenants, where they need support, but where they, the banks, do not have confidence in the management or the chairman to get the company out of trouble. What do they do then?

Replacing the executive management is not always the whole answer; often the banks need outsiders too, as guarantors, as it were, to give them comfort. The non-executive is the obvious solution, a device their venture capital arms have often used in the past when making investments in companies.

The banks may not like it but a combination of the recession and political pressures to avoid job-destroying liquidations, is forcing them into the world of company governance.

The institutions

The power of the institutions

A survey quoted in *The Independent* newspaper in November 1991 reckoned that private individuals owned only 16.1 per cent of the equities on the London stock exchange in 1991 (down from 18 per cent in 1990 and 28 per cent at the start of the decade). Every major company's report and accounts confirms this. Looking at random at the 1990 annual reports of British companies we note that 117 shareholder accounts control 55 per cent of BTR's share capital; 500 control 77 per cent of BP, enough to carry an AGM; 353 control 63 per cent of Shell; barely 100, practically half of ICI, and 450, 70 per cent of Hanson. Eleven per cent of SKB's shares are owned or managed by just three institutions: Barclays Bank, Postel Investment Management Nominees and Prudential Corporation. Prudential, with 4.95 per cent, is the largest holder in Barclays, and it is a name that recurs again and again in share registers. The Prudential also owns 3.55 per cent of ICI, for instance, which is greater than the total owned by some 160,000 of the smallest holdings. The Prudential is said to control nearly 4 per cent of British publicly quoted shares and is the largest single shareholder in many of its 250 disclosed holdings. The 'Pru', with some £20 billion invested in ordinary shares, follows the fortunes of its investments and its stated policy is to invest in companies that have at least three non-executive directors on their boards. It was this policy which, reportedly, kept the Pru away from investing in Maxwell Communications Corporation.

Of course, the annual reports of companies do not give many details of which individual institutions own their shares: moreover, holdings need not necessarily be British-owned, particularly in world companies such as Shell (which is only 40 per cent British-owned in any case), nor do they necessarily equate with individuals or single organisations. An individual or organisation might have several holdings for instance. But it is a good indication of the balance. Most big companies find that some 25 institutions can exercise majority control.

In the latter half of the 1980s the government sold its stake in BP, but because of the unfortunate timing of the sale the Kuwait Investment Office was able to acquire much of the tranche. BP then felt it necessary to spend some £4 billion to buy in this stake. The subsequent effect of this may turn out to be very damaging indeed because the money so spent was not available for investment in acquiring oil reserves and developing the business.

We carried out a survey of the shareholding of the British clearing banks as revealed in their 1990 accounts. The four clearers have just under half a million shareholders. The split of their shareholdings is set out in Table 5.1.

The institutions and takeovers
The myth of a shareholder democracy is one thing, the reality is that it is not only that the institutions own the majority of the major quoted companies' equity, but it is also that this majority holding is held by, perhaps, no more than a relatively small number of the major institutions. It is they who

determine a company's fate when it comes to takeovers. The part played by the takeover culture in Anglophone countries, and the short-term business climate that is both a cause and effect, are subjects of a fierce debate which we do not propose to enter into here, but we need to be aware of it because it is so central to corporate thinking in Britain, and therefore impacts on governance. The feeling is that because of the influence of short-term pressures on their thinking the institutions do not really understand the long-term worth of companies. Certainly hostile takeovers are still virtually unknown in the more successful economies of Germany, Japan, Switzerland and the Netherlands, whose company managements do not have to concern themselves with poison pills and golden parachutes and the ever-changing names on the share register, matters which in Britain (and the USA) can cause such friction between managements and shareholders, and where the financial world is conditioned to taking a long-term view of business.

Bank	Percentage of shares owned by top 1% of shareholders	Percentage of shareholders owning bottom 10% of shares
Lloyds	78	85
Barclays	81	75
Midland	84	85
NatWest	72	89

Table 5.1   Bank shareholdings
Source: Company accounts

Hostile takeovers are, by their very nature, antagonistic affairs, and in Britain both sides to a takeover bid often spend large sums of money to demonstrate the incompetence of the other side and broadcast this incompetence to the widest possible audience. That must have an impact on confidence in the managements concerned. Continental managers watched the ICI–Hanson quadrille in the second half of 1991 with amazement as both sides were seen to waste money (and management energy and time) on specialist consultants and merchant banks in attacking each other rather than concentrating on their businesses. The Redland–Steetley battle in Spring 1992 was another example of this trend. All good fun, no doubt, and very profitable to the merchant banks involved, but did the mudslinging really help either company?

Speaking before the House of Commons Trade and Industry Select Committee early in 1991, Sir John Clark, formerly of Plessey, savaged the role of the City fund managers for their part in the 1989 take-over of Plessey by GEC and Siemens. He claimed that Plessey's fate had been determined by 35 fund managers,

who did not know one end of a shop floor from another, who had no interest in the company or any knowledge of what it did, who had no interest in the employees of the company. Thirty-five people who had one interest and one interest alone: short-term gain. Thus was the fate of a great company sealed.

Plessey is only one of many leading British companies to have disappeared in the last few years, often into foreign ownership: Rowntree Mackintosh, Hawker Siddeley, Yorkshire Bank, Pearl Assurance, Morgan Grenfell, Clydesdale Bank, The Northern Bank, Jaguar Motors, Eagle Star; the list is endless. A clearing bank study has reckoned that over a quarter of British manufacturing will be in foreign hands by the end of the century leaving even fewer quoted shares available for the institutions to invest in.

The truth is that the institutions have the same power in Britain as in Germany and Japan, only they have not understood (or accepted?) their responsibilities. They are agitating for more recognition and information, but it is legitimate to ask what they bring to the companies they have invested in, in return. They still act as if the small shareholder rules, and that everything can be solved through share transfers. But to whom? Only to another institution, of course. One fund manager's ex-growth fund is another's recovery share. The big funds are locked in: why sell ICI to get more Hanson paper which they already had? The fewer companies in existence, the fewer opportunities to balance their risks.

The institutions have only two sanctions against bad management: action to remove the management, or at least the chairman, which as we pointed out in Chapter 1 is growing in popularity; and an assent to a takeover. But, though these catch the headlines, they still reflect the minority of cases. In general, as long as things go reasonably well, there is no shareholder control at all. The shareholders are free riders and management has it all its own way, though to be sure the published accounts will be full of references to working on behalf of the shareholders.

What we have attempted in Britain is to organise the governance of companies through the scissors and paste compromise of loading responsibility on to the non-executive director. The fact that this code of conduct is voluntary means that the compromise is basically only accepted by those who want to accept it. Is it therefore workable?

What have the institutions done with their power?
Increased intervention by the institutions, says Mr Michael Sandland, head of the Institutional Shareholders' Committee and chief investment manager

of Norwich Union, 'is a historical inevitability' (*Financial Times* 11 June 1991), and indeed the institutions are beginning to flex their muscles. Their attitude is still, however, that intervention is the last resort. The starting point is, as we have already indicated, to understand that the institutions are investors, and see themselves as such, not as owners. Their interest is in their funds and the performance of the funds, rather than the companies they have invested in, and they are judged, publicly, on their funds' performance. Their aim has to be to maximise returns to their own shareholdings by constantly adjusting their investment portfolios. Underperformance to them means underperforming shares, while to a German or Japanese bank, it means underperforming companies. The two may not necessarily be the same thing. British institutions still take a financial view of the company, German and Japanese ones take an industrial view. The answer to problem shares in Britain has for long been to sell them in the same way as companies seek to sell underperforming assets, or at worst, to hold them in the hope of a bid. On the continent the preference is much more to get rid of under-performing managers rather than selling or breaking up businesses, a practice which is regarded as almost obscene. It is interesting that institutions are always seeking to outperform, yet the British economy as a whole does not outperform those of most of the other EC countries.

The institutions were able to take full advantage of the takeover boom of the 1980s. It could perhaps be said that there are better ways of disciplining companies and encouraging performance than by takeovers or the threat of them. Such an approach might not have been inappropriate in the boom years of the 1980s, but it became less appropriate as the recession of the late 1980s and early 1990s limited the number of takeovers, though whether this reflects a permanent change in corporate attitudes, or whether it is only a temporary blip until business picks up again, is anyone's guess. We feel it could well be more than a temporary phenomenon, however, not just because of a changed business climate but also because the institutions' holdings in industry are now approaching saturation point. There is very little further they can go.

The result is that latterly they have had to concern themselves more with the companies they have investments in and, as Mr Sandland pointed out, they are having to intervene more often. The interventions are episodic, however; they are for specific reasons and they occur on specific occasions, rather than being a constant pressure on managements to perform. The institutions lack the necessary expertise for this business approach, nor perhaps do they have the staff and the specialised technical departments. The Tace intervention by Norwich Union and Framlington, another fund manager (between them they owned 20 per cent of the company), is significant in that they attacked the board for financial mismanagement, corporate extravagance and lack of strategy (see p. 10). Norwich Union explained that it felt that it had a responsibility to all the shareholders, which is why it held on to its shares and did not sell them, seeking to make management changes instead.

This could be a sign of a beginning of a change of heart on the part of some institutions at least, or, cynically, one could say that in the climate of mid-1991 Norwich Union could not sell the shares at a profit anyway, and had to make the best of the situation. Georg Siemens, founder of Deutsche Bank put it succinctly 150 years ago when talking of shareholdings: 'If one can't sell, one must care.' In general, however, the institutions still appear to be not so much concerned with corporate planning, marketing strategies, organisational developments, succession planning, R & D, technological developments and strategic alliances, which is the essence of what companies are *really* about. Instead, they concentrate on management style, as with Professor Sir Roland Smith in his days at British Aerospace and Gerald Ratner of the Ratner jewellery group, or on high levels of remuneration combined with a perceived lack of success, as with Sir Ralph Halpern of Burton. They are particularly concerned to separate the roles of chairman and chief executive.

It is still not easy for them. Pressure in a continental supervisory council can be exercised discreetly. If there is to be a row it will be behind closed doors. Unless they act behind the scenes through some of the directors, the British institutions have to do so more publicly with the final act (if they cannot get their way in private) at a general meeting. This can put them under the glare of publicity as with Norwich Union and Tace, and lead to a public confrontation, much to the delight of the press.

The institutions are looking for a way out

The institutions are in a dilemma. They are being pulled in different directions. They have big stakes in major companies; they are the real owners. Yet they do not have the experience or the experienced staff to act as owners in all the different situations they have invested in. They are at a disadvantage against an expert and entrenched management. They will face confrontation if they have to, but confrontation is costly and an exercise in damage limitation rather than in profit increase. Nobody wants the unpleasantness, and the unpleasant publicity of public rows. The institutions hanker after the flexibility and the freedom to act as they were set up to act, as investing bodies relying on financial information provided by the companies they have invested in. They already receive such information of course, and major (and sensible) companies have very effective shareholder liaison departments to do just that. But how far can all this information be relied on? There have been problems enough recently with audited company accounts of companies that have hit difficulties soon after the annual audit, to keep the lawyers busy for many years to come. The institutions need an interface they can rely on, a proxy to enable them to feel comfortable so that they can continue to act as if they were private shareholders. In other words, they need someone to supervise the executive directors on their behalf.

Who better than the non-executive director? It is therefore no surprise that the institutions have enthusiastically promoted the role of the non-executive director. Even Hanson had to placate them by appointing more non-executives to the board in autumn 1991 at the time of the stand-off with ICI.

The non-executives fill the role of supervisory (or controlling) intermediaries to perfection. They are directors, and therefore part of a company's top policy-making body, but, in a subtle way, they are also independent of the executive. They are ideally placed to monitor the three aspects of corporate governance the institutions want to focus on: the accounting principles, reporting and controls through the medium of an audit committee; the remuneration and benefits of the chairman and executive through an emoluments committee; and a counterbalance to an over-powerful chairman, getting rid of him or her if needs be. Non-executives could also play a particularly useful role in selecting a chairman. If pressure had to be put on a company's management, a powerful group of independent non-executives would be exactly the right way to apply such pressure.

Indeed, so beguiling is this picture that a non-executive director industry has grown up. Books are published on their duties, conferences are held explaining their role, organisations such as Pro-Ned (Promotion of Non-Executive Directors) are seeking to find them for companies in need, there are proposals to train them, and you can write off for checklists of their duties. One prominent non-executive director of our acquaintance, a very senior ex-public servant, told us that on retiring from the civil service and being appointed to the boards of several major companies, he was inundated with letters from consultants offering to train him.

It is clear that with the non-executive director the institutions have found the ideal theoretical answer to their problems. But does such an ideal exist in practice? And, furthermore, even if such an ideal exists, is the structure workable?

THE NON-EXECUTIVE DIRECTOR
AS *DEUS EX MACHINA*

How does the non-executive match up to requirements?

It will be apparent to the reader by now that non-executive directors are expected to be supermen (and superwomen) to fulfil all the requirements of the job description that has been thrust upon them. They have to be at one and the same time wise, all knowing and experienced. They must have good contacts and be able to play their full part in board matters so as to add weight to its counsels, and yet be independent and able to stand apart and monitor performance and behaviour, and – if necessary – act to depose a chairman. The board has to work together, and yet one part of it has, in a subtle way, to monitor and watch over the other. It is not easy to exercise a supervisory function over your colleagues when sitting on the same board. The non-executives are therefore subjected to a lot of pressures. At the same time they are regarded in law exactly like any other director, but must expect far less remuneration, not surprisingly, because they have to do all this on about two dozen days a year. Few such individuals exist, yet the institutions have been obliged to invent them because they need some body of representatives to stand in their place as institutional shareholders. Absentee landlords have to have their agents, but the institutions dare not be seen to get too close to the non-executives, far less give them instructions, for fear of being caught in the shadow director trap, which is a real worry in the case of small or medium-sized companies that can hit trouble so easily and so quickly.

Hence too the fund managers' continual preoccupation with the non-executives' independence, defined as 'freedom from bias, involvement or partiality'. (Report of the Institutional Shareholders' Committee, 'The Role and Duties of Directors – A Statement of Best Practice 18 April 1991'). But if they are not involved and committed, what is the point of having them? If we are really to expect boardroom monitoring by truly independent and disinterested parties, why not go to the logical extreme and have persons on the level of regulators, such as those of the telecommunications, electricity or gas industries? Independence is all very well but it must be independence of mind, of thinking, not disinterest in the company. Outside directors must have a commitment to the companies they are directors of. They must have a concern for the company and an attachment to it. Other countries too have outside directors on their boards, but they are there for very specific reasons, as representatives of major shareholders, bankers, lenders, suppliers, customers, allies and partners, and in the German and Dutch cases, employees.

The Japanese, for instance, have great difficulties in understanding the role of the outside director. They take a very down-to-earth attitude. 'Surely', they say,' the non-executive director could not have enough knowledge of the business, be sufficiently sensitive to the corporate culture or appreciate the subtleties of the group and its relationships to be of much use? With their lack of knowledge they might destroy the company's social fabric and harmonies.'

It is necessary to be clear as to what we mean by the word independence. We certainly do not advocate that directors have personal interests, such as business contracts, in their relationships with the company. They must be in a position to resign, if necessary on points of principle, if they feel it necessary. The institutions are also pressing for the chairman, too, to be independent and not combine the job with that of chief executive. It has become quite the fashion. We do not disagree with this in principle, but feel it unwise to insist on it as an absolute rule, in a unitary board. It depends on circumstances and there are many successful companies where the two roles are combined in one outstanding person. The moment a company loses its aura of success, of course, as BP did when it hit trouble in early 1992, it will be under heavy pressure from its institutional shareholders to split the job of chairman and chief executive. On the continent, on the other hand, there appear to be no such inhibitions in those countries that have unitary boards: Alex Krauer is chairman and chief executive of Ciba-Geigy; Jean Gandois, of Péchiney; Gabriele Cagliari, of ENI; Helmut Maucher, of Nestlé; Oscar Fanjul, of Repsol. These are all successful companies where the two posts are held by the same man. What the institutions should be doing in such situations in the UK is to ensure the effectiveness of the management team, and to see that there is a proper succession, instead of carping about the combination of the roles of chairman and chief executive in one single person. It goes without saying that in the supervisory council structure the position of the CEO (on the managing board) is automatically separated from that of the chairman (of the supervisory council).

Selection and Training

Our surveys bear out the general impression that even in the biggest companies, fully two-thirds of the non-executives were appointed because they were personally known to members of the board, usually to the chairman, and therefore acceptable to him or her and to them. Nor is it surprising that boards act to ensure that they choose newcomers who will fit in. It would be astonishing if it were otherwise.

Our surveys also show that new non-executive directors mostly grow into their jobs, learning as they go along from the old hands, as it were. Often they do not get even informal induction into their jobs unless they press for this. Those who are already directors of other companies will still have to adapt themselves to the culture of their new companies but given their experience of working at board level they will hardly be going in cold. On the other hand we have found that when looking at companies in *The Times* top 1,000, up to four-fifths of non-executives are appointed without a clear definition of what it is that they are required to do, and, of course, there is no training as such. We find that non-executives who are academics, ex-civil servants or politicians most of all need to have some form of instruction, not least in their legal responsibilities and liabilities.

AUDIT COMMITTEES

There is an accelerating trend for major British companies to set up audit committees. A study by the Institute of Chartered Accountants of England and Wales ('Audit Committees in large UK Companies') reported in May 1992 that two-thirds of the 202 companies and 88 per cent of the 44 financial institutions polled had audit committees, compared with only 17 per cent of large companies polled in 1985. In the USA they are already mandatory for companies seeking a listing on the New York stock exchange. It should be remembered, however, that in most US states the auditors report to the board of directors, not to the shareholders as in the UK.

We discussed the matter of audit committees with a very distinguished, long serving non-executive of a number of companies. He admitted that it was easier for him because of his years of experience, both as an executive director and chairman and, latterly, as non-executive of several companies. Experience, and a nose for trouble, come with having done the job for a long time. Not everyone is in this situation.

So what are the average non-executives to do, without a staff of their own, devoting perhaps two days a month to the company in question and faced with a very determined and well documented finance function?

Decisions in big companies are made down the line and there have been enough cases brought before the courts to show that the executive – let alone the non-executive – directors of even the most well-known companies are on occasion unaware of some of their senior managers' actions.

The *Financial Times* of 15 July 1991 printed an extraordinarily revealing, and brave, article by Mr Jerry Shively, a former non-executive director of Sketchley, who was involved in the board room changes there when the company hit problems. He did not hide the fact that he felt, in retrospect, that he should have been more critical of the well-produced pieces of financial information he was given at board meetings, and which he (and, to be fair, the executive directors as well) accepted too readily. At one point he was receiving reports that everything was all right, and then, quite suddenly the situation deteriorated. In a revealing aside he commented that his experiences led him 'to wonder if fund managers and bankers really know anything about operating a company. I wondered why the fund would own 20 per cent of one company – and then not have a single director on its board.' Why indeed!

The advocates of audit committees seldom point out the dilemma of directors in a public company who suspect – but cannot be certain – that something is amiss. They can ask questions and may receive answers they are not very happy with; they can raise the matter at board level, but to no avail. What do they do then? Should they publicise their doubts? If it is a public company the media attention could well bring about the very result they were striving to avoid, such as a fall in the share price and a collapse of confidence. Shareholders who felt aggrieved at losing money could well sue them, and the directors could find themselves having to pay out – personally – considerable sums in damages. In this litigious age there seem to be legal consequences to everything. Even though it must be clear that audit committees cannot be the perfect solution we are in favour of them, but we have come to the reluctant conclusion that to work satisfactorily they will entail the setting up of some elements of a bureaucracy.

Not every non-executive can handle the matter as elegantly as ex-cabinet minister Mr Peter Walker, who declined the offer of the chairmanship of the Maxwell Communications Corporation in mid-1991, giving a reason that was just plausible enough to pass muster. Even so his action hit confidence in the group and, in retrospect, can be seen as the beginning of the end for it.

EMOLUMENTS COMMITTEES

Graef Crystal is a poacher turned gamekeeper. In his book *In Search of Excess* (1991), he gives an apologia for his time spent as a compensation consultant advising boards on executive pay. It is true that his comments refer to the USA, but they are equally relevant to Britain. Companies may make a lot of the fact that their non-executives fix the remuneration of the executives and, often, the senior managers as well. In practice this means taking the advice of specialist remuneration and recruitment consultants, and no consultant would be likely to suggest to his or her clients that in their case the remuneration levels ought to be in the lowest quartile! It is only natural to look at comparable pay rates in similar companies and try to equal if not to exceed them. There is therefore a ratchet effect. Compensation levels ought to be fixed not on comparability, thus putting every company into the top quartile out of pride if nothing else, but on what a management team actually succeeds in accomplishing. If a company's performance puts it into the bottom quartile of its industry group, its management should be paid accordingly.

In real life, however, it is the executives who fix the pay of the non-executives, just as the non-executives fix the executives' pay. The circle is complete and this reality becomes apparent when you look at the actual composition of boards of directors. In ICI's 1990 annual report the chairman and chief executive was Sir Denys Henderson. The role of chairman was subsequently split from that of chief executive. Ten non-executive directors are given, five British and five foreign. Every single one of the British non-executives is chairman of at least one major company, sometimes more, and therefore presumably has his own non-executives in their turn scrutinising and determining his own remuneration. At least four of the non British directors are also executives in their own companies.

Sir Denys Henderson is, himself, a non-executive director of two organisations, Barclays Bank and RTZ, on which latter board he sits with one of the deputy chairmen of Barclays Bank. The 1990 accounts of RTZ list seven non-executive directors, two of whom (including Sir Denys) are company chairmen, and three are deputy chairmen. The chief executive and deputy chairman of RTZ is, in his turn, a non-executive director of Barclays Bank.

The German two-tier supervisory structure makes it easier for two reasons: the position of the non-executives, that is the supervisory council, is protected and therefore its members are less susceptible to any pressure from the executives; moreover, German law, by stipulating that practically half the supervisory council members must be company employees, ensures that there is some restraint on the more extravagant remuneration packages that have caused such comment in Britain.

THE STRUCTURE WORKS BEST WHERE IT IS LEAST NEEDED

Perhaps we reviewed the wrong companies when we looked at corporate governance in the major corporations. By definition most of these would want to respect best practice, even if the code were only voluntary. There are some variations – idiosyncratic but successful companies, and companies owned by private shareholders – but all have outside directors; most have audit and emoluments committees, or pass that role to the non-executives; they are careful to liaise with their shareholders and communicate with the City.

It may be that we should have reviewed not the large and reputable, but the large and perhaps more questionable companies, which would not feel bound by any voluntary code. Considered coldly and logically, the situation is really most extraordinary. Non-executive directors are the subject of an intense debate in Britain: yet they have no distinct legal status as they would if they were separate from the executive board. Nor, we might add, has their presence on boards prevented the many scandals that surfaced in 1990–91.

Readers might be amused at a little case of how a continental group of managers reacted to this example of British illogicality, set out in Appendix 5.1. It is taken from an article written by one of this book's authors in *Management Accounting* magazine, and is reprinted here by kind permission of the magazine.

ANGLO-SAXON ATTITUDES

In mid-February 1992 the working party set up by the Institute of Chartered Accountants of Scotland on governance reported. It concentrated on directors' responsibilities for financial statements. It is an interesting document as it reflects so many of the points we have been highlighting in this book.

The report focuses on the importance of the audit committee: it expands its functions so that in our view the committee is close to becoming a separate department of the company with its own staff and working arrangements. The committee members should be non-executive (with which we agree) and would have to give considerable time to their committee work if the working party's recommendations are to be followed. We thus have a supervisory – even control – structure almost in place, and yet the working party baulks at the mention of the dreaded word 'supervisory council'.

That, perhaps, is our biggest criticism of the report: its myopia. United States, Australian and Canadian practices are carefully examined in the appendices, but the committee has not thought it worthwhile to look at what they can learn from Britain's EC colleagues just across the Channel.

THE SYSTEM IS NOT WORKING ANYWAY

1991, a year of scandals

Perhaps it was the sheer number of the scandals in 1991 that gave such an impetus to the pressure for better governance. The two biggest were the BCCI and Maxwell affairs, and both were still unfolding a year later as this book was going to press. The collapse of the Bank of Credit and Commerce International was, of course, much more than merely a British scandal, and it had implications for banking supervision just as much as for actual corporate governance itself. Nonetheless, it is worth noting that in the bank's heyday the regulators and central bankers always drew comfort from the fact that the BCCI board contained four experienced and respected Western bankers. With the benefit of hindsight – always 20/20 vision – it is now widely felt that these outsiders were not questioning enough about the bank's lending practices. We have already commented on the weakness of outside 'governance' in BCCI in Chapter 1. Would insiders, on a supervisory council, take the same attitude, we wonder? The Mirror Group pensions saga tells the same story. As reported in the press, the minutes of the Mirror Group pension trustee meetings show that the trustees appointed by management never ever voted against Mr Maxwell. Some of them, it is said, never even spoke at the meetings. All this bears out the points that Mr Shively made about his time with Sketchley.

In February 1992 the auditing firm Price Waterhouse gave a detailed account of its role as auditor to BCCI. The point it made was that all significant power was in the hands of the founder, Mr Agha Hasan Abedi, and his chief executive officer, Mr Swaleh Naqvi. All the outside directors did was to give credibility to the bank's loan portfolio.

In contrast to BCCI the collapse of the Maxwell business empire at the end of 1991 was largely a British affair, and was particularly relevant to the corporate governance debate. The matter is still, at the time of writing, *sub judice* and we need to be careful when making comments, but it is clear that while the non-executive directors conferred respectability on the publicly quoted Maxwell companies, they were, on the other hand, unable to check his actions or even on occasion to be aware of them. Mirror Group Newspapers (MGM) and Maxwell Communications Corporation contained many members of the Whitehall and City establishments, and, as with BCCI, their presence gave comfort to investors, lenders and business commentators alike. Robert Maxwell ran the companies himself, in his own way, regardless of both non-executives and senior executives. When his finance director discovered that funds from MGN had gone to the private companies, Robert Maxwell simply brushed him aside, demoted him and bugged his office to boot.

The House of Commons Social Services Committee's report on the Maxwell pension fund in March 1992 was damning in its condemnation of voluntary good practice by professionals: 'Pontius Pilate', it said, 'would have blushed at the spectacle of so many witnesses washing their hands of their responsibility in this affair in public before the Committee.'

All this has given ammunition to the detractors and critics of the governance concept. The deputy chairman of Lonrho, Mr Paul Spicer, had an easy defence for his company against the charge of not having independent outside directors when under attack early in 1992: 'I would ask you to look at Polly Peck, Brent Walker and Maxwell Communications Corporation. They had a long list of non-executives, but it did not seem to make much difference when it came to corporate governance' (*Sunday Times*, 9 February 1992). And who could say that he was wrong?

There have been foreign scandals, too, which reflect on a critical breakdown in other countries' corporate governance, such as the US investment bank, Salomon Brothers, being caught bidding illegally for US treasury notes, and the Japanese brokerage house, Nomura, being caught out in a series of financial malpractices that have been dubbed Nomuragate. Britain saw the collapse of the Levitt Group, Polly Peck, International Leisure, and the continuing problems at Lloyd's, all of which have had and will have repercussions in the form of legal actions, if not fraud cases. All these revolve round the doings of individuals who appear to have been unconstrained by any form of corporate control. In the background we have had the Blue Arrow and Guinness trials, and public outrage at the high salary increases top business people continue to be paid even in recessionary times in companies such as BT, British Airways, British Gas and Tesco.

All in all, 1991 was not a good year for governance.

The myth of better people

Despite everything, there is still the feeling that having better people on company boards could prevent excesses and rein in idiosyncratic business dictators. Certainly the quality of the non-executives on the BCCI and Maxwell boards was high enough, but as we have seen their scope for action was limited.

Turning from the scandals to the heart of the financial world, the banks, we note that their boards contain the great and the good of the establishment. We compared the non-executive directors on the boards of the four British clearing banks with the composition of the supervisory councils of the three big German banks (Deutsche, Dresdner and Commerzbank). The results are set out in Table 5.2.

There can be no doubt that the British banks have a much greater array of eminent people on their boards than the German banks, half of whose boards are made up of representatives of employees and trade unions. Yet it cannot be said that either the governance or the performance of the British banks is any better than that of the German banks. There are many analysts who would say that exactly the reverse is true. The 1991 results of the British clearing banks were dismal. Every one of the seven major German banks, on the other hand, increased both its business volume and its operating profits: the lowest increase in profits being 10 per cent, the highest, 43 per cent.

1. British banks	
Members of the House of Lords	3
Ex-cabinet ministers	1
Knights (most of them company chairmen, chief executives or directors)	25
Chairmen or chief executives	14
Retired senior employees	2
Representing Hong Kong & Shanghai Bank (on the Midland board)	1
Others	4
Total	50
2. German banks	
Elected by the employees	22
Trade union representatives	8
Academics	5
Chairmen or chief executives	16
Unspecified (most probably representing the shareholders)	10
Total	61

Table 5.2   Composition of bank boards: Britain and Germany

Source: Annual reports and accounts

British banks, in fact, have been under sustained attack for their attitudes to their customers, particularly the smaller businesses, and have been busy publicising fair play charters to combat this accusation. Does this mean, we wonder, that they had not been playing fair with their clients before? Nor has their performance been particularly inspiring: over several decades the share prices of the clearing and merchant banks have underperformed in the market, and they have started the 1990s in deep trouble with serious losses and bad debt problems.

The answer is not having better people, or more distinguished and important people on the board. Even if they existed, supermen (or women) as non-executives would not solve the problem. Ordinary people will do provided they are involved in the company and committed to its success. What is important, if governance is to be made effective, is not to confuse the different roles, but to spell out very clearly what is expected of the executives and what the non-executives have to do, who monitors whose performance, and against what criteria. If this has to be enshrined in law to make it effective, and if there have to be separate structures to make it work, surely that is no insuperable problem?

It is disappointing that the fund managers appear to be taking such a narrow line in the governance debate. In their search for the right formula for the ideal non-executive they are almost completely ignoring the successful experience of other countries, not least just across the Channel, just as the Institute of Chartered Accountants of Scotland appears to have done. It seems to be a British disease to avert the gaze from the continent. Fund managers have two fears: they are concerned at the danger of being sucked into long-term commitments with the companies they have invested in, and they are frightened that a two-tier board with enshrined responsibilities would encourage a whole number of interest groups, not least the employees and trade unions. They still remember the Bullock Report of the late 1970s. Perhaps the prospect of a Conservative government throughout the bulk of the 1990s will finally convince them that the trade union dragon has at last been laid to rest.

The system they hanker after, however, is unworkable. Is it logical to have a unitary board working as a team to manage the company, but with one half supervising or controlling the other half? There has to be another approach, but it has to be a solution that will suit British conditions.

TOWARDS A COMPROMISE

The approach that is currently being propagated in Britain is clearly so full of contradictions that it is hard to see how it can work effectively. What we must now do is to look for an acceptable compromise that combines other countries' successful experience (where it is successful) with the distinctive British business culture, and which is at the same time in tune with business trends and the likely thrust of EC legislation. We emphasise that we are talking throughout of major companies, the plcs, particularly the international ones, not the small or medium-sized companies and the family companies.

There are certain elements that have to be part of any solution:

(i) Company managements must be free to manage. Their operational freedom must not be unnecessarily or needlessly constrained. Being set specific performance objectives and having their contribution regularly appraised is not incompatible with such operational freedom.

(ii) While not supporting the wilder salary excesses that have been so criticised lately, we would certainly advocate payment at market rates and linked to results, according to criteria that can and should be justified at AGMs.

(iii) There has to be accounting transparency and there must be a monitoring of the financial controls and a check on balance sheet engineering.

(iv) Outside directors, that is persons without an executive role in the company, are the people who should be involved in such checks. Outside directors are essential to prevent company managements from becoming too introverted and inbred. Not only can they bring a breath of fresh air to the boardroom, but they are also valued for the advice that they give as well as their connections in the City, in business and in government. But the involvement of outside directors has to be properly thought through.

(v) At the same time we appreciate the issues of legal liability that these outside directors can face, and any proposed solution must take account of this fact, which is why the involvement of these outside directors has to be properly organised.

(vi) We also have to recognise the fact that the companies we are talking about – the major ones – do not work in isolation, existing, as it were, merely between suppliers and customers. They are living in a world of alliances, business networks, interrelationships and obligations to other businesses, to those who have lent them money, to their employees, to local and central governments and to the wider social world, not only in Britain but wherever the company operates. The company's relationship with its employees is an especially important one, and there is pressure from the EC to formalise it.

(vii) The interests of the stakeholders must be carefully balanced with those of the shareholders. We must never lose sight of the fact that the shareholders own the company, and therefore any scheme must allow them a key role in governance.

(viii) The principal shareholders in today's major companies are much more permanently involved than ever before and it is in their interest to eschew short termism and the financial window dressing that so often accompanied the presentation of company results in the roaring eighties.

(ix) It is also our firm conviction that any system must eventually be regulated to make it work. Voluntary codes are all very well, but while the 'my word is my bond' culture might have been applicable to the former coffee house atmosphere of the trading room, it is no longer so in the days of electronic trading from terminal to terminal, when such large amounts of money can be invested passively by computer formulae and embedded software, almost without manual intervention.

Partly it is a question of a change of culture. The institutions have to realise that their world is changing. On the one hand they have a predominant, majority stake in industry – certainly not contemplated in British company law – and on the other there are fewer and fewer companies available to invest in. Perhaps they realised this when they were considering the ICI–Hanson situation in the second half of 1991. They cannot, of course, invest in their traditional way in businesses acquired by foreign owners. The fund managers must take responsibility as shareholders and act as owners, and – yes – they should bite on the bullet and put directors into companies to represent their interests where needs be. If Deutsche Bank can do it, why can the British institutions and banks not follow suit? A *de facto* division between executive and non-executive directors already exists in many British companies, and others, such as Reuters and the Anglo-French CMB, have a two-tier system already. The practice of supervision is already plain for all to see and every working party looking into the subject recommends more and more controls. Perhaps a two-tier system is not so outrageously outlandish after all!

We realise that the current company law provisions could well be an impediment to some of the changes we will recommend. All we can hope is that pressure can be put on government to change some of the restrictive legislation we have identified.

In the rest of this book we seek to explain what a new system could consist of, what its components should be, how it could work, and to judge it against the changes in corporate life that are currently taking place and which we are sure will lead to new forms of corporate organisation over time. Nor do we intend to leave the discussion at a theoretical level only: we aim also to present some practical things companies could and should do to improve their governance.

We set out our ideas of how companies can work to improve their governance in Chapter 10, where we give the outline of a programme for companies to undertake, including our view of how non-executives should be trained.

APPENDIX 5.1

Czechmate

We have just completed a finance course for senior financial managers from Czechoslovakia. They sent their first team: a man from the ministry, a sprinkling of academics; but the majority were finance directors from the major industrial companies. The acknowledged leader was Frantisek, a finance director from the armaments industry. Like most of his colleagues he was a qualified engineer, and was a bit surprised and disappointed to find out that we were only mere accountants.

'We invented the bren gun,' he told us proudly. We forbore to ask about semtex.

The purpose of the week's course was to give them a grounding into how Western companies organise their finance functions and explain our financial view of business so that they would be helped in forming alliances and joint ventures with Western organisations. The programme, however, took on a life of its own, and we found ourselves discussing the points they wanted to discuss, not the ones we had prepared. Frantisek was the ringleader in derailing our carefully prepared programme. The sessions on management accounting and costing went off without incident. Apart from activity-based costing the topics were old hat to them, and we had many a learned discussion on fixed and variable costs, directs and indirects and breakeven points. They did not appear to have many problems with overheads. 'You will', we joked with them, 'once you adopt Western business and organisational practices.'

Taxation enthralled them. They had naïvely assumed that taxes were one of those unavoidable inevitabilities of life. You simply paid them. We initiated them into the mysteries of tax avoidance, of routeing investments in and dividends out in the most tax efficient way. They were not slow to get the point and realise that they should set up international holding companies in those countries that have the largest network of double taxation agreements. Somewhat to our chagrin they plumped for the Netherlands.

And then we got on to the topic nearest to their hearts: how to organise their companies. The discussion centred round the role of the board of directors, and we had prepared for this, bringing in a senior executive from one of the more prestigious City institutions to lead the debate.

He explained best practice in Britain, how boards were in effect divided into two components, the executive directors, who were the company's operational managers, and the non-executives. Frantisek was puzzled when we explained that this was voluntary and had no foundation in law. 'You mean it is not compulsory?' he asked. He found voluntary codes of conduct difficult to understand. We put his bewilderment down to the fact that he was from Mitteleuropa after all, as well as having the drawback of being an engineer. Our City man went on and explained the role of the non-exectuve director: to participate fully in the affairs of the company, yes, but also to monitor the remuneration of the chairman and the executives as well as to control the standards and quality of the accounting through the audit com- mittee of the board. 'All on 20 days' service a year', muttered the Czechs, 'but then you British always were a race of supermen.'

'Who do they report to?' asked Frantisek. Why, we answered, the share- holders of course. But, he went on remorselessly, as the institutions own two-thirds of the shares on the market, surely these non-executives are in reality the nominees of the institutions? Our City man was appalled. 'They are independent,' he thundered. The Czechs were surprised. What is the point, they asked, of getting independent directors in? Surely you must have people who are fully involved? How else can they give proper advice?

There was clearly a culture clash here. How could we expect these people, with their sad history, to understand? It was explained to them that the non-executive directors have to be independent so as better to check the executives.

The Czechs were clearly bewildered: could it be the quality of the simul- taneous translation that was confusing everything? Who chooses the non- executives? The shareholders of course, well . . . if you insist, it is the chairman and the executive directors really. Who determines their pay? Well, the executives of course. And then they in turn are meant to control the executives' pay? The Czechs looked at us as if we had gone mad. Was this perhaps some elaborate British joke we were playing on them?

The man from the ministry, who had been taking careful notes, was completely at a loss: 'We do not see the logic of this,' he said in his precise English, 'if some of them are, as you say, executive directors in one com- pany, and non-executives in another, surely it is in their interest to help each other in the matter of pay and not cause difficulties for each other.' Lamely our City man fell back on the audit committee and its controls. 'On two days a month', hooted Frantisek, 'and without a staff. I bet I could run rings round any non-executive.'

None of them could understand how we could call one group of directors independent, who in some vague way controlled the others – who had selected them in the first place – and how all of them were regarded at the same time as having the same obligations in law.

Frantisek summed up their perplexities:

You are telling us that the owners of British companies, the institutions, act through non-executive directors who they have not chosen. That these men are selected by the people they have to at the same time work with and monitor. That they are usually directors of other companies or ex-civil servants whose salaries are fixed by those whose salaries they fix. They have to be independent even though fully responsible, yet also give good advice and be good company men. And they are part-time. This is voluntary, and all the papers are full of British company scandals where it seems the non-executives either did nothing or were not aware of what was happening.

The Czechs asked how the Germans get round this difficulty. 'They have these supervisory boards,' said the City man dismissively, 'which stifle initiative, and slow things up.' 'If only we were as stifled or as slow as Siemens, BMW or Daimler-Benz', said one of the academics innocently. The conversation got round to a comparison of the British and German economies and before we knew it we were explaining the German and Dutch two-tier board structure, where the different rights are enshrined by law, where directors have to be qualified, and where the rights of employees are protected. The Czechs clearly preferred their directors committed and qualified rather than independent.

They took copious notes and it was clear that at the first opportunity they would cross over the border into Germany and see how a successful economy managed its corporate governance. They were nice about it though: 'Provided you have a race of geniuses', said Frantisek, 'your system will work perfectly. Unfortunately we Czechs are just ordinary people, so we shall have to take lessons from the likes of Volkswagen.'

Source: Reprinted by kind permission of *Management Accounting* magazine.

6 THE COMPANY AND ITS STAKEHOLDERS

A WIDER VIEW OF GOVERNANCE

The management perspective

So far we have been looking at governance from a legal and regulatory point of view, focusing very much on the top board of directors. Indeed, up to this point, despite ourselves, we have been treating governance almost as something on its own, as a means of ensuring balance between the various interested parties in a company's affairs: a way of making sure that the chairman or chief executive is under control, producing transparency in reporting or curbing excessively generous remuneration packages. But we have not concerned ourselves with the essence of what business is all about.

All these checks are not ends in themselves; they are means to an end, which is to be successful in business. Different organisations define success in different ways, but the definition always includes words such as growth, market share, innovation, product leadership and, above all else, profitability. It is therefore appropriate to look at the large multinational companies that are the subject of our book, from a purely practical point of view: how best should the constitutional structure of the company, the governance of the corporation, be put together so that it adds value to the business?

We shall therefore now take a much wider perspective so as to examine the main factors that influence the application of governance in a company from an operational point of view. And in this chapter we shall examine the topic under three broad headings:

(i) *Management and its perspective*. Management personalities and their culture are important drivers, as is the inevitable interplay between the centripetal pull of the centre against the centrifugal tendencies of the business units.
(ii) *The business itself*. Operating management considerations shade into governance as you look at the business from the point of view of the

divisions or the geographical organisation. Vertically too, the two considerations merge. Thus main board directors of a multinational company may be executive directors with divisional, functional or regional responsibilities at main board level. At a subsidiary level, however, they may well act in the role of a non-executive chairman, with the divisional managers taking the part of executive directors.

(iii) *The stakeholders in a company*. 'Governance is too important to be left to the shareholders,' was how one non-executive director put it to us, only half jokingly. The bigger and the more widespread the companies are, the more people they affect and the more communities are affected by them.

Having defined the outside interests in a company in this chapter we can take it one stage further, in Chapter 7, and make our recomendations for a British approach to the subject. But before we can pull our philosophy together we shall need to look at the subject from a number of different angles. To do this we shall have to take a brief look at how companies are organised, and the implications for governance, exploring the wider world of the multinational corporation and examining the two essential aspects of corporate relationships: the internal relationships; and how corporations face the outside world. This latter reflects the new pressures from the outside world that are impacting on the way companies are governed and that provide us with pointers as to the direction current practice is moving in.

The relationship between companies and the wider outside constituency is a double-facing one: companies need to influence key decision-makers in the outside world, and at the same time there are many groups and communities that have an interest in the company and its fortunes and will want to influence it.

BP and BOC: two different approaches

Companies themselves have no doubt that they serve a wider world. In its annual report, BP states: 'In everything BP does, it is committed to creating wealth – always with integrity – for its shareholders, employees, customers, and suppliers, and the community in which it operates.' BP, like many other companies, recognises it owes a duty to more people than just its shareholders. Other companies try to depict this relationship in financial terms. British Oxygen Company (BOC) expresses the concept in a different way by showing who benefited in 1990 from the added value of £1,053.5 million earned by the company. This is set out in Table 6.1.

	£ million	%
To employees as pay or as contribution to pensions and welfare schemes	653.8	62.1
To banks and other lenders as interest	71.9	6.8
To governments as taxes on profits	90.9	8.6
To partners in companies not wholly owned by the Group	5.0	0.5
To shareholders	88.8	8.4
Amount retained within the group	143.1	13.6

Table 6.1   Distribution of BOC added value 1990

Source: BOC annual report

The internal dynamics of multinational organisations: the driving factors

The organisation structure quite clearly must also impact on the way a company's governance is constituted. There is no one answer as to how multinationals, or any other company, should be organised. It depends not only on the industry but also on the culture, the shareholding, the point in time, the leadership and management style, and, most importantly but perhaps surprisingly, the company's history. Over a quarter of a century after his death, the style of AGIP SpA, the Italian oil exploration and production giant, is still dominated by the legacy of Enrico Mattei, the man who started the group on the road to successful growth; the founding fathers of the Marks & Spencer retail chain may have quit the scene a long time ago, but they have left an indelible mark on a company that is renowned for its unique blend of community, employee and social care.

   Different types of organisations have different governance profiles, which depend on such factors as:

   (i)   The size of the head office and its role.
  (ii)   The type of organisation structure: divisional, geographical or a mixture of the two.
 (iii)   The type of company and its legal structure, e.g. state company, conglomerate, subsidiaries with a minority outside shareholding, and so on.

It must be clear that we are not just referring to one board, the main board, but to a whole family of boards, some of which could be of large companies in places other than the parent company's home country.

The eternal triangle

The role of the centre

At this point in history companies are having to grapple with change as they have never experienced it before. Company after company that we talked to was either going through a major merger, such as ABN-AMRO or SKB, retrenching on core businesses as with Midland and NatWest Banks or BAT, or, and this was the most common, reorganising to push accountability from the centre down to the divisions or business units: BP, Hoechst, Rhône-Poulenc, Solvay, Ciba-Geigy and Akzo are just a few of the companies that are trying to resolve the eternal problem of balancing the synergy that can be achieved from the headquarters' co-ordination role with the need for the operating flexibility of stand-alone, autonomous divisions.

From a governance point of view there are three components of a multi-national: the centre, a geographically-based organisation, and a product based organisation. The balance of power between the three varies according to time, circumstances and management fashion.

The current trend is to pass managerial responsibility downwards, and to leave the head offices as small units with carefully defined functions. In conglomerates in particular, head offices are very small indeed: starting in 1990 BP, under Bob Horton, began a reorganisation and a process of culture change intended to reduce its central staff down to a few hundred and pass more autonomy to the operating divisions; BTR with a world-wide turnover in 1990 of £6.7 billion, makes do with about 50 head office staff as befits its reputation as a notoriously lean and mean conglomerate. BTR consists of eight management and holding companies and about 70 principal subsidiaries organised in five big divisions, which are mini-conglomerates in their own right.

A headquarters has three roles: strategic at main board level, which also includes top level personnel planning, financial management and government relations. Strategy is the most important role, finance and accounting staff are the most numerous. Electrolux is typical. The headquarters corporate staff cover the following functions:

(i) Administration
(ii) Financial management
    (a) control;
    (b) treasury;
    (c) risk;
    (d) administration.
(iii) Audit.
(iv) Mergers and acquisitions.

(v) Technical R & D.

(vi) Legal counsel.

With Electrolux as with so many multinationals, the business areas, such as Zanussi, are mighty organisations in their own right, with their own headquarters and staff functions. They handle the operations while the performance reporting is centralised on a pan-company data base. Electrolux had a turnover of some £9 billion in 1990, employing 151,000 people. It was the 155th largest European company by market capitalisation in 1991. It follows a divisional organisation and is divided into 19 product lines within five business areas.

Business area or country management?

Historically, before the days of advanced information technology and before the concept of global products, it was most common to have an organisation based almost entirely on geographical lines. Small companies might have executives at head office with geographical responsibilities but the larger companies tended to supplement their corporate headquarters with regional or national local head offices. Thus it is not unusual for many US organisations to have European or European, Middle East and Africa head offices: really large ones such as Citibank in the UK, would also have national head offices in those countries where they had a really significant presence.

From the national, cultural and control points of view there is much to be said for the concept of a geographical organisation. The problem is that in a multiproduct company – and few multinationals are not multiproduct – business units have more in common with their fellow subsidiaries in the same market sector, even though they might be in different countries. Aggregating country units for geographical reasons would therefore result in an aggregation of businesses in different market sectors.

In today's era of world-wide products and global competition, the product division concept is finding favour with very many companies. The key organisational aspect here is the division or business unit which is where the technical and product expertise resides. The subsidiary units report to the division regardless of their location, so that in any one country the company may have several units. They could all be in different divisions, and therefore they would report to different divisional headquarters, often located in other countries. The advantage is the operational advantage of putting like with like, but there are governance problems in that companies would find it difficult to mobilise themselves effectively on a national or regional stage. Globalisation and the EC may be powerful forces but one should never ignore nationalism and provincialism. As we know from our consultancy experience, woe betide the consulting firm that has only one national Belgian office in Brussels, without another in Antwerp: or in Italy: Rome and not Milan; in Spain: Madrid and not Barcelona, and Lisbon and not Oporto in Portugal.

In practice companies have to adopt a compromise, matrix arrangement, balancing product divisions with country organisations, a difficult balance to maintain without conflicts or bureaucracy. Figure 6.1 sets out how one company, the French chemical company Rhône-Poulenc (R-P), with a turnover in 1990 of some £8 billion, and a world-wide workforce of 92,000 (of whom 50,000 are outside France), manages the organisational balance. The business area dominates in R-P's case, but even so it is not clear cut. The centre exerts a powerful pull on key service functions such as finance and human resources (HR), and senior financial and HR executives find themselves reporting to both their divisional and the central functional management. Major divisions such as health and agrochemicals themselves also contain regional management, while at the same time there are country delegations for the main countries R-P operates in. Local nationals fill these posts in Germany, the USA, Brazil, Spain and the UK. Many companies follow the same policy, but whatever they do, one thing is almost universal standard practice: the country representative for the USA is nearly always a US citizen.

The matrix

Rhône-Poulenc is not unusual in having a matrix organisation. Most major international organisations follow the same pattern. The balance depends on circumstances and people. Shell has traditionally given great power and prestige to its country general managers, while BP has put more emphasis on the divisional structure. Even so, two of BP's main board directors have regional responsibilities, and are located in Singapore and the USA, to oversee the corporation's interests there. Other companies, such as Hoechst and ICI, for instance, allocate portfolios to their main board members, some of whom will therefore have regional responsibilities to add to their other jobs.

Some companies find that their actual situation is a big determinant in defining their organisation structure. Thus the Belgian chemical group, Solvay, the European number 171 in 1991, has to have a great regard for national susceptibilities: it has higher sales in France, Germany, the USA and even Spain than in Belgium, and indeed recognises its internationalism by publishing its accounts in English, Flemish, French and German. On the other hand, BAT, is typical of many holding companies which have major

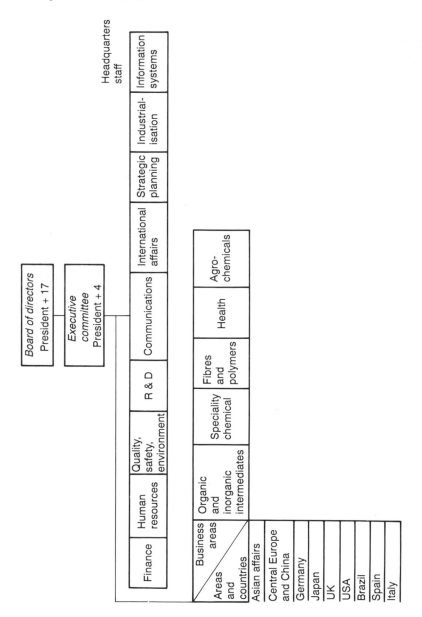

Figure 6.1   Rhône-Poulenc organisation chart

Source: Rhône-Poulenc annual accounts, 1990

industrial groups under its wing. It has Farmers Group, Eagle Star, Allied Dunbar, British-American Tobacco, and so on. Nestlé, with a less diversified product range, neatly balances regional with divisional imperatives in the case of its major subsidiaries Barilla and Nestec (the former Rowntree-Mackintosh), each of which has its allotted role in Nestlé's product strategy, though they are less important than previously. The intention appears to be for the company's minerals water strategy to be centred round Perrier, and it will be interesting to see how the eventual organisation restructuring will develop if Nestlé's acquisition of Perrier is allowed to go ahead.

Inchcape, the former colonial trading house, reorganised itself in 1991 away from the former country-style organisation. It had found that one of the drawbacks to a country structure was that the business remained parochial in its outlook, with people bounded by their national frontiers. A reorganisation on product lines also cut out several layers of management – always a potent consideration in the cost-cutting era of the 1990s. The result has been a matrix structure. Interviewed by the *Financial Times*, (27 January 1992), the company's chief executive gave it as his view that the new structure was four-fifths product globalisation, and one-fifth country. The latter could not be completely abolished, and was still important in certain countries such as Singapore and Hong Kong which were separate markets in their own right. For that reason country management was usually allocated to a marketing executive. Even so, Inchcape has some way to go in governance: though an international trading company, there was at that time only one non-British non-executive member of the board, a French national.

The point to emphasise is that just as management and control are adapted to the organisation structure and the company's business sector, so governance is not just a rigid formula to be applied in an identical way in every single case. Its application, too, has to be sensitive to the organisation and the business. However, there are some fixed points. Whatever the subsidiary structure, there has to be a top board which has the ultimate responsibility for the business. It is therefore appropriate that we have a look at the main board from a management perspective.

The role of the main board

The legal structure of any group of companies is often as complicated as its management structure. There is a pyramid of boards of directors in multi-national companies, some of the subsidiaries being major operating companies, others nameplate companies for tax or fiscal or other reasons. Some of the subsidiaries can also be public companies with outside shareholding. One thing is certain, however, and that is that the top board is the most important. Main board directors, therefore, have a special responsibility.

A main board director of a multinational company is not just a divisional or functional director writ large. It is a different job. There is a special quality of direction that looks at the situation as a whole, takes a longer-term and strategic view of the business. What distinguishes direction from management is that there has to be a strategic awareness combined with lateral thinking and the power of delegation. The directors, and no one else, have the ultimate responsibility for the company to the shareholders and stakeholders. Their role is to:

(i) Define the company's business and long-term objectives and to identify the strategic opportunities.

(ii) Make sure that the company has access to the right quality of people, technology and organisation.

(iii) Set the cultural and moral tone of the company.

(iv) Evaluate and monitor the chairman and the chief executive, and, if necessary, to replace them.

(v) Evaluate the internal controls to ensure the protection of the shareholders' assets and to validate the financial statements issued by the company.

(vi) Take care that the company has effective management processes for making sure that its resources are applied to the profitable exploitation of business opportunities.

(vii) Oversee the process of management development to provide an adequate succession.

Big international companies rely on flexibility in their directors who have to combine several roles at different levels: executive main board director, non executive subsidiary board director, non-executive or executive subsidiary board chairman, and so on. They have to show a broader and longer-term strategic awareness and perception; they have to set the style of the organisation, be able to look ahead, and not be bound by the confines of the present, and of their business unit. A tall order indeed!

The board of a multinational has to be able to rely on support from a high quality management team, but there are two critical factors outside this management team that have to be present. The first is a creative and stimulating chairman who carries weight and respect throughout the company, not just at board level. To listen to the governance debate you might be forgiven for imagining that boardroom business is dominated by controversy and confrontation. On the contrary, such a situation is not the norm and is, furthermore, a sign of a failure of governance. The chairmen's role is critical. They have to build a team and to weld it together. To do that they also need the vision and independent perspective of directors who are not part of the operating management of the business. To us, independence means independence of thought and of attitudes, rather than independence of the company they are directors of.

Having outside directors, therefore, is very important as they can best provide this independent perspective. They should also add lustre to the business and, it goes without saying, they need to be selected with care. In Britain the regulatory authorities will vet the persons to be appointed to the boards of banks and building societies. One building society director told us that when he was checked out by the regulator before becoming a director of the society it was like filling out an application form for employment. In a sense that is what it is. There are six business, as opposed to regulatory, criteria for the selection of independent outsiders to the board:

(i) To obtain specialist experience.
(ii) To give access to governments, authorities, opinion leaders, specialist sources of information, etc.
(iii) To provide an independent appraisal and check on management.
(iv) To strengthen the board.
(v) To give a new perspective on the company's direction.
(vi) To provide status.

An outside director, like any other director, is part of a team. We cannot emphasise enough the importance of team-building. It is one thing to bring the most talented people into the company, but if they cannot or will not work together, the result will be chaos. There is a small and very successful British company that we have worked with and very much admire. The chairman is also the majority shareholder but he has deliberately created a two-board structure, as it were. He has built up the executive team as the management of the main operating company. He chairs its meetings and monitors overall progress. But, basically, he leaves it alone to get on with the job of running the company that makes the majority of the profits for the group. It is not easy for a majority shareholder to have such a hands-off attitude. It is his money, after all. There is also the group board, which he calls the supervisory board, and which we would call the supervisory council. This board consists of himself, the group finance director (the group controller is the finance director of the operating company), and an outside director who is also the minority shareholder. The top board concentrates on strategy and succession planning, group cash and managing the property subsidiaries. The outside director is the chairman's *alter ego* (as well as being his brother-in-law!), who can give him advice or criticism without fear or favour, and who can, as an outside director, also deal with such emotive matters as the senior managers' pay and bonus and the car scheme – the latter always a delicate matter in British companies.

It is a small-scale example of good practice, of how boardroom relationships should be handled.

Subsidiary boards

So far we have been talking of the main board directors. The same reasoning applies to the boards of subsidiary companies in a group. Subsidiary boards are an underutilised resource and are often ignored by global companies when considering their strategic relationships. Companies fill their annual reports with their expressed determination to be good citizens in every country they operate in, and yet it is all too common for them to regard the organisation of the many subsidiary boards as a regrettable necessity and therefore merely a paper exercise, a chore at best, and to hand out the directorships of these subsidiary boards to head office staffers without any thought of the resentment that such an attitude could cause locally. Just as importantly, careful selection of the directors of major subsidiary boards could be a very useful way of strengthening the company and cementing local relationships, and all without burdening the top board with too many members and thus devaluing its importance.

We discussed this point with a senior executive of one of Britain's major companies – in the top 50 – that had just established an important operation in a foreign country. The local board was a 'paper' board, set up to satisfy local legal requirements. All its members were British, from head office. The company had never considered the benefits it could derive from having local representation on the board.

Every multinational has large numbers of legal entities in its family. Electrolux, for instance, has 609 companies in some 40 countries (per the 1990 Annual Report). It is important to exploit this resource to benefit the company. But care has to be taken to ensure that the right corporate vehicle is used. Some companies are nameplate companies and exist only on paper, to manage a property or for tax reasons. These companies are not appropriate for the type of networking we are describing here. Multinationals need to concentrate their efforts on companies in countries or regions of importance to them where either local control needs are significant or where there is a special situation because of, say, the high incidence of local shareholding. The really aware organisation, such as Shell, Unilever or IBM for instance, will use the local subsidiary board as a kind of strategic radar so that the parent can be informed as to what is going on in the host country or business area.

Outsiders are needed at the subsidiary level in just the same way as at the top board level: to lobby governments and the authorities, to give the company a high profile among local business leaders and people of influence, to cement alliances, to tap into local/national thinking and sources of information. Good citizenship in a country also entails having representatives of the great and the good of that country on the board. That is a powerful reason why companies are loath completely to abandon the country delegation concept despite all their talk of the globalisation of the business.

There is a very practical reason for all this. An international company will be big in many countries. Much as it may want to it cannot appoint all the key opinion leaders from all of its host countries on to its main board. The result would be hopelessly unwieldy. There has to be a limit if the board is to work effectively. Appointment to subsidiary boards, therefore, can be an important means of having the best of both worlds.

Siemens is an interesting example of the effective use of subsidiaries. Siemens is the ninth largest European company, employing 365,000 personnel and having a turnover of some £21 billion in 1990. It is very much organised on divisional lines, every division being the size of a multinational in its own right. There is also a parallel national organisation in the countries in which Siemens operates. One such country is the UK, and we set out Siemens UK organisation in Figure 6.2.

Siemens had a turnover of £360 million in the UK in 1990, and employed just under 3,200 persons. This was not a very large proportion of the corporation's total business, but nonetheless it was sizeable in its own right and, moreover, it was in a country of strategic importance from Siemens' point of view.

Siemens produces a very high quality annual report for its British operations. From this we note that there are several German members of top management, as you would expect, but that the 10 person board has a British chairman, and half its members are British.

The price to be paid for all this

Of course it is not as simple as all that. There is a price to be paid for this. It is not just a question of seeking out distinguished local opinion leaders and inviting them on to the board and leaving it at that. It will also be necessary to define what the subsidiary board is responsible for and what it should do. It has to be consulted, it has to make decisions, and it has to be seen to have influence on the parent. There are two dangers: over-complication with too many rules will merely stifle initiative and create the monster of a time-consuming bureaucracy. Giving the subsidiary board no powers, on the other hand, could result in the resignation from the board of just those influential people the company was hoping to enlist to its side. It is very

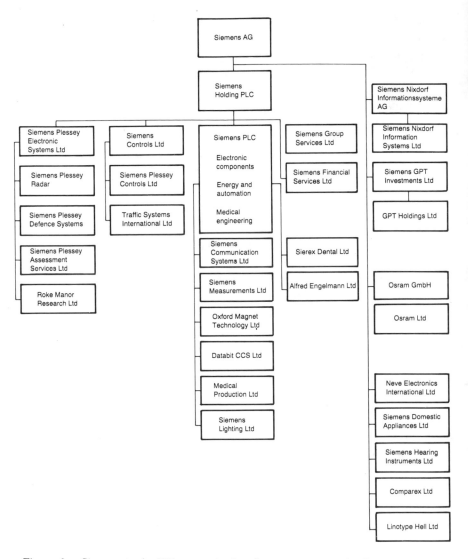

Figure 6.2 Siemens in the UK – organisational structure as at 1 April 1991
Source: Report and Accounts, Siemens PLC, 1989/90

tempting to go for a cosmetic solution and create an impressive-sounding
organisation, and attract people to it by offering fancy titles, while the reality
is that all the really important decisions are made by two or three persons at
the centre. That is not the way to build up influence in a country. There is no
point in having a series of country or regional boards if the company does not
take the trouble to consult them and use them properly, to listen to them and

to be seen to listen to them as well as to take their advice where relevant. Better do nothing than to do something and get it wrong.

Each company should think through its requirements from its subsidiary board and work out the boundaries between the different boards. We have to add that it is not just a matter of cost benefit for the company. There is intense pressure on the global company to be seen to be a good citizen of every country it is in. And what better way of demonstrating this than by having local directors? Japanese companies are under particular pressure which, we feel, will get more and more relentless with time. Already by the start of the 1990s Japanese car companies have begun to set up design centres in Europe, and Honda for one, claims that it is trying to establish Honda North America as an equal partner to the Japanese parent, while Nomura, in the banking industry, says it eventually wants to have three equal head offices: Tokyo, London and New York. Product globalisation is being followed by management globalisation. Management itself is moving from the hierarchical control models of past generations to a much more partnership-oriented approach.

THE STAKEHOLDERS

The community and the company

Multinational companies, as we have shown, have an interest in making themselves good citizens of every country and every community in which they operate. There is another side to this too. There is intense competition between countries, provinces and localities to attract strong, reputable companies because they bring employment, whether Disneyland to Paris, Nissan to Tyneside, or Volkswagen to Czechoslovakian West Bohemia. Countries and communities have a strong interest in the success of the companies they play host to, and are only too aware of how they are affected by the companies' corporate decisions. They are affected at all levels, from entire countries such as Brunei, virtually depending on a single company, Brunei Shell Oil, to towns such as Scunthorpe, which is essentially a company town for British Steel. Works closures affect much more than the direct employment; there is also the knock-on effect on indirect employment as evidenced by the closure of the steel mills around Corby or the coal mines in South Wales. When British Steel closed its plants in Lanarkshire in 1991, some 1,200 jobs were lost. The Allander Institute, Scotland's leading forecasting body, has estimated that a further 5,500 indirect jobs will also be lost over the following four years as a result of those closures. Similarly, the closure of the Ravenscraig plant, announced early in 1992, has been estimated to cost some 1,200 direct jobs and, eventually, a further 5,000 indirect jobs.

Companies are being forced to recognise their responsibilities. 'Companies of the Royal Dutch Shell Group', says Shell in its annual report, 'are members of the societies within which they operate'. And indeed Shell takes care to spread its munificence around widely. Other companies, even some of the very biggest international ones, still, regrettably, concentrate a disproportionate amount of their largesse on their home countries rather than on the other areas in which they operate. This social pressure has latterly been powerfully influenced also by the green movement, and companies are now very concerned at the environmental pressures they are under. This takes many forms. The Swiss chemical companies have a special love/hate relationship with the city of Basle, and are particularly sensitive after the spillage of chemicals into the Rhine in the late 1980s, which affected communities right down to the mouth of the river in The Netherlands. A more humble example would be the ICI works in Huddersfield. The biggest employer in Huddersfield, ICI's chemical plant is bounded on two sides by private housing. The householders have a very definite interest in ICI's anti-pollution control measures, and so the company takes care to hold regular meetings with them or their representatives, to discuss its anti-pollution measures and explain to them what it is doing. Those householders may not have shares in ICI, but nobody can deny that they have a very great stake in the local company and its actions: greater perhaps than that of most of the private shareholders.

Companies' actions take various forms: Midland Bank seconds managers to work on local enterprise agencies, Sainsbury gives priority to environmental concerns in its store development projects, and Marks & Spencer, typically, ensures that companies selling it goods, packing or transport services, take environmental concerns into consideration.

The company and its corporate partners

The intelligent use of the family of subsidiary boards, allied to the regional board structure used by some companies, is one example of how companies have developed the board mechanism into a means of gathering together their business network or partners. The word business partner is coming into vogue: Renault talks of its partnership with suppliers who account for half the cost of its vehicles. Very few multinationals are so big and powerful that they can exist alone, outside a business network of alliances and partners, and even those that are big enough find that it pays them to work within such networks.

Partnership is different from the old-fashioned relationship with suppliers and dealers or agents: it means working together rather than each one trying to get the upper hand over the other. The Japanese car industry and its relationship with its component suppliers and its agents, has provided any number of examples, but Britain's very efficient retail industry also demonstrates how companies can work together for their common good.

Marks & Spencer prides itself on working with its suppliers, but it also imposes its stringent quality and cost control standards on them. The company is so important because of the sheer size of its buying power. It is reckoned that in 1992 M & S will have purchased more than £4.5 million worth of goods from its suppliers, making it the biggest purchaser of clothing in the UK. It is the purchaser of at least a quarter of all the clothing made in the country. The company is criticised for being a hard taskmaster, but, for its own part, it feels that it has saved the British clothing industry from the fate of, say, the British motor cycle industry. Businesses have been built up on the back of M & S with links going back even as far as 100 years! The connection between M & S and its suppliers is technical at one level, with the use of such devices as electronic data exchange, thus allowing M & S to manage its supply chain more effectively. For the companies concerned, this co-operation with their overwhelmingly important customer also exists at another level. Their strategy and investment programmes have to take account of M & S and its requirements. Marks & Spencer may not have its executives on the boards of supplier companies but no one can deny that it has an influence over their governance, using that term in its widest sense.

Purchasing links

There is a growing trend in certain industries for products to be purchased within the framework of such partnerships. Close customer and supplier relationships are being developed, helped by the strong interdependence between companies as a result of processes like just-in-time (JIT). Buyers are organising networks of contractors and subcontractors among their suppliers, like the pyramid-shaped organisations of Japanese automobile producers. These relationships extend to collaboration in distribution and even the siting of warehouses and plants. Such relationships also have to involve the greater circulation of information among the partners and more openness in information between them. Renault's *Information Achat* programme, for instance, periodically brings together the CEOs of some 80 of Renault's best suppliers. One of the objectives is to develop control procedures with the intention of reducing costs for everyone.

Purchasing collaboration, or 'co-makership' in the popular business jargon phrase, is now a key element in the business strategy of many companies. You have only to look at your personal computer, or under the bonnet of your car to realise that an increasing number of manufacturing companies themselves produce fewer and fewer of the parts that go into their products. The proportion of their costs that goes into their wages bill is shrinking at the expense of the amount that goes into purchases from third parties. It is the accepted wisdom that companies should stick to their core businesses and expertise and not try to attempt to compete in peripheral areas where they do not have the know-how.

They are therefore having to purchase more from third parties as the shift in their manufacturing balance has impacted on their purchasing strategies. The toughness is still there, but the old adversarial buyer–seller relationship has changed: dual sourcing is less common. More of a supplier's business is going to a single customer, and vice versa. The talk is of 'partnership purchasing' linked to a JIT philosophy to remove the traditional barriers. The goal is a perfect fit between supplier and customer. In practice this means technical and planning co-operation. The customer defines the supplier's role as closely as possible, also setting out the performance criteria that must be satisfied, leaving it to the supplier to identify the best way to accomplish this at the lowest cost. Marks & Spencer even gives its suppliers consultancy-type assistance to help them achieve this goal. The collaboration goes as far as transport arrangements: it is not only Toyota in Japan (and in the north of England) that has its suppliers sited next door to its plants, IBM has been doing the same at Havant on the south coast since 1988. The aerospace industry is another sector where the huge development costs make partnership a business essential. The Boeing 747 has 6 million parts purchased from 1,500 suppliers in 15 different countries. Manufacturing of such complexity has to be organised quite differently from the arrangements traditionally provided by the classical purchasing departments of the past with their armies of buyers and clerks.

Other types of links

British Aerospace (BAe) quite openly states that its future will have to lie in global alliances. Its competitor across the Channel, Aerospatiale, says its policy is to encourage alliances so as to give the company strategic advantage in each of the sectors and for each of the programmes in which it is engaged. A network of partnerships is seen as enabling it to broaden its market access and make it possible for R & D to be shared. It envisages a wide range of legal structures to do this: for tactical missiles there is the Euromissile, a Franco-German consortium; the EMDG group on the other hand, is an arrangement between BAe, MBB (from Germany), the Italian Alenia and the French Thomson, as well as Aerospatiale itself. Early in 1992 Aerospatiale announced that it had linked its helicopter interests with those of MBB in the so-called Eurocopter Group. The next stage could well be further links with Alenia and Deutsche Aerospace. The airlines, too, are now busily seeking partners, and it is accepted wisdom that Europe will be dominated by no more than four to six groupings within the next five years.

There are any number of corporate structures to accommodate such links. It could be through joint subsidiaries, as above, it could be through cross-shareholdings as between Renault and Volvo, or between the Royal Bank of Scotland and Banco de Santander, or it could be a simple investment in a company as is the French Groupe Victoire's stake in the Danish insurer Baltica, which earns it one seat on Baltica's board; whatever the arrangement, this is a new and growing trend.

French, Italian and Spanish groupings work on an extended family – you might almost call them hunting pack – basis, where whole empires are constructed through cross-shareholdings and directorships between friends and allies. Figure 6.3 sets out one such grouping, the alliance in the French food industry between the Agnelli family, of Fiat fame, their friend Mr Mentzelopoulos and his family interests, and the link with Mr Antoine Riboud, chairman of the French BSN food group. The situation shown is that at the turn of the year 1991–92, which formed the background to the byzantine manoeuvres round the takeover target, Source Perrier, with the Agnelli interests on one side, Nestlé and its allies from the Indosuez bank on the other, and BSN, apparently, in between. Mr Giovanni Agnelli is a director of Lazard Frères, while his younger brother, Umberto, is a director of BSN, whose business interests the Agnellis have pushed in Italy. On the other side, Mr M. David-Weill and Mr A. Riboud, chairmen of Lazard Frères and of BSN, respectively, are on the boards of several Agnelli-controlled companies. Despite all this, the Agnellis were still worsted in the battle.

Readers will notice not only the complexity of the relationship, but also what powerful allies it is necessary even for the Agnelli family to try to secure for themselves in France. Even though they have for years been involved in French business, they have still been seen as outsiders as against the Swiss Nestlé company.

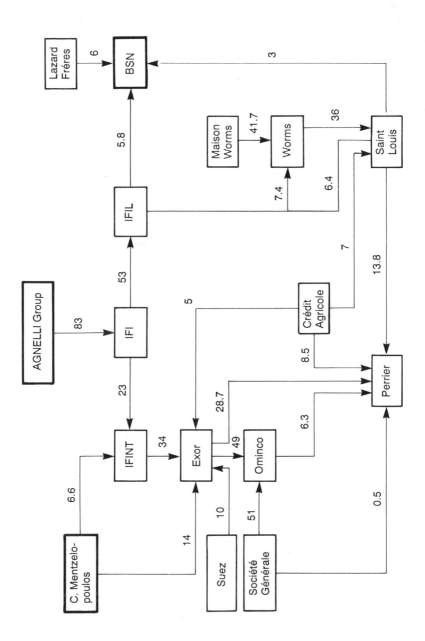

Figure 6.3   The Agnellis and their French allies, January 1992

Source: Les Echos

Note: All figures are percentages

The Japanese approach

The kairetsu *network*

In Japan there are basically two forms of company grouping: horizontal and vertical. The horizontal groups consist of a sizeable number of large companies, in different industrial sectors, held together by cross-shareholdings and old-boy networks. It can almost be likened it to a gathering of the clans, the objective being to beat the other clans! At the centre there will be a bank or a company that is well endowed with cash and which can provide the other members of the group with capital at low cost. It has been estimated that the Sumitomo, Sanwa, Mitsui, Mitsubishi and Dai Ichi Kangyo groups account for about one quarter of Japan's total business assets and revenues.

It is possible to get the feel for such a network by looking at the accounts of a major Japanese company such as Nissan, which reported that it had just over 133,000 shareholders in 1990: the key ones are set out in Table 6.2.

The Dai-Ichi Mutual Life Assurance Co.	5.7
The Industrial Bank of Japan	4.6
The Fuji Bank	4.6
Nippon Life Insurance Co.	4.2
The Sumitomo Bank	2.6
The Yasuda Trust and Banking Co.	2.5
The Kyowa Bank	2.4
Sumitomo Life Insurance	2.2
The Nissan Fire and Marine Insurance Co.	2.0
The Meiji Mutual Life Insurance Co.	2.0

Table 6.2   Major shareholdings in Nissan, 1990 (%)

Source: Nissan annual report (1990)

There are also vertical groupings. These are pyramids of companies that serve a single end manufacturer who dictates virtually everything, including the prices it will pay, to the hundreds of suppliers that make up the supply pyramid. These suppliers are often prohibited from selling outside the grouping of companies.

The banks as partners

Readers will notice that in both the above cases banks are featured as business partners, not just as sources of term finance. It is well known how effectively the German banks are able to network throughout German business as investors, owners and allies: when Morgan Grenfell was purchased by Deutsche Bank, MG's senior executives could not believe how easily Deutsche Bank's network opened almost any door in Germany to them. The introductions came from the Deutsche Bank's directors on the companies' supervisory councils. We have commented earlier on how business failures such as those of the Maxwell companies or Brent Walker have resulted in British banks virtually owning these companies, but such ownership does not come easily to them, unlike the favourable attitude of the German, Japanese, and, latterly, French banks.

A stunning illustration of what partnership is all about in the banking relationship is illustrated by the story of British Leyland (BL) and Toyo Kogyo (TK), the manufacturer of Mazda cars. At the time of the oil shock of 1974, TK's production of 800,000 units was two-thirds that of BL. British Leyland's debts were one-quarter of TK's, which were approaching $1.4 billion. The oil shock hit the car industry badly as finance was needed to develop a whole new generation of energy efficient cars. The consortium of the British clearers refused to help BL (the risk was too high and the returns too uncertain), leaving it to the government to step in, with its preference for spending money on redundancy payments rather than on investment.

Sumitomo, on the other hand, stood steadfastly by its ally. It sent in a crisis task force which cut production (of the gas-guzzling rotary engine), froze pay and cut dividends (imagine British reactions to that!), but made a huge investment in products and equipment. By 1980 TK had launched five new models and had cut the labour force by 27 per cent. The rest is history.

Toyo Kogyo's board was the place where it rallied its partners. Sumitomo was one such. It held 5 per cent of TK's equity. It shared the risks, but it also had access to the detailed figures. It had an intimate knowledge of the company and knew which managers it would have to replace, for instance. Sumitomo had been watching and taking notes for years. Of course Sumitomo also had the expertise and managerial competence to deal with such a situation from an industrial rather than a financial viewpoint. The British banks simply do not have staff with such skills. As Herbert Levinstein, the Victorian founder of the British dyestuffs industry, and himself a German, wrote: 'In England we have always suffered from a lack of educated money.'

A concern for people

The employee as stakeholder
It has been usual for a long time for companies to thank their workforce in their annual accounts. Would it be cynical to suggest that perhaps now they are beginning to mean it?

Corporate managers, busy with their calculations of shareholder value and portfolio analysis, often forget that a company is only as good as its people, and that the staff have a much greater stake in the company than most of the shareholders. They depend on it for their careers, their livelihoods, and eventually, their pensions. In 1991 the spotlight in Britain was very much on the pensions.

Americans are continually surprised at the difficulty in dismissing employees in continental Europe (we exclude the UK quite specifically). On the continent the company is seen not as a piece of financial real estate, as it were, but from the industrial point of view, as a living organism, of concern to the community (or communities) that houses it and the employees that work in it, one of its main objectives being to ensure that it gives those employees the scope and the space to develop and to live useful, fulfilling and rewarding lives.

North European companies have always emphasised their concern to involve the staff in the company. This is much more than just having employees on the board, though that is very important. Deutsche Bank takes great care to co-operate with employee representatives in staff councils both at local and at group level. The main topics discussed with the general staff council and the group staff council in 1990 were fairly contentious matters: the effects of restructuring, the development of the appraisal system, environmental protection, and the increase in the number of positions open to the disabled. In 1990, also, as a result of changes in German law, for the first time a committee of spokesmen for senior executives and a group committee of spokesmen were elected. These committees discussed such matters as business and personnel policy.

Nor should we be surprised. At a time of unprecedented change in working conditions and corporate organisation, when companies are merging and reorganising, hiving off divisions and acquiring new ones almost as a matter of routine, it is only natural that the employees should feel concerned if not alarmed at what is happening to their company and to their jobs. The works councils in Germany and The Netherlands serve as a very useful communications channel to ensure that they are informed and that their views are at least heard.

Both ABB and SKB used teams of many hundreds of executives in total to cement the detail of their mergers, and both groups say they were very pleased with the results. Apart from anything else it was the best way to gain their commitment. At the time of their merger, ABN and AMRO agreed a social plan with the workforce. It is obvious that the merger of the two banks will have to result in staff reductions over the years. The staff reductions will be subject to the social plan, the main principles of which have been agreed as:

(i) No redundancies for permanent staff as a result of reorganisations.
(ii) Preferential treatment in the internal labour market for staff whose jobs are lost or undergo significant change.
(iii) An obligation on staff to accept suitable alternative employment offered.

Works councils in British companies tend to be much more at a plant – trade union level, but companies are increasingly realising the need for communication at all levels and the more advanced companies are investing time and effort in this process: ICI has a three-tier consultation system with its employees, including formal committees. Staff share schemes are also another popular method of involving the staff in their company's fortunes.

Recently, the first large UK employer to set up a formal worker participation scheme since the ill-fated attempts in the 1970s, was Royal Mail. It announced in March 1992 that it planned to give union representatives a say in a wide range of business issues including prices, standards of service, and new technology. It was emphasised, however, that this did not amount to co-management, and, we note, the announcement referred to 'union' not employee representatives. We repeat again, and cannot repeat too often, that workers' representation on supervisory councils in Germany and The Netherlands, and the workers councils of Belgium and France does not constitute an involvement in management. Supervision and consultation are not management.

There is a further area which has often been neglected in the past, but which has come to public attention as a result of the Mirror Group Newspapers affair, and that is that companies need to have concern not just for their present employees, but for past employees as well. German companies take care to honour their retired staff but they do not have the same legal relationships with them through the pension funds that British companies do. We believe very strongly that past employees, too, are important stakeholders in a concern, that companies need to consider them, and that caring for pensioners (and properly caring for the pension funds) is a significant aspect of governance.

Training
Training goes hand in hand with a concern for the employee. International companies are working hard to build up an international staff cadre, and most major companies are investing heavily in management training and management development. For example, BP prides itself on having nearly 2,000 staff from 30 BP companies working in over 50 locations. German

companies are tackling the task of bringing their employees in what was formerly East Germany up to Western standards, treating this almost as a crusade. German companies have always invested heavily in training. In 1990 Deutsche Bank had some 5,060 apprentices in the group out of 68,500 staff. French companies have by law to report on their training policies and to quote the amount they have spent on training. In Britain some companies, such as Shell and ICI, are well known for the quality of the training they have offered their staffs. ICI boasts of the fact that about a quarter of its employees are graduates. Almost imperceptibly, companies are accepting that training for the job, development for the next job, training for better qualifications, and even language training, are things they have to provide their employees with, almost as of right, and they will have to account for this to the outside world. This concern lasts right through to the retirement stage and companies increasingly see the necessity of taking care of their pensioners too.

A SYNTHESIS IS WHAT IS REQUIRED

In this chapter we have attempted to delineate the boundaries of governance by identifying all the different organisational factors that impact on it, by looking at the pressures a company is under, and by identifying the key interested parties that have a stake in the enterprise. In this way we are beginning to identify the elements of a new philosophy and to suggest a way out of the dead-end we seem to have arrived at in Britain in our approach to governance.

The first stage is to understand the world of the company. Board structures depend on organisations, whether synergistic world wide ones such as airlines, banks or oil and chemical companies, or completely decentralised conglomerates with tiny head offices. Different situations require different approaches to boardroom management. A conglomerate such as BSN, which has many different national companies, has to be governed in one way, while one with only a few but very major subsidiaries in different industry sectors, such as BAT, will require quite a different approach.

Then we have to realise that governance cascades downwards, and affects not only the top board but also the whole family of boards that report to it. Executive directors on the main board may also be in a 'supervisory' role as non-executive directors on important subsidiary boards and will have to change their roles accordingly. These subsidiary boards can be very important indeed if they relate to major companies, and especially if there is outside shareholding.

Structure is one thing, but understanding and accepting the importance of the stakeholders is just as important. Readers will have realised by now our deep conviction that a company is not just a piece of property owned by its shareholders but a community with obligations to others such as the employees, business partners, lenders of finance, customers and the surrounding community.

There are several caveats of course. Stakeholders are very different from pressure groups, and companies will have to take care to distinguish the one from the other. Nor are we suggesting an uncritical acceptance of other countries' solutions and practices. We agree most emphatically with the Institute of Directors, for instance, in its criticism of the growing practice among US companies of electing to their boards of directors persons who have particular affinities with various social groupings such as racial minorities, women and consumers. Not only are such actions insulting to the persons concerned, but such a direct representation of special interests could well result in the breakdown of the boardroom consensus that is so essential for the effective governance of a company. The politicisation of business on Italian and even French lines is not on the agenda either, nor is the *kairetsu* system, admirably though it appears to serve Japanese companies. We can learn from some of its aspects, such as co-makership, but we accept that as a whole it would not fit into the British business culture. The downside smacks too much of cronyism, insider pressures and even corruption. However, we have also to accept that other stakeholders, too, have an interest besides the shareholders, and we have tried to show that this principle is becoming accepted by British companies.

Employee participation is still a sticking point for most British companies fearful of falling into the hands of what they regard as aggressive trade unions. The lesson from north Europe that employee involvement is not such an insuperable danger could not be more positive, and surely the British employee is no less reasonable than the Germans or Dutch? We were discussing this with a senior British manager who wondered why the last few mayors of the city of Peterborough were, apparently, fairly junior British Rail employees, and yet such employees could not be trusted with British Rail board portfolios! Our view is that it will take time to build up trust but that employee involvement in governance (not management!) is not only necessary, it is also inevitable.

Any structure of corporate governance must assist in furthering the interests of a company in continuity in a manner which abides by the rules of government – of course – but which also is consistent with the interests of the existing stakeholders as well as of the shareholders. This system of accountability must not, quite clearly, attempt to replace or hinder management's judgement and right to manage the operations, but should rather provide the checks and balances, and test that judgement and that management in terms of the legitimate interests of all the different parties that have a relationship with the enterprise as well as an interest in it.

TOWARDS A NEW PHILOSOPHY

The emerging organisation

A new type of multinational organisation is emerging to shape the governance of the 1990s. Such an organisation is being characterised by an emphasis on:

  (i) Flexibility and adaptability: a willingness to experiment with new structural models, and not adhering to past structures simply because of history.

 (ii) Management through networks rather than bureaucracy, and with delegation, devolution and decentralisation, all of which make for a fitter, leaner and certainly meaner organisation.

(iii) A concern for the individual and the recognition of a duty towards the employees and past employees.

(iv) The recognition that responsibility carries accountability with it, not just for subsidiary managements, but also top management as well.

 (v) A blurring of boundaries between the company and customers, suppliers and partners (in the widest sense).

It is the last two that concern us the most. The influence of Japanese ideas and Japanese competition has focused on the need for a partnership mode of operation, with a high level of involvement from suppliers, customers and business partners as well as the workforce (influenced also by EC social pressures). In Japan this works usefully also to prevent a concentration of powers in a company.

If Japan appears too esoteric for British tastes, we have only to look across the North Sea to the German system. This depends on mutual confidence between investors, providers of finance and company managements. A useful by-product is that such confidence can allow for companies having larger quantities of long-term debt. The amount of bank lending to the top 100 companies is roughly equal in Germany and Britain. In Germany, however, a higher proportion of this is in the form of long-term investment which is cheaper for the company than a straight loan: an investment means that the bank is a business partner rather than just a straight commercial creditor. When German banks lend to the small and medium sized businesses they do not force the directors to pledge their houses and their life savings in exchange for loan finance: instead they sell some of the equity in their businesses. The German banks see this equity not as a stake to be traded on at a profit (unlike the venture capitalists) but as a token of the continuity of their involvement in the business that will allow them more information over time to further support their lending: hence their role on the supervisory councils of the companies they have invested in. This role is no sinecure. Nor is it easy for the companies concerned: there is unremitting pressure for performance in a whole variety of areas, not just financial but also in social relationships and in employee relations. This business partnership is at the same time successfully accompanied by the involvement of the workforce in the companies that employ them which is certainly being enviously regarded by the British trade unions. We do not deny that there is a downside to the German business culture: cartels, over-dominance by the banks, deals behind closed doors, a lack of openness and transparency. What is important is to take the best elements of the culture, not to copy it blindly.

The elements of a new philosophy

Figure 6.4 sets out the different pressures that impact on the governance of a company, from the internal management to the external stakeholders and interest groups. It is, of course, not strictly correct to talk of this as if it were an element of a new philosophy. It is absolutely standard in many continental countries, and the pattern set out in the figure would be recognisable and accepted by very many British companies today. They all refer to stakeholders, partners, employees and the social imperative. Indeed a large number of them talk openly in these terms in their annual reports. What we do not have – overtly – in Britain is a supervisory council structure. Instead we have non-executive directors as a kind of half-way house. British companies are already having to move in the direction of closer informal (and even formal) links with partners, customers and suppliers: they are looking for commitment from their employees, providers of finance and suppliers. What place is there in such a world – we wonder – for the here-today gone-tomorrow shareholder and the outside director hired for his or her disinterest and independence of the company?

A supervisory council where a company rallies its allies, as it were, makes the organisational issues of governance very clear. It achieves a balance through which the professionals are allowed to get on with the job of running the company but at the same time there is a formal system whereby they

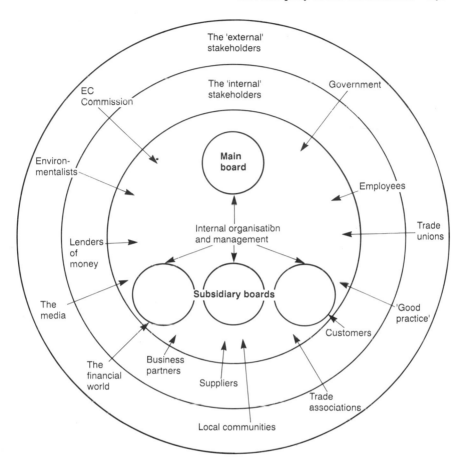

Figure 6.4 The pressures on a company

have to account for their actions to the interest groups and obtain support for major new initiatives. This seems to us to be a much neater and more effective solution than only going so far as to set up audit committees of non-executive directors, that is of directors who have originally had no interest in the company, or trying to control the executive directors by increasing the number of these outsiders, all of them sitting on the same board, with, theoretically, the same responsibilities.

One of the most important interest groups is the employees. Their role in governance is as a distinct interest group. They have no role in the professional management of a company through its board, though we should point out that the professional management of any company is also composed of persons who are employees!

The danger in Britain is that we will produce an unsatisfactory half-and-half solution relying on concepts of 'good practice' and voluntary codes and slide towards a messy compromise. We believe it is time for the job of professional management to be clearly distinguished from those whose role it is (or should be) to hold professional managers accountable, and that the different roles should be confirmed by regulation and law.

Before British readers throw up their hands in horror at this suggestion they might care to reflect on the fact that many British companies are not so very far from this solution themselves, and that it would not be so very difficult for them to institutionalise their *de facto* current executive and non-executive groupings into two boards, with the supervisory element being carried out formally by directors who are not executive directors of the company.

The John Lewis Partnership is a successful retailing organisation that has increased its turnover in every one of the last five years and whose turnover as a percentage of fixed assets has been consistently better than that of Marks & Spencer for the last 20 years. The company not only practises a very open communications policy with regard to its employees, but since 1929, when John Spedan Lewis put the family company assets into a trust for the benefit of past, current and future employees, the company has operated as a partnership with its employees who not only participate in the affairs of the company through elected councils, but also through elected membership of the board. Under the partnership's constitution five of the 12 directors hold office by annual election of the partnership's central council. In 1991 these included a senior systems analyst, a buyer and a sales assistant from the group's Peter Jones store in Chelsea, London. Management has great operating freedom, but it is held strictly accountable by the employees (or partners as they are called). As John Spedan Lewis put it, 'The supreme purpose of the John Lewis Partnership is simply the happiness of its members.' (*Business Performance in the Retail Sector, the Experience of the John Lewis Partnership*, Keith Bradley and Simon Taylor, Clarendon Press, Oxford, 1992). It really is not very different from Hoechst or any other German company. And it appears to work just as well.

7 A FORMULA FOR BRITAIN

A MOUSE ROARS

The long awaited report of the Cadbury Committee finally saw the light of day at the end of May 1992. The committee, chaired by Sir Adrian Cadbury, was set up by the Financial Reporting Council, the Stock Exchange, and the accountancy profession to report on 'The Financial Aspects of Corporate Government', and it produced the draft report a year after being set up. The report fairly set out the safe, establishment view of best practice in governance and gave a nudge to the non-executive director movement, but no more. It has been criticised by the business press for not being radical enough. We regard it as an opportunity missed.

The report accepts the current, unitary board structure, where all directors have the same responsibilities, but reinforces the position of the non-executives: listed, or to-be-listed companies, must have non-executives and these are to fill the audit committees and be a majority on the remuneration committees. There are also useful recommendations for strengthening AGMs (regarding directors' contracts) and improvement in the reporting of accounting information. The recommendations separating company management from its pensions fund management are particularly to be welcomed.

The report's timidity comes out in the fact that all this is a voluntry code of practice and therefore not mandatory. Linking it to a new listing requirement for the Stock Exchange is not strong enough. The self regulation of the financial markets is preferred to the more formal, and stringent disciplines backed up by the force of law. After all the scandals of the past few years the committee has a touching faith in humanity, though it says that if this code of best practice does not work, then legislation will have to be enacted: surely giving the game away as to its view of the difference between codes of practice and legal enforcement! We would refer the committee to the comments on codes of voluntary good practice made by the House of Commons Social Services Committee, which we reproduce in Chapter 5. In our view this unwillingness to consider legal enforcement will have four important negative results:

- it is all very well to increase the powers of the non-executive directors. In practice this will also increase their separateness from the executive directors, and, as long as there is a unitary board, this will surely only serve to exacerbate tensions on the board;
- a major opportunity for change has been missed. It could be argued on the one hand that the recommendations follow the traditional British process of gradual evolution: we see it, on the other hand, as leading to the equally traditional process of drift;
- the preference for a voluntary code of good practice will only encourage the British government in its lack of enthusiasm for enacting the necessary legislation, but;
- it will not deter the EC Commission from legislating on the subject, which will affect Britain in any case. Britain could thus have the worst of all worlds: a voluntary code of practice coupled with dirigiste Directives from Brussels.

In a sense much of the criticism the Cadbury Commission has been subjected to is unfair. Public comment appears to have regarded the committee as reporting on corporate governance in general. That is not strictly the case. The committee's terms of reference were to report on 'good financial corporate governance', focusing on 'the control and reporting functions of boards, and on the role of auditors'. The committee was, therefore, heavily biased towards the accounting profession, and it is no surprise that its report centred on the negative and inward aspects of accounting, reporting and control. The opportunity that was missed was to broaden out the remit of the committee to cover the outward looking, business and profit-generating aspects of governance. We would recommend readers to compare the comments of the committee with the attitudes and reports of Hoechst's and ABN-AMRO's supervisory councils quoted in Chapter 3, and Siemens' in Chapter 7.

A COMPROMISE SOLUTION

Objectives

The Cadbury Committee does not go far enough, and therefore in this chapter we set out our view of the structure of governance for British companies, and how they should organise themselves for it. There are two approaches: the ideal to be achieved in the long term, and the short- to medium-term compromise. In this situation the best is very much the enemy of the good, and we have therefore concentrated on what companies can achieve practically, by themselves, in the immediate future, without any changes in company law. At the end of this chapter we shall set out our ideas as to what the long-term 'solution' entails. We see the immediate structure as an interim arrangement from which companies will easily be able to move on to the longer-term solution, and therefore the two are totally compatible with each other. However, as this long-term solution involves changes in the law and the regulatory regime, there is little doubt that it will take time to achieve.

We have set ourselves six objectives in developing our ideas:

  (i) To improve the standard of governance in companies.
 (ii) To ensure a balance of all the stakeholders' interests in the governance of companies. When we refer to stakeholders we are specifically referring to partners as well.
(iii) To separate governance clearly from management as being two distinct aspects in the direction of companies.
 (iv) To protect the advisory directors: that is those the company wants to use because of their knowledge or contacts rather than their managerial abilities.
  (v) To improve financial transparency in reporting company results.
 (vi) To ensure that what we are recommending is in line with the growing trend of what companies are actually doing in Britain and abroad.

This latter point is an important one. Though the short- to medium-term solution contains no legislative changes, it does involve cultural change which could be quite considerable and daunting for some organisations. Before they baulk at this, we would point out that what we are recommending is nothing basically new: every one of our proposals has already been implemented by companies in Britain and abroad, and as we go on to point out in Chapters 8 and 9, our ideas are also in keeping with the way the governance of major companies is developing. Until the necessary legislation can be enacted, what we are recommending can be no more, alas, than a voluntary code of good practice for major companies. It is not meant to be a rigid bureaucratic requirement, to be followed to the last detail. Flexibility in the implementation of our ideas is very important, and the application of the detail will depend on companies' special situations and circumstances. Small and medium-sized companies, in particular, will find the total application of our recommendations too expensive and heavy for their organisations. With them in mind we have added an appendix on governance for the smaller company (Appendix 7.1).

The fundamental concepts

Directors fulfil several different roles in most companies, and many of the governance problems encountered by businesses result from their corporate failure to understand and distinguish between directors as executives, as stakeholders and as advisers.

The executive directors

The executives of a company are not just a single monolithic group. While some of them will also be main board directors, it is not unusual in major companies for the majority of the topmost executives not to be main board directors. They will of course be directors of subsidiaries, whether in an executive or non-executive and supervisory capacity, and could well also be non-executive members of the boards of outside companies. Senior managers of high calibre are quite used to working in many different roles, in a variety of situations.

Whether on the main board or not they will also attend the board meetings, or parts of them, as well as the relevant board committees. Thus a corporate planning director could attend board meetings concerned with strategy and planning as well as any specific strategy subcommittees of the board, while personnel directors, say, would be present when personnel policies were being discussed, as well as attending specialised board personnel committees.

There is thus no hard and fast dividing line at the top of major corporations – as opposed to the smaller company – between main board directors and everyone else. A company succeeds through the quality of its management team. A capable and cohesive management team is essential for the successful management of a company. Readers will note that we have used the word management: management is not the same as governance. Management is concerned with the company's operations, governance with ensuring that the executives do their jobs properly.

The stakeholders or partners

The stakeholders (or partners as they are often now called), are persons or corporate bodies who have a valid and critical interest in the well-being and success of the company. It is easy to make checklists of all potential stakeholders, and to include a wide variety of interests, but two undoubtedly predominate: the shareholders and the employees, and both have to be involved in governance.

Where families, individuals or industrial and commercial bodies have significant shareholdings in companies, it is usual for them also to be represented on that company's board of directors. What is not usual in Britain, however, is for the group that overwhelmingly has such a majority stake in British industry to be represented on the boards. We are, of course, referring to the institutional investors. We believe it is time for the institutions to accept their corporate responsibilities and actively pull their weight in industry rather than intervene only when they feel things have got to such a pass that they must make a stand. To misquote the popular phrase: they have to put their mouth where their money is! We appreciate that not all the institutional investors can be represented on each and every company's board. It has to be the lead institution or institutions, exactly as in Germany, where not every bank can find a place on every supervisory council. This will put pressure on the top institutions such as the Prudential Assurance. We have already suggested that the Prudential should consider accepting a range of board representation in Britain much as Deutsche Bank does in Germany. It could be argued that having directors on company boards with their access to board papers would put the investing institution so favoured in a privileged position as against everyone else. We would reply that shareholders who are currently represented have been in that same position for some time, and in any case directors and those linked to them are prevented from dealing in their company's shares at certain times in the company's financial year. Above all, the fact that an institution is represented on a company's board must be seen as a signal to the financial world that the institution in question does not regard itself as an in-and-out short-term buyer and seller of that company's shares, but as its partner. It is there for the long term and is therefore less interested in short-term share price movements and capital gains. The point about board representation is that it means that the investor is not an uncritical shareholder but one who is in a position to press for sound management. That is what governance is all about.

The employees, too, have an abiding interest in the company. British companies write a lot in their annual reports about their enlightened staff relations: they consult with their employees, communicate with them, take endless pains to recruit, train and develop them, and devise share schemes for them, and are even beginning to provide crèches for their children: everything it seems but actually include them in the governance of the company, perhaps because governance is confused with management and they are terrified that the employees (or worse, the unions) may become involved in management. There is a community of interest in the well-being of the enterprise between management and employees, but power is quite another thing. Power lies in the hands of those who have access to an understanding of the relevant facts. Power cannot be shared, but the right to accountability can be. That is the lesson that can be learnt from successful joint ventures across the North Sea. There can be only one operator, but that operator is accountable to his or her partners.

It may well be that the deep rooted hostility to employee involvement in governance is due to such a confusion in business executives' minds between management and governance. In Germany or The Netherlands the two sides of industry are not referred to as in Britain as if they were locked in a never-ending battle. The talk is in partnership terms. Be that as it may, it is obvious to us that some confidence-building measures will have to be necessary before we in Britain can aspire to continental levels of enthusiasm for employee involvement in governance (or supervision). As a start, perhaps, employees could be invited on to advisory boards. We shall discuss this point further later on in this chapter.

The lesson from the dealings of the Swedish company, Electrolux, with Zanussi's unions when it took over that company, is that employee hostility can be overcome, though it may take a lot of hard work. When Electrolux was poised to take over the Italian company, the trade unions were initially extremely hostile to the sale of the company to the 'Vikings from the North'. Electrolux had to guarantee that all of Zanussi's important functions would be retained in Italy. Twenty union leaders were sent from Sweden to reassure the Italian unions about the Swedish company's policies regarding its workforce, and, to ram the point home, 20 Italian union representatives were taken to Sweden to observe for themselves how things were managed there. The resulting retrenchment was not easy, but certainly the careful preparation undertaken by Electrolux helped to make things smoother than they would otherwise have been.

Banks, too, can be stakeholders, and if their stake is a major one they ought also to accept their responsibilities and act as partners. The British clearing and other banks will not relish the thought of acting like real business partners in the way that continental and Japanese banks do, but it might be that if they had understood some of their major customers in this way in the recent past, they would not have started the last decade of the twentieth century saddled with the weight of the non-performing loans and bad debts that they have found themselves with. This will mean a significant culture change for the banks as with the institutions. They will have to recruit or develop people who can act as directors on company boards, and they will have to build up the necessary organisation structures to support them.

There may well be other stakeholder/partners as well: local interests, business allies or co-makership partners, suppliers, pensioners, even major customers. There are no hard and fast rules: it all depends on a company's special circumstances.

The chairman should be selected from the ranks of the stakeholders. It is right in normal circumstances for the role of chairman in major companies to be quite distinct from that of chief executive, who will, of course, be one of the executive directors. The chairman's role in welding the various elements of the board together and providing leadership, is a critical one. It cannot be a part-time job in a big company.

The advisers

The third type of people who can currently be elected to UK company boards, the advisers, are in a different category from the executive directors and the stakeholders. These latter two groups are insiders, who have a personal concern for the company's success. The outside advisers have had no previous relationship with the company (unless coincidentally they owned some shares in it) but are brought in by the insiders because of specific qualities or knowledge that they can bring to the company. It might be specialised knowledge, experience, contacts or influence. The company wants to make use of them, but we have to be clear how such outsiders can best be used. An ex-permanent secretary could well help a company enormously in its business in, say, the health care sector, but might be quite useless in managing it because he or she lacks the necessary experience of management. So why insist that such an individual be a director with all the pressures of a main board directorship? Surely a suitable place for such people in the organisation can be devised? We have taken our formula from firms of accountants or solicitors who bring in outside experts and opinion leaders but have been debarred (so far) from making them partners (i.e. main board directors in our terminology, when we apply this to companies) because these experts do not have the right professional qualifications. They are called something like 'associate directors', to signal the fact that they are important but cannot participate formally in the management of the partnership.

Non-executive directors currently straddle what we have defined as the stakeholder and the adviser categories. The two roles are quite separate, and bringing them together as companies currently do in their unitary boards only serves to confuse their role.

THE BOARD STRUCTURE

The directors

Though the laws remain unchanged, there is nothing to prevent companies from amending their articles to codify the *de facto* separation, which exists already in many companies, between the executive directors (the executive board) and the others, who will form the supervisory section of the board: in other words the supervisory 'council' in all but legal name, which is why we have to put it in inverted commas.

In legal terms there will have to be a unitary board until the law is changed, but *de facto* the executive (section of the) board will consist of the executive directors who manage the operations of the company, and the supervisory (section of the) board will consist of the stakeholders. It is surely right that supervision should be carried out by interested parties such as the stakeholders. The stakeholders should be in a majority: thus of a typical board of 15 persons, the stakeholders ought to number eight or nine. We would like to see employee representation on the supervisory part of the board, but, given the deep-rooted British prejudices, we have to accept that in the short term the employee representatives may well have to content themselves with membership of the advisory board (this is discussed below). The chairman should be elected (and can be voted out of office) by the stakeholders meeting together as the supervisory 'council', and they will also furnish several committees of the directorate, and dominate others, as we go on to describe later in this chapter. This is, of course, our interim solution, pending a change in the law.

The real agenda of the supervisory 'council' section of the unitary board is the same as that of a continental supervisory council. It is as follows:

   (i) Watching out for trouble.
  (ii) Preparing for a crisis (and often taking over the reins in a crisis of confidence or of leadership).
 (iii) Appraising the CEO.
  (iv) Forming a judgement about the next CEO.
   (v) Setting standards of performance, and the culture of the company.
  (vi) Influencing and being involved in strategy.

There will also be two specifically British items:

   (i) Overseeing compliance.
  (ii) Overseeing and controlling the pension fund arrangements.

In the rest of this chapter we shall assume that while companies have unitary boards in the legal sense, for all practical purposes these are divided between executive boards of management and supervisory councils, and that the latter are staffed by stakeholders who are not executive directors of the company. There will be more stakeholders than executive directors. The executive directors will of course meet separately as a management board to run the company. In normal circumstances none of the stakeholder directors will attend these meetings, which in some companies take place as often as once a week.

We draw a sharp distinction between stakeholders, that is persons who have a very positive interest in the company's success, but who do not have an executive post in the company, and non-executive directors as currently defined in the UK business culture. These latter are persons who have no executive post in the company but who also have had no link with the company or interest in it, until their appointment as directors. We would question the benefit they bring to companies *as directors*. Of course as advisory directors they can add a considerable amount to a company. We discuss their contribution below.

The advisory board

The advisory board (or boards) is very different from the supervisory 'council'. Here we are deliberately borrowing from the structure of advisory boards of US and continental companies. In a way they are not boards at all in the legal, managing sense. For one thing they would be appointed by the company and not elected by the shareholders. The advisory directors, who could also have the title of associate directors, do not have legal responsibility for company management as company directors currently do. They are in essence committees of distinguished, eminent, knowledgeable and influential people, brought together to provide some specific benefit for the company. The chairman will have to take great pains to ensure that this group does not degenerate into a talking shop, and it will not consist of people who can just be accessed for their opinions as a sort of telephone panel. They will advise the company – and indeed make policy – on specialist matters such as public affairs, R&D, technology and the environment. This is why we have deliberately used the title of advisory or associate director for them. Individually they will also be used to assist the company in various ways. Together, because of their eminence, they will form a powerful grouping and having set up an advisory structure it will be difficult for a company to ignore them. They certainly are not lower in status than main board directors. They may even be much more distinguished! Their functions are different, that is all. They will also have a significant role in board committees, thus strengthening their power and influence. In this sense they parallel the executives, who are not directors, but who also attend board committees. It could be that British companies should start by appointing the elected representatives of the employees to the advisory boards so that both sides, the company and the employees, become accustomed to employee participation in management deliberations and get used to each other. This could be a confidence building measure acting as a prelude to eventually having the employee representatives on the stakeholders' section of the main board.

A well-known British service company has just recently set up an advisory council of employees to underpin its main board. The company made two classic mistakes: first of all the members of the council were selected by the chief executive, and secondly the members were all senior members of management, just below board level. The members should have been elected by the employees for them to have any credibility and they should have been at different (and indeed, at any and every) level. Clearly British managements have still a lot to learn in the matter of staff relations.

The members of the advisory board (or boards) can be consulted individually, in committee or collectively. Good practice is for them to meet together at least twice a year, preferably with the stakeholder main board directors, the meeting to be chaired by the company's chairman. As always the pressure will be on him/her to ensure that the meetings are fruitful and to the company's benefit. We would expect the advisory directors to make a particularly useful contribution to the company's strategic thinking and would expect them to meet with the executive board and supervisory 'council' (and with other very senior executives) at key times in the strategic planning cycle, much on the lines of the internal annual planning meeting held by the Dutch chemical company Akzo. This meeting, called the 'scrum meeting', is not a formal board meeting, but a structured day (or two day) long meeting of the two dozen key decision-makers to talk over where the company is going and to set the direction for the future. The British company Grand Metropolitan follows much the same approach.

Advisory directors will have many roles:

(i) They can provide an entré into administrative and governmental circles, which is why newly retired ex-senior civil servants are snapped up so quickly by companies.
(ii) They can provide specific expertise: thus a state company seeking to commercialise its operations might bring prominent retailers on to its advisory board to draw on their experience.
(iii) A company with a strong Scottish or regional or foreign investment

would bring local nationals on to its advisory board, or have a local advisory board.

(iv) Well-known persons, academics or business school professors can be brought in for what they personally can add to the company's thinking.

(v) Specialists can be appointed for their specific expertise.

The numbers of advisers depend on the company and its circumstances. There can be different groups according to geography or expertise, there can be advisers at different levels of the company. Some can be very part time, some can be almost full time. There is only one set rule: the company must have thought through the role of its advisory directors. It cannot afford to waste either its or their time. There should also not be too many. We would be surprised if a company in the top European 500 (apart from a bank) would require more than six to 10 at most. We have talked all along of an 'advisory board', and certainly for the largest companies we would expect a formal board on the lines of say IBM or a Swiss bank. Companies not of that size might well have no more than three or four such advisers, but there can be no set rule. It depends on the circumstances.

There is of course nothing to prevent companies from appointing distinguished outsiders to their executive boards or supervisory 'councils' as full directors in the legal sense, should they so choose, and should the outsiders so agree. However, both sides would do well to reflect on the rationale for this. What is the purpose, what does the company gain, and could not the objective be achieved by a route other than election to the main board? We shall discuss the committees of the board later on in this chapter. The associate directors should in any case take part in the committee structure of the company, attending the key committees concerned with governance and their special areas of expertise. In this way they can be involved in the company without taking on the legal obligations that go with the position of main board director.

This is exactly the structure of the successful Anglo-Dutch Unilever. Unilever has advisory directors, whose function is to give 'advice to the board in general and to special committees in particular, on business, social and economic issues' (Unilever annual report). The advisory directors are 'invited' to serve on at least one of three key committees: the remuneration committee (remuneration policy for directors and senior executives), audit committee (financial reporting and control arrangements), and external affairs committee. This is exactly the policy we are recommending.

As you would expect, Unilever's advisory directors are extremely distinguished: the nine members include François-Xavier Ortoli, a former French government minister; the former chief executive of Ford, Mr D. E.

Petersen; Romano Prodi, a former Italian government minister and chair-man of IRI; a former Dutch finance minister, Mr H. O. Ruding, and Mr Spethmann, the chairman of Thyssen. Sir Patrick Wright, the former head of the British diplomatic service, was also appointed as an advisory director in 1991.

THE COMMITTEES OF THE BOARD

The committee structure

We set out in Figure 7.1 a board and committee structure for a major organisation. It has the following features:

(i) A directorate consisting of a management board and a supervisory council with the stakeholders in the majority. Under current law, of course, the members of both 'boards' are regarded as directors with equal responsibilities.

(ii) Advisory board.

(iii) Subsidiary boards, with varying membership according to circum-stances, but in all cases a large part of the members will be senior executives who are not main board directors. There may well also be stakeholder directors and advisory directors: either persons who are also on the main boards, or persons with regional or specialist local expertise and interests, again, according to the circumstances.

(iv) The committees of the board. There should always be an audit, an emoluments and an executive committee. Whether a company has other committees, and what committees, depends on individual cir-cumstances. The committees break down into three categories:

(a) Management committees such as executive and finance. These are staffed virtually entirely by executives, both directors and senior managers, though it is possible that a stakeholder director from the supervisory 'council' may be a member of the finance committee.

(b) Advisory committees such as the employee development, public affairs, R & D, and environment committees. Here we would expect to find as members anyone who can contribute to the company. We would expect the stakeholders to take a particular interest in employee development, and the advisory directors to contribute particularly to R & D, environment and public affairs.

(c) The 'governance' committees: emoluments and audit. These should be composed entirely of directors (both stakeholders and advisers) who have no executive posts or responsibilities of any sort

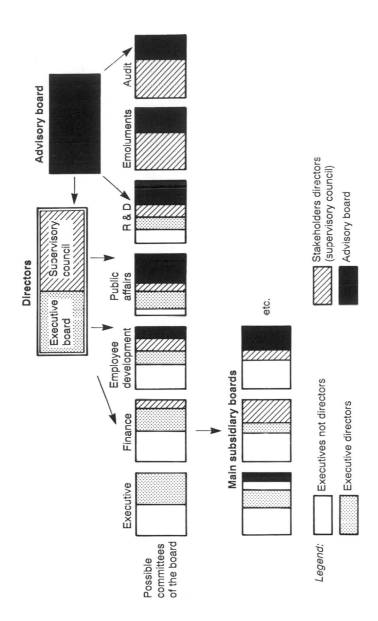

Figure 7.1 Board and committee structure for a major organisation

in the company and who also do not sit on the finance committee. The supervisory directors will be in the majority. Company officers and executive directors can and will be in attendance on these committees, but by invitation, not by right.

Ad hoc committees can be formed to meet specific requirements, such as an acquisitions committee, if the company does not already have one. Such a committee would consist of executives, executive directors and stakeholders as well as advisers with special expertise, if any. Readers may be somewhat surprised that we have come out so strongly in favour of the audit and emoluments committees after criticising them so strongly in Chapter 5. There are three reasons for this:

(i) Our criticism was based on the committees existing in the framework of a unitary board system in which a supervisory role sits uneasily on the non-executive directors. The work of these committees can be focused much more easily in a two-tier system in which the supervisory function can be established and defined more clearly. In a unitary system there is always the danger of setting one half of the board against the other half.

(ii) There is a perceived need for the type of control provided by audit and emoluments committees, and which cannot be so satisfactorily carried out by any other function in the company.

(iii) The concept of these committees is already well established in big company thinking and practice. It makes sense to build on this, even though it may involve some extra bureaucracy. Indeed, one of the penalties of the extra pressures on the audit and emoluments committees, on the supervisory and advisory directors and on the requirement for more disclosure, will be extra, and costly bureaucracy.

The governance committees

We believe that it should eventually be mandatory for every publicly quoted company to have the two key governance committees of the board: the audit and the emoluments committees. The names of the members of these committees should be stated in the annual report and accounts and they should also report on their stewardship as part of the stakeholders' report, which we describe later on.

It is important to be very clear about these committees. Such committees are already in place in many (most?) major British companies, and the need for such committees is certainly regarded as best practice. But we must underline the fact that the existence of such committees, and the bureaucracy that they inevitably entail, is nothing more or less than the adoption of the supervisory system, albeit within the unitary board structure. Our argument is that if companies have the supervisory system in essence, why not formalise and clarify it through the setting up of the supervisory council? It would make the boardroom organisation much tidier.

The audit committee

It is important to appreciate the difference between an audit committee and a finance committee. The finance committee is responsible to the shareholders (through the board) for monitoring the company's financial health and for assuring that its financial viability is maintained. It deals with matters such as cash management policies, risk management, funding, dividend policies and investor relations. The finance committee deals with the financial management of the company. The audit committee's concern is with governance and compliance.

The audit committee has four objectives:

  (i) To ensure that the published financial statements are not misleading and accord with good practice.
 (ii) To ensure that the internal controls are adequate.
(iii) To follow up on allegations of material, financial, ethical and legal irregularities.
(iv) To recommend the selection of the external auditor.

The audit committee serves as a means of opening up communications between stakeholder directors, assisted by the advisory directors, and the auditors, both internal and external, the compliance officer and the regulatory authorities by:

  (i) Giving the supervisory 'council' directors the mechanism and the right to pursue matters of concern.
 (ii) Providing the auditors and compliance authorities with an interface with the company that is an alternative to the executive managers and directors.

Its task is to comment on the efficacy, and to safeguard the credibility, of financial statements published for the shareholders and the outside world, and to ensure that in putting their name to the figures, the directors have exercised the care, diligence and skill required by the law. The committee will therefore have contact with the external and internal auditors, and will meet them on its own with no company executive or executive director present, unless by invitation. It will receive all internal audit reports and the external auditors' management letters, as well as following them up to see that they have been acted on by the company. Both the internal and external auditors will have the right of unfettered access to the committee at all times, and it will also be up to the audit committee to recommend the choice of external auditors (or change of auditors if necessary) to the board.

Audit committees are already common in British blue chip companies and in the USA where they are a requirement for any company seeking a listing on the New York stock exchange. There have been four main drivers: the reaction to the financial engineering devices which were such a feature of the 1980s; the wave of company failures at the end of the decade; the tightening of the accounting regulatory regime (which we wholeheartedly welcome); and the need for managements to demonstrate accounting transparency to the outside world. It will be noted that the ambit of the audit committees goes beyond the outputs, the reports and the statements, and extends to the systems and controls that input the information.

The work of the audit committees is therefore most definitely not a sinecure. We would expect its members, though not executives, to have to spend an appreciable time on company business, and we wonder if eventually, in the major companies, it may require a small staff to assist it.

We have already set out some of the signs of incipient trouble in a company in our book *Finanzmeister* (1991). The two key ones are:

(i) Consistently missed cash flow forecasts and/or a declining cash flow, even if the company is still profitable. This is probably the most important single indicator that there is something wrong with performance.
(ii) Profit and return on assets targets consistently missed. Our experience as consultants examining company accounts is that a sure sign of trouble is where there is a large (negative) extraordinary item which the company does its best to ignore by focusing on its earnings before that item.

Appendix 7.2 sets out some more detailed guidelines on audit committees.

The emoluments committee

Like the audit committee, the board's emoluments (or remuneration) committee should be made up of supervisory and advisory directors, in other words, directors who have no executive role in the company. As with the audit committee, this committee would normally meet by itself with no company executives or executive directors present, though we would expect that the personnel director could well be in attendance at times. This committee should not include any bankers, lawyers or solicitors who draw fees from the company, whether supervisory or advisory directors or not.

There is a lot of merit in the suggestion that no chief executive officers of any company should sit on this committee at all.

The purpose of this committee is to determine the remuneration policy regarding the executive directors and senior executives. There are three terms that have to be emphasised: remuneration, policy and senior executives. The committee deals with wider topics than pay. It includes bonus schemes, pension arrangements, stock options and fringe benefits. We emphasise the word 'policy' because in this difficult area of remuneration it is critically important for there to be a laid down policy, a standard which can be referred to. And we have specifically used the term 'senior executives'. The work of the emoluments committee will need to cover not only the remuneration of the chairman and the executive directors but also that of the members of the company's senior management echelon. It is not unknown for some of these – particularly where located outside the UK – to be paid more than the chairman and highest paid director.

Appendix 7.3 sets out some guidelines on the structure and function of the emoluments committee.

THE SUPERVISORY DIRECTORS' REPORT

The directors of the supervisory 'council' need to produce a report on their activities, to be included in the company's annual report. This is already standard practice in Germany where the supervisory councils report on what they have done during the year. In the USA too, the audit committee reports in some detail on its role, its activities and its contacts with the external and internal auditors.

In one or two cases British companies, too, are inserting a report on governance in their accounts: we have already commented on two such cases, Thorn EMI and Grand Metropolitan. Inevitably at this stage in the evolution of governance in British companies, these two companies have concentrated on explaining how seriously governance is regarded in their companies, the company policy concerning governance, and the role of the non-executive directors on the board. Eventually we envisage a report much more on the lines of a continental supervisory council's report. For readers' information, a good example of that would be the report of the supervisory council of Siemens AG. The main contents of its 1990 report are:

(i) Contacts with the management board.
(ii) Review of:
    (a) business development:

   (b) major capital investments and the financial position;
   (c) opportunities in Eastern Europe;
   (d) expansion in the USA;
   (e) current developments in microelectronics.
(iii) Special attention was paid to the acquisition of Nixdorf.
(iv) Visit to the corporate R & D facilities.

The supervisory council also confirms its belief that the recent company reorganisation was successful, and in approving the annual financial statements the council affirms that it is satisfied with the company's accounting procedures and controls. It has examined the accounting records and concurs with the results of the audit.

Our view of best practice is that UK companies should include a report by the stakeholder members of the board who constitute the supervisory 'council' on the above lines. To cater for current British concerns and pressures it also ought to give the following specific details:

  (i) The membership of the audit and the emoluments committees, with a specific statement that the members hold no executive posts in the company, its subsidiaries or associates.
 (ii) The remuneration policy as determined by the emoluments committee: the pay, bonus and options gained by directors should be set out in an easy-to-read table.
(iii) An explanation of how the bonus or performance-related element of pay (if any) has been calculated, and when a new option plan is adopted a statement should set out the potential value of the plan to the senior management if the stock annually appreciates by 5 per cent, 10 per cent, etc., over the period of the grant.
 (iv) A specific statement that the audit committee has a completely free right of access to the internal and external auditors as well as the compliance officer, has sight of all their reports, and has followed up those reports where it has sought to.
  (v) Any other comments by the audit and emoluments committees.
 (vi) Report on the management of the pension fund.
(vii) Report on compliance.

Where appropriate the audit committee should report on the following:

  (i) Changes in accounting policies where material and their effect. It must be emphasised, however, that it is not normally the audit committee's role to identify accounting policies that require revision.
 (ii) Major areas of judgement in the financial statements that had to be resolved.

(iii) Significant adjustments that had to be made in the published accounts as presented by the company management as a result of the annual audit and pressure from the external auditors.

(iv) Significant departures from accounting standards, the reasons, and the effect.

A SUPERVISORY SYSTEM OR UNITARY BOARDS?

We have made it very clear that we believe that the supervisory system is preferable to the unitary board, and that the right approach to governance is to separate management from supervision (i.e. governance), with the interest groups, the stakeholders, represented on a supervisory council. In the short term the supervisory structure will have to be voluntary but it is the two-tier board, established by law, that we see as the eventual solution. It is a long-term aim only because it will take time to change the law in the UK, but we do not believe such a structure can be firmly established by a voluntary code of practice, only by changes in the law. We are not, we must stress, talking of power-sharing between capital and labour, which is how the argument is sometimes represented in Britain. It is also not a question of management, though it can be one of offering advice and of obtaining information. The system should work, as it does in Germany and The Netherlands, on the accountability of management (i.e. of the executive directors on the management board). The most important function of a supervisory council is to appoint and dismiss members of the management board (given justification for such action) and to maintain a continuous watching brief over the executives' management of the company's affairs. It is a matter of checks and balances, however. The tenure of office of the members of the management board is secured for a period, giving them freedom of action for that period, within their prescribed duties.

There are six reasons why we favour a supervisory over a unitary structure:

(i) Even if we have a unitary board it would still be composed of two types of director in Britain; executive and non-executive, with all the disadvantages that we have already pointed out. It is easier to set out clear legal obligations and requirements as between the executives and the non-executives when there are two separate board organisations. There is an uncomfortable untidiness in having one group of directors supervising or controlling another group on the same board, which is meant to be the collective for managing the company.

(ii) The argument against a two-tier system is that it is unnecessarily bureaucratic. We would reply that there virtually is a *de facto* two-tier board system anyway, already, in many companies in the UK, and that the board committee structure that has come into vogue has already introduced an element of bureaucracy. A large board, such as can occur with a unitary system, may tend to turn into a senate-type talking shop. Two focused boards with their separate roles spelt out are more manageable.

(iii) Supervision (such as through the audit and emoluments committees) can best be carried out by interested parties such as the stakeholders, rather than by disinterested outsiders, however distinguished. Dare we say that the existence of disinterested and independent names has not prevented the commercial scandals that have so disfigured British business life in the late 1980s and early 1990s?

(iv) The separation of the roles of chairman and CEO is smoothly handled, as described later on.

(v) It affords stability in the face of takeover bids. This, too, is described below.

(vi) Above all, the two board system works, and it is beginning to be introduced into Britain. Separating the stakeholders from the managers makes the role of management easier and more clear cut.

Though there would be two boards with two separate functions, they would in practice work closely together, and often have joint meetings, such as for strategy briefings.

THE LONG TERM

In the long term the biggest change we are looking to would be the mandatory establishment by law of the two-tier system, which we see as inevitable given the EC pressures and the direction governance in continental European companies (as well as many British companies) is taking. At present British companies may establish it voluntarily, but as the law with regard to all directors having equal responsibilities still obtains in Britain, companies at least should insert clauses in their Articles to set up an advisory board and decouple it from the main boards.

In the long term, British law needs to be amended to separate the roles of the stakeholders from the management boards with a specific requirement to have employee representation on the supervisory council, which we consider should be no less than one-third. This would still leave the shareholders with a majority of the supervisory council members as well as leaving some room for other stakeholder representatives if elected at the AGM. The supervisory council would be the forum for recommending to the AGM the dismissal, if needs be, of executive directors, the CEO and, if necessary the chairman. The supervisory council would also elect the chairman. It will be noted that the company chairman will be the chairman of the supervisory council, while the CEO will preside over the executive, thus formalising the separation of the two top roles in the company.

The law would also need to be changed to confirm the supervisory council's role in audit and emoluments (i.e. the present audit and emoluments committees), and to confirm the requirement of the supervisory council to present an annual report to the shareholders in the annual statement and accounts. The supervisory council would have the key relationship with the internal and external auditors and the compliance officers. It would also oversee the management of a company's pension arrangements. In this way our short-term proposals lead logically into the long-term ones, the difference being that the latter will be enforced by law.

In the case of takeovers, the acquirer would still be able to dominate the supervisory council through the majority of the shareholder directors, but it will be a bare majority only, and before acquirers in, say, a hostile takeover, can dismiss the executive directors, they will have to convince the other stakeholders. The law should be changed to allow companies to amend their articles so that a three-quarters majority of the supervisory council is required to dismiss the executive directors in cases of a take-over, or change of articles. This, and a fixed term of office for executive directors may be some protection against the excessively short-term takeover climate that prevailed in the UK in the 1980s. While not recommending inertia, there is a lot to be said for stability. In Germany the executive directors on the management boards are under just as much pressure as in Britain, but the pressure comes not from the threat of takeovers, but from the owners (partners) of the company sitting on the supervisory councils. If something goes wrong, it is the management that is changed, rather than the ownership of the company. That is taking a long-term view of the company. That is the sort of regime we would like to see in Britain.

APPENDIX 7.1

Governance for the smaller company – a practical example

The background

We appreciate that much of what we have written so far could appear to be somewhat remote and academic. We shall therefore give a specific example of interest to practitioners. In order to give our example a human dimension, we shall look at a medium-sized company with some 3,000 employees. We discussed governance in that company with its chairman, who is himself a non-executive, nominally working one day a week for the company. We look at governance through his eyes.

He took over as chairman some time ago, having first served as an ordinary non-executive director. His predecessor was an autocrat who brooked no question, let alone opposition, to his authority, and he sees his role very much as one of changing the culture of the company to bring it up to date, as well as to wean the directors away from being cowed yes-men to becoming contributors to the company's development. As he sees it, his key relationship is with the chief executive, and he regards it as essential that their two roles are clearly defined and the differences clearly demarcated. He says he has to be very careful to keep to his 'side of the fence' when dealing with the CEO, which his predecessor did not do.

The CEO is the undisputed operational boss of the company, and the chairman's most important job is to select the right CEO and to give him or her enough space to run the company. It varies with the circumstances, of course. There are no fixed parameters and rules in the chairman's relationship with the CEO. It is a question of two people getting together to agree how they will work together. But whatever their agreement, there are certain fundamentals. One is the job descriptions of the chairman and CEO. They have to be agreed from the start, and the boundaries between them defined. Without this there is chaos.

The board

The chairman in the company we are looking at sees his main job as dealing with the shareholders, the outside world and, from the governance point of view, shaping the board. He was not happy with the board that he had inherited. There were a lot of people on it who did not contribute very much to the company. His main concerns were succession planning (which went hand in hand with choosing the right CEO), ensuring the right mix of directors so that they could work harmoniously together, and coping with the growing weight of regulation in the industry concerned.

From the lay person's point of view an appointment to the board may appear to be the final accolade of success. This chairman sees it differently. The company is fairly large, but even so it cannot compare with the majors. It is therefore surprisingly difficult to attract persons of sufficient calibre to the board. The company needs persons of vision to assist the chairman in planning for the future. He notes that whenever it comes to really hard work, such as attendance at board committees, he always has to rely on the same small group of directors. There can be no room for directors who do not contribute. He is currently looking for an additional non-executive director and has gone to a specialist recruitment agency to find one. There is an audit committee which is taken very seriously and means a lot of hard work. The company has put the audit out to tender which has forced the auditors to justify themselves. The committee takes great care to go through all the internal audit reports. Just to read and understand them takes time and is not easy. The emoluments committee (which the company calls the remuneration committee) is less firmly established and is still in the running-in stage.

The company has just made a friendly takeover of another organisation in a part of the country known for its local traditions and its separateness. Even though it is a wholly-owned subsidiary with no outside shareholding, the chairman has deliberately used the local board as a focal point for establishing good relations in the local community. Some of the main board directors sit on this board and one of them is the chairman, but he has deliberately brought in local outsiders, persons of standing in the local community, to sit on the board as well. The chief executive of this subsidiary has been invited to sit as a non-executive director on the main board.

The non-executives are in a 3–2 majority on the board. The chairman feels that in this way he has a supervisory council and an executive board in all but name. The difference between the executive and the non-executive directors is very clear to everyone, if only because the executives are on the premises all the time, while the non-executives' presence is intermittent. The chairman takes an old-fashioned view of advisory directors. His view is that when there is a need for specialist outside advice it will be obtained from the company's professional advisers such as solicitors, accountants and tax experts. They are there to give advice and so are outside the decision-making core. To be inside that decision-making core as a non-executive director you have to be able to contribute to the strategic process. Our view is that he has not understood the value of advisory directors and how they could be used to the company's advantage.

The job of the chairman

The chairman is a non-executive with a 'full time' job in another company. But what is a non-executive? It might amount to 20 days a year for some directors who do not take the job seriously and who will have to be weeded out eventually, but it cannot be restricted like that for persons who are chairmen of public companies and who want to do the job properly.

Though nominally a one day a week job, it does not work out like that in practice for our chairman. Hardly a day goes by without him having to do something for the company he is chairman of. For instance, he is on the telephone to his CEO almost every day, people write to him asking for something or just complaining about the company, he has to meet other chairmen in the industry, and he has to talk to the authorities (as well as being summoned to meetings by them). He cannot excuse himself by saying he is part-time and that on that specific day in question he is not scheduled to work for the company. A chairman represents the company all the time and so has to do this full time. It is not easy to keep two jobs going at the same time and he does not understand how people can be non-executive directors or, worse, chairmen, of several companies in parallel. There are just not enough hours in the day. Our view is even more emphatic, and we feel that he has demonstrated very clearly why a chairman of such a company (let alone of bigger ones) cannot be part-time.

Consensus is very important: there has to be a unanimous vote to get rid of a director, for instance. However, it is very serious if things get to such a pass that the board has to take formal votes like that. That is why our chairman is vehemently against employee representatives on the board. He is clear that the company's duty is to its shareholders and though it has to consider the employees, of course, he feels it would be divisive to have them on the board. They would either be a disruptive force, in his view, and therefore break up the constructive harmony that has been built up, or else they would cower in a corner and be overawed by the board. In both cases they would not contribute. Our recommendations with regard to appointing employee representatives to the advisory boards as a start are designed to deal with such prejudices.

The system of employee directors works for two main reasons in Germany that do not obtain in Britain:

(i) It is based on several generations of experience and test: the law has therefore followed the business culture and practice.
(ii) The employee directors sit on the supervisory councils and are therefore not involved in management.

Because of the unitary board structure in Britain it is not possible to do that.

Employee directors (as *directors*), if any, would have to sit on the single board and therefore would as a matter of course be involved in management. It is precisely for that reason that we recommend that in the initial phase, they be appointed to the advisory boards.

APPENDIX 7.2

The audit committee

This appendix sets out the role of the audit committee. This committee will be formed by directors from the supervisory council, assisted by associate directors from the advisory board. In some companies the audit committee could well be composed of the entire supervisory council.

What it is

It should be a requirement that all listed companies have an audit committee. This is a committee of the main board, and of any subsidiary boards that produce accounts for outside shareholders such as minority shareholders. It will consist only of directors who have no executive posts in the company. It will therefore consist of stakeholder directors from the supervisory council and also associate directors from the advisory board, with a clear majority of stakeholders. They will elect a committee chairman.

   Audit committees have the following features:

  (i) They are committees of the supervisory council and are answerable to it.
 (ii) Their job is to review the financial statements and the effectiveness of internal controls, including controls on the treasury operation. The committee most emphatically is not concerned with financial management or with second guessing the executive management.
(iii) They can have an important influence on the presentation of the financial reports to the outside world, to ensure quality reporting, that is clarity and comprehensiveness, lucidity and unambiguousness in the presentation of facts.
 (iv) They can call on any item of information they require from anywhere in the company and have the right of access to all persons and all files.
  (v) The number of meetings held during the year varies according to circumstances. We would expect the committee to meet at least quarterly, but no more than six times a year at the maximum.
 (vi) The committee reports to the supervisory council: it should report formally annually, and the key points of its report should be incorporated in the 'governance' report.

Scope of audit committees

The scope and role of the audit committee needs to be spelt out by the company. It must have clear terms of reference and effective chairmanship. In general, the role of audit committees is as follows:

(i)   They discuss with the external auditors their problems in completing the audit and their views.
(ii) They discuss the scope and timing of the outside audit.
(iii) They discuss with the outside auditors the effectiveness of internal controls. They will have sight of the auditors' 'management letter' and will review the company's reply to the points made by the auditors in this letter.
(iv) They will pay particular attention to the notes to the accounts and their meaning.
(v)   The outside auditors will have free access to them at all times.
(vi) They will recommend the appointment of the outside auditors.
(vii) With regard to the internal auditors:
    (a) they will meet regularly with them;
    (b) they will see all the internal audit reports;
    (c) they will check that the internal audit reports are followed up and acted on;
    (d) the internal auditors will have free and confidential access to them at all times;
    (e) they will comment on the internal audit programme: is it concentrating on the right areas, is it reporting to the right level of management?
    (f) they will give their views as to whether internal audit is adequately resourced, or if there is no internal audit, whether there is need for such a function.
(viii) They will meet with the company's compliance officer and discuss regulatory matters with him/her in the same way as with the internal and external auditors.

It is our view that the internal audit function should usually report to the audit committee. Care has to be taken here as internal audit often also covers internal consultancy and operational audit. These should most definitely not report to the audit committee.

It is also our view that the external auditors should be invited to attend the majority of the meetings of the audit committee. The CEO and executive directors have no right to attend the audit committee's meetings, but we would expect them to be invited to be present on certain occasions, particularly the chief executive, finance director, controller and treasurer, and particularly at times when documents such as annual reports are to be issued.

The items the committee will concentrate on depend on circumstances, and the business situation of the company. Thus we would expect the audit committee of a homogeneous UK business, say a building society, to concentrate on specific problems affecting the business, while that of a diversified international group would be more interested in consolidation issues to ensure that outsiders obtain a clear picture of the group and its activities.

We should emphasise that the purview of the audit committee extends beyond the sometimes narrow boundaries of purely financial reporting of the areas that are actually audited by the statutory auditors. The audit committee must therefore also interest itself in matters such as:

   (i) Non-financial information, for example the chairman's statement in the annual report and accounts, physical information such as health and safety data, etc.

  (ii) Interim statements, circulars etc.

 (iii) Control information: the board is interested in making business judgements on that information; the audit committee, on the other hand, in whether it is the right information, of the right quality, in due time.

 (iv) Good practice in general.

  (v) Keeping its members up to date with regulatory matters and with good practice. The auditors may well be of assistance here.

APPENDIX 7.3
The emoluments committee

What it is

The emoluments committee consists entirely of supervisory council members, though in its deliberations it will naturally have to deal with the chairman and senior directors and managers such as the personnel director and company secretary. We would remind readers that we are discussing the short-term situation when, legally, there is still a unitary board, and companies may have the same person as chairman and chief executive (though we would counsel against this).

The remit of the committee covers all the remuneration of the members of the board and of senior management, whether in cash or kind. The emoluments of the supervisory council members are far less contentious as these are far smaller than for the executives, and do not contain share options. It is good practice for the emoluments of the supervisory council to be fixed by the executives against established outside standards, using outside specialist advisers to check the amounts. There will, of course, be extra payments for extra duties such as service on the committees.

In the USA there is a movement to reduce the pay of part-time directors by the number of meetings they do not attend. We would not go so far as this, but, clearly, if a director regularly and without good cause consistently fails to attend board meetings, then he or she can have no place on the board, and would have to go.

Scope of the emoluments committee

The purview of the committee covers the members of top management. The size of this group varies from company to company but:

(i) It will certainly cover all the main (management or executive) board directors.
(ii) It will usually cover all the heads of the main functions and divisions even if they are not formally members of the main board.
(iii) It will cover all persons who share in the top management share option and/or share incentive scheme, as well as any bonus scheme.
(iv) It will also cover any family or associates of the above if they too receive benefits from the company.

In a company, we know well, with some £7–8 billion turnover, the size of the top management grouping is around 40–50 persons. In a mega-corporation such as Shell, it could be as high as 200–250 persons.

What are emoluments?

Emoluments cover all pay and benefits that accrue to the beneficiary by virtue of his/her employment with the company, such as:

  (i) Salary.
  (ii) Bonus.
 (iii) Shares and share options.
 (iv) Pension and any other arrangements for payment after retirement.
  (v) Severance compensation package.
 (vi) Fringe benefits, including special arrangements for payment of expenses.
(vii) Any other benefits.

It should be noted that the committee will be interested not only in UK payments, but also in those made world-wide.

Policy

The emoluments committee is concerned to ensure that there is an agreed and laid down emoluments policy which can be justified and explained. The committee will want to make comparisons with other, comparable, firms. It will also need to be mindful of the comparison between the top management's emoluments and average salary rates in the company, as well as between average salary increases, and the increases for the top management. If there are divergencies the committee will need to have an explanation, as it will be its job to justify this to the outside world.

Reports

The supervisory council will report on remuneration as part of its annual report. The remuneration element of the report will cover:

  (i) The package and what has been paid.
 (ii) The criteria for the payment (and any increases).
(iii) Total remuneration (shown together in one place and not scattered around the report, as sometimes happens (and only serves to confuse).
(iv) Share options in total, and granted during the year.

(v) The bonus element and how this is justified (for instance, comparing the bonus increase with the profits increase).

(vi) Any unusual or exceptional payments or benefits paid or granted, and the justification.

8 GOVERNANCE IN A WORLD OF CHANGE

A WORLD OF CHANGE

Change as a constant

At a recent workshop we held for company chief executives we asked them what they saw as their current biggest business challenges. There was a fair unanimity in their naming the top 10 as:

  (i) The global market place.
 (ii) Liberalisation and competition.
(iii) The need for differentiation and, at the same time, focus.
 (iv) The pressures on management.
  (v) The scarcity of the right human resources.
 (vi) Delivering quality.
(vii) Ever more demanding customers.
(viii) Managing international teamwork.
 (ix) Information technology.
  (x) Transitional organisations.

They summed it up in one word, 'change'.

Managers are having to accept change as a constant. In writing this book we have been very well aware of the fact that we are not discussing a static world, but are trying to keep abreast of changes that are taking place at an ever faster and ever more bewildering rate. It is hardly an exaggeration to say that we are almost frightened to praise a company for fear of reading some disaster or scandal about it in tomorrow's newspaper!

Our 100-company review of the annual reports and accounts of the majors brought home to us the extent of the changes that have taken place. One has only to compare their latest reports with those they issued a decade earlier, at the start of the 1980s, to appreciate the enormous corporate cultural changes that companies have undergone. We are not referring to the way the figures are set out, but to the words that describe them: what they report on and how they feel they have to present themselves to the outside world. The guidelines as to what is socially acceptable for companies are becoming tighter and tighter, and best practice is ahead of regulation. Companies that seek a reputation must not only act within best practice, but must demonstrate publicly that they have done so.

Organisational implications

In every discussion with chief executives the biggest worry that emerges is how to cope with the pace of change, not just change on its own, but its sheer unpredictability: the Gulf War and the aftermath – or lack of it – the collapse of communism, to be replaced by, what? Nearer home, their concerns are being able to recognise where competition will come from, let alone meeting it; to understand technology, let alone using it. There is so much going on that managements in major companies are suffering from initiative overload.

In his book *Competition in Global Industries* (1986), Michael Porter identifies half a dozen cross-currents that will make the pattern of international competition more complex in the next decade, and will consequently demand a subtler and more responsive approach from companies looking for a true multinational strategy:

(i) Decreasing rates of economic growth, coupled with intense competitive rivalry.
(ii) Eroding types of competitive advantage: labour costs will decline in importance and companies will be unable to maintain a technological edge for long because knowledge of it spreads so quickly.
(iii) New forms of protectionism, e.g. demands for local content and local ownership, with, we would add, clear implications for governance.
(iv) New types of government inducement, as well as governments (and regions, and provinces) being increasingly aggressive in helping national firms to compete abroad.
(v) Proliferating coalitions among firms from different countries: competition will be between clusters of companies rather than companies on their own, especially in the fields of motor vehicles, communications, electronics and computers.
(vi) Growing technological ability to tailor products and services to local conditions.

Michael Porter's book was written in 1986 but his points remain as valid today as ever. With the benefit of a further six years' hindsight, however, we would say that the key issues are how to manage diversity in a Europe with fewer boundaries than ever before, environmental problems, a growing shortage of world capital, and (the opportunities in?) Eastern Europe.

All of this will impact on companies' organisation structures. Considerations of governance are central to most of these points because the common answer to any problem seems to be to restructure the organisation and the universal goal is to achieve flexibility through decentralisation. When in doubt, reorganise. A *Harvard Business Review* article (May–June 1991) surveyed major US corporations between 1989 and1991 and found that in companies with over 10,000 employees 70 per cent had undergone a major restructuring within the last two years, 45 per cent a major divestiture and/or acquisition, 45 per cent had expanded substantially internationally, and 36 per cent had significantly reduced the number of their employees. These figures are borne out by our survey of 100 international companies. Annual reorganisations have almost become a fact of life. In view of this background we concentrate in this chapter on four key areas: regulation, the environment, the wider world of the company, and human relations.

INCREASING REGULATION

A new climate of regulation

On 3 February 1992 it was announced that the Italian parliament had finally approved rules for takeover bids of stock market quoted companies. These rules which, *inter alia*, were designed to protect the rights of minority shareholders by putting an end to the previous practice of Italian companies exchanging crucial stakes in listed companies at premium prices without offering the same terms to small investors, finally brought Italy, formally at least, into line with market practice in other major industrialised countries. Whether these new rules will be effective is another question, but who can doubt that the rules and regulations regarding good governance and good corporate practice are beginning to tighten if even the Italian stock exchanges are forced to take notice?

Mr Attilio Ventura, head of the stockbrokers' committee which runs the Milan bourse, said the law represented 'a decisive step forward for the market'. The reason is obvious, and it is why the regulations are also being tightened in other European bourses such as Paris and Frankfurt: they want to expand their business as major financial centres to rival London. They can only do so if they are seen to move their regulations up to the level of best international practice. The Nestlé–Agnelli battle over the company that owned Source Perrier revealed how the regulatory authorities in France are beginning to take account of minority interests and international best practice in takeovers.

There are interesting developments in Germany, too. Recognising its international position, Deutsche Bank moved in early 1992 to institute a strict Anglo-Saxon-type compliance regime within the bank, the first of the big German banks to do so. This move came hard on the heels of the German government's announcement of its plan to set up a regulatory body for the German securities industry and to introduce tough penalties against insider dealing, which is still not illegal in Germany. In announcing the Deutsche Bank's decision, Hilmar Kopper, its chief executive, exhorted the other German banks to follow suit, saying this would help Frankfurt's status as a financial centre.

In Britain, too, the regulations are becoming more strict and it could be that the turn of the decade saw the high-water mark of the charismatic financial buccaneers who so dominated the imagination of the business press in the eighties. It is not just the scandals, the business collapses, the worries about the security of pension fund management, the failure of governance in Lloyd's of London, but also the subtle change in the climate of opinion that we noticed shifting against Hanson plc in its trial of strength against ICI in autumn 1991.

We are not betting men but there is a fair certainty that before the decade is half over there will be a major scandal and financial collapse in Eastern Europe that will further concentrate people's minds on international regulation and governance and will add weight to the operation of the regulatory regime. One more major scandal, of course, could well be the final nail in the coffin of the reliance on voluntary codes of practice school of corporate governance.

The financial regulations tighten as well

We are only being a little bit unfair if we say that British companies in the past took a strictly legalistic view of the accounting standards. If they could get away with a favourable interpretation by so construing the rules so that they benefited from them, they did so. P-E International, a management consultancy, was reported in the press (*Financial Times* 10 May 1991) as calculating that the overall balance of extraordinary charges in the UK's top 250 companies in 1990 amounted to a negative £2.5 billion. Under the Accounting Standards Board (ASB) proposals these would in future have to be set off against reported earnings. The result will be much nearer to US GAAP. Had Polly Peck been required to comply with the rules now being proposed so that it had made a full cash flow statement available to shareholders, its situation would have been all too clear much earlier on than actually happened. An almost legendary example is provided by Midland Bank, which in July 1987 showed provisions of £916 million against Third World debt as an extraordinary item, of all things. It was thus able to claim a pretax profit of £216 million for the first six months. Why it did so is another matter. Who did the board (all of them – non-executives as well as executives!) think it was fooling?

However much they may disagree about the details, there is broad agreement between the accounting profession, business people and the institutions, that fundamental reforms are required. The new regime that has been proposed is much less legalistic and more in line with what the financial world's equivalent of the man on the Clapham omnibus would regard as reasonable. There is therefore now no excuse for audit committees abdicating from their jobs and being overawed by financial jargon from the company accountants. One thing is certain, if they will not take action, the ASB is disposed to take a heavy-handed line and has publicly said it will do so.

The work of the ASB will give more power to audit committees by emphasising the commonsense approach to reported figures, concentrating on cash flow for instance, and virtually abolishing extraordinary items, that great alibi for British companies for so long. It should have happened a long time ago. The whole thrust of the new proposals has been to shift the balance away from the producer of the accounts, the company, to the user, especially the investor. Companies, moreover, must expect that the new requirements, such as the more complicated profit and loss accounts with the division between continuing and acquired businesses, will cost more money, and that as audit committees become more formalised and established in their work routines, they too will cost more money to maintain and to service. This is, in fact, a point to be emphasised in general. Compliance and regulation will not be cheap, and companies will have to pay the price. Already in early 1992 the Financial Reporting Review Panel publicly reprimanded two large companies for their accounting policies, Williams Holdings, an industrial conglomerate, and Ultramar, an oil and gas group. If this is a sign of things to come, we would expect that in the case of future reprimands the spotlight will be on the auditors (if they gave the company concerned a clean audit certificate) and any audit committees in such companies.

THE ENVIRONMENTAL PRESSURES WILL NOT GO AWAY

A challenge for industry

Referring to the importance of a regard for health, safety and the environment, BP comments in its annual report: 'Industry's licence to operate is becoming more and more dependent on its HSE performance.' Strong words indeed, but they emphasise one of every chief executive's growing fears, that the all-pervasiveness of environmental issues could not only cost their company its profitability and competitive edge against less scrupulous firms in less strict countries, but that the sheer unpredictability of the pressures and the interpretation by the law courts could make business planning more difficult. In BP itself, the environmental committee is one of the main board's committees. And it has not escaped the attention of certain industry lobbies in countries such as Germany, that strict environmental legislation could be an acceptable way of keeping cheaper Third World and south-east Asian products at bay.

Whatever the outcome, business life will certainly become more expensive, particularly for firms in exposed industries such as oil and chemicals. The USA again takes the lead: US firms have long been forced by regulators to think about the environmental impact of their businesses. Monsanto, for instance, made a pledge in the late 1980s that the company would reduce its worldwide emissions of its over 300 chemicals by 90 per cent by the end of 1992. After that it would work towards the target of zero emissions. All this is expensive. Monsanto's investment in environmental protection alone more than doubled in the two years to 1990, to $85 million.

In Switzerland, too, the events of November 1986, when the dousing of a fire at a Sandoz warehouse caused several tonnes of poisonous chemicals to be washed into the river Rhine, have left their impact on the city of Basle despite its favoured situation as the home town of the Swiss chemical and pharmaceutical industry. Environmental pressures from the city and a feeling of hostility forced Ciba-Geigy and Sandoz in 1991 to announce that they were making investments outside Basle and, indeed, outside Switzerland.

The legal framework

The shape of the legal framework which will govern European industry's environmental responsibilities in the next century is becoming clearer following the completion, in the summer of 1991, of a new draft of the EC's Directive for civil liability for damage caused by waste. This is the centrepiece of the European legal regime which could well become law within a year or two and has already been submitted to the European parliament and council. This new draft reflects the two principles which also underpin the US legal framework: strict liability (which means that the plaintiff does not have to prove either negligence or causation on the part of the defendant), and 'the polluter pays'. The new draft extends primary liability to carriers as well as to producers of waste. It also increases the power of the environmental pressure groups, such as Greenpeace and Friends of the Earth, making it easier for them to take legal action against environmentally sensitive operators. Such groups are becoming increasingly willing to take out private prosecutions against companies and their directors. The EC draft Directive also argues in favour of a compulsory environmental insurance, bonding or guarantee arrangement. The implications are enormous, particularly for the UK insurance industry which is not yet sure whether 'old' pollution is covered – as the environmentalists want.

The UK, too, has not been idle. The 1990 Environmental Protection Act introduced the now familiar term 'integrated pollution control'. This is defined as a single system which assesses on an integrated basis the impact on the environment of all the releases and emissions from any one plant, whether into air, or water, or on to land. The intention is to establish a European environmental agency and there are also proposals for measures on municipal water waste, hazardous waste, civil liability for damage and environmental degradation caused by waste, classification, packaging and labelling, and vehicle emissions, as well as proposals for economic and physical measures to back up EC environmental policy. Even eco-audits are proposed. The Maastricht deal of December 1991 boosted Brussels' 'green' powers even further, by paving the way for the EC Commission to have greater environmental influence. Some 'green' laws will be able to be passed in future by majority voting.

A report produced early in 1991 by Environmental Policy Consultants estimated that Community environmental legislation in general may cost British business as much as £15 billion per annum. A clear sign of the times was provided by the UK pharmaceutical company, Fisons, which had to announce in December 1991 that a regulatory foul-up in the USA had cost it a quarter of the year's profits, which was accompanied by a drop of about a third in its share price over a few months.

Every business will be affected

It is not just that the obvious targets, e.g. chemicals, rubber, heavy industry, will be affected. *Every* industry and business could be affected, often in a roundabout and a surprising way.

The lay person could well ask what banking has to do with the environment apart from the recycling of waste paper and the proper siting of banking establishments. Again the USA leads the way! The US Bankers Association, in a survey carried out in 1991, stated that US banks now faced another risk besides bad loans: having to shoulder the cost of expensive clean-up operations at polluted industrial sites. The Association reported in its survey that almost two-thirds of US community banks (i.e. those with assets under $500 million) have rejected loan applications or potential borrowers because of concerns about environmental liability. Despite this, one in eight of the banks had still had to pay pollution clean-up costs at polluted industrial sites. The result has been a tightening of loans to industries such as scrap merchants, businesses dealing with hazardous chemicals, pulp and paper mills, and even filling stations. Well over four-fifths of the banks have changed and tightened their lending procedures to avoid environmental liability and nearly half said that they had discontinued loans to customers because of the fear of environmental liability.

The trend is already crossing the Atlantic. British banks have become fearful that they too might find themselves liable for penalties incurred by a client when they foreclose on its assets. In such a situation the bank will become the owner of the failed company's property and could therefore be responsible for any pollution caused by the company. There is even a fear that they could become liable through the simple lending relationship, a fear inspired by a notorious US court case at the turn of the decade, involving a company called Fleet Factors. This set a general precedent for a bank's liability for clean-up costs. Such concepts have a habit of being transmitted from the USA to Britain because of the similarities in the legal regimes. Such worries are much less prevalent outside the Anglophone world.

Banks are therefore finding a policing role in environmental matters being thrust on them, forcing them to curtail lending to just those companies that, arguably, need it most. In their lending operations banks are finding that they need to scrutinise property for environmental sensitivity. All the UK clearing banks already have established environmental procedures to check out their customers' environmental situation and records before advancing a loan, and monitoring them until that loan is repaid. This scrutiny is bound to become more severe over time. The British Co-operative Bank has for a long time had a policy of not lending to companies in industries it disapproves of, such as armaments or tobacco.

Customer satisfaction

Customer satisfaction is linked in a general way to the environmental concern for the outside world. What quality was to the 1980s, so customer satisfaction will be to the 1990s. The reader will note that even British Rail and the London Underground are protesting their interest in their customers and will feel that this is a breakthrough too important to be ignored. We would expect to see companies installing customer satisfaction monitoring measures and customer satisfaction departments, especially in public monopolies, perhaps going so far as to regard customer user groups as one of the stakeholders in their businesses. Regulatory pressures are already bringing this about in the utilities in the UK.

This could have quite far-reaching effects. Companies will still measure quality on the basis of internally generated numbers, but they will also begin to evaluate their performance by collecting data directly from their customers. Competitive benchmarking has developed greatly in the past few years. This involves identifying competitors and/or companies in other industries that exemplify best practice in some activity, function or process. Internal yardsticks rarely have such an eye-opening effect. It will not have escaped our readers' notice that to do this properly companies will have to collaborate and exchange data more.

BUSINESS PARTNERSHIPS

International networking

Global competition, high R & D costs, shorter product life-cycles and more complex distribution channels (such as cash dispensers in banking) as well as the pressure of ever higher environmental expenditure is increasingly forcing firms – even if they are competitors – to pool their experience and resources in a variety of co-operative arrangements. Such alliances have embraced R & D, production, distribution and marketing. There are many types of alliance, for example joint ventures, co-operation agreements such as licensing in pharmaceuticals, market alliances, even collaborative export groups of small companies as in Italian cities.

European business is gradually changing its structure. According to the European Commission, the number of mergers and acquisitions made by Europe's leading 1,000 companies doubled between 1986/7 and 1988/9, and in the 12 months to June 1990 the number of cross-border mergers and acquisitions in Europe exceeded domestic ones for the first time. The number of joint ventures involving companies from two different EC states rose from 16 in 1986/7 to 55 in 1989/90. The most acquisitive tended to be engineering groups such as France's Alcatel-Alsthom and food groups such as Unilever. Mergers are getting bigger as well. In 1986/7 there were 88 deals in Europe that created new companies with a turnover of over five billion ccus. In 1989/90 there were 257.

Some alliances are half-way stations on the road to mergers, that is the strong taking over the weak as with Honda and Rover. At the other end of the scale, there are outright transnational mergers like Asea Brown Boveri (ABB), a fascinating and much-admired company that deserves to succeed. A lot of thought has gone into its organisation and operating structure. It has no natural centre. It has a networked structure of 65 business areas, 1,300 companies and more than 200,000 employees. Each business area has a world-wide responsibility to allocate its resources. Coherence is ensured by the holding company and ABB has taken deliberate action to reinforce common values throughout the organisation by three main methods: forcing the establishment of multinational teams, pushing for international transfers of staff and fighting national biases. Smith Kline Beecham too, is a merger with much the same philosophy, except that being an Anglo-American merger (as against ABB's Swedish–Swiss merger) there were perhaps fewer national cultural and linguistic differences to overcome. The Dutch and the British also appear to be able to work together amicably as the two long-standing Anglo-Dutch alliances, Unilever and Shell, testify.

The oil industry, a global high cost industry, has a long tradition of joint ventures – a basic form of strategic alliance for a specific and circumscribed purpose. It is a fiercely competitive industry, yet it is renowned for the way companies also work with each other. This collaboration takes many forms. Companies may have crude oil and product swap agreements so that they can minimise the distances they have to transport the crude oil and the products; they can share refinery capacity, and above all, they can go into partnership to spread the risk of that most expensive operation of all, oil exploration, as in the North Sea.

What is new is the extent to which this practice is spreading to other industrial sectors, such as the aircraft industry. The drivers are, as always, cost and competition. The French company Aerospatiale is quite open in the way it has had to co-operate in R & D and in production, a policy that has been heavily backed by the French government. The Airbus A320's development costs were $6 billion, the equivalent of Aerospatiale's annual turnover. Therefore some 80 per cent of its production has been undertaken co-operatively with other firms. As with planes, so with helicopters. In January 1992 Aerospatiale and Deutsche Aerospace merged their helicopter interests to form Eurocopter, the world's second biggest helicopter manufacturer after the US Sikorsky company, with a combined turnover of FFr12.65 billion (£1.3 billion). Though the other helicopter companies, Westland of the UK and Agusta of Italy, were in collaboration with Sikorsky, Eurocopter's stated intention was to expand this merger to include both Agusta and Westland as well as to negotiate alliances eventually with Asian and even Russian partners. The reason for what can only be called a global rationalisation was the depressed state of the helicopter industry in the face of shrinking defence budgets and a depressed civil helicopter market.

Mergers and alliances are not an easy option

While there are successes, there are many failures too, and cross-border link-ups, whether acquisitions, mergers or alliances, have a very high failure rate for which the problem of blending cultures is the greatest single cause. Dunlop–Pirelli was only one of the most spectacular collapses of an era that saw such disasters as Générale de Banque–Amro, Fiat–Citroën, Olivetti–AT&T and many others. The British Motor Corporation, later renamed British Leyland, was another catastrophe, a domestic merger of warring groups that never properly allied with each other, and which unravelled during the 1980s. British Leyland, like the UK group AEI two decades earlier, was composed of companies which, though all British, still had different cultures, and that alone was enough to cause critical problems. Perhaps as Austin-Rover, and backed by Honda, it has a chance of survival.

Industry watchers are looking on with interest at the merger of US banks such as Manufacturers Hanover with Chemical Bank to see how they will resolve their different business approaches: Manufacturers Hanover had centralised management; Chemical Bank took a more decentralised approach. In addition, they had very different software systems. As British building societies have found out, software differences can be sufficiently critical to kill a merger. Change will involve mergers, but the pressures to make them succeed will cause companies severe strains and tax their managements' abilities to the limit.

Cross-frontier culture problems are the most serious of all. More recently the unlucky Pirelli again came unstuck, this time in its abortive 'bid' for Continental in 1991, when it was clear that it did not quite understand German business. The Anglo-French merger of the Metal Box and Carnaud canning companies (CMB) also hit severe culture problems which resulted in the departure of the chief executive, Jean-Marie Descarpentries, in autumn 1991. Other Anglo-French links, however, appear to be more successful, such as Wiggins Teape and Arjomari and GEC–Alsthom.

Perhaps the secret is that in these two, one side is in definite control: the British in the former, the French in the latter.

The Western world's version of the *kairetsu*

Purchasing collaboration
In its 1990 annual report, Marks & Spencer says:

> We could not have moved forward as we did without the full co-operation of our suppliers, using that word in its widest sense to include providers of services, buildings and equipment as well as merchandise. These suppliers have made substantial investments in plant, technology and people on our behalf. They realise that through working closely with us they can expand their businesses by meeting the needs of a vast and growing number of customers.

Marks & Spencer refers specifically to its suppliers as partners and says that it has thought of them in this way since the 1930s. Marks & Spencer is no longer the exception it once may have been. Purchasing collaboration between companies is already not unusual and will become more and more common. One has only to look behind the brand name of one's home appliance or computer and find out where the parts were actually made, to appreciate the extent of the existing manufacturing–supply network.

We have already pointed out in Chapter 6 that though they may not be actual shareholders in each other, they are partners in every other way. The extent of the partnership can be surprisingly wide: at Deere & Co. in the USA, for instance, workers are solving problems directly with their counterparts at suppliers such as McLaughlin Body Co. In some cases companies are actual shareholders in their suppliers: IBM and Digital have gone so far as to take equity stakes in strategic suppliers or in high technology start-ups that could benefit them. In other cases financing help is available: IBM for instance sometimes pays its suppliers up-front instead of on delivery, for research or product development work.

United States companies have learnt the lesson from the Japanese. In industries as diverse as computers, farm implements and motorcycles, they have rethought their business approach and planning to form links that extend both vertically down the supply chain, and horizontally to sister companies, universities and professional institutes. Since the early 1980s US industry has been busy pooling so-called precompetitive research on product technology and formed over 250 R & D consortia in the decade.

One of the best examples of these developments is the world motor industry, which in a curious way has come full circle. People sometimes forget the fact that Henry Ford started out totally reliant on outsiders who supplied the chassis, engines, gearboxes and other parts for his motor cars. All his company originally did was to bolt on a body and wheels. By the 1930s it was fully integrated, however. Now the company is returning to the past. We set out in Table 8.1 Ford's complex series of alliances as it entered the 1990s.

---

1.   VEHICLES

Mazda: Ford stake 25%

The Tracer is based on a Mazda design and built by Ford. Mazda has engineered the Escort subcompact. As this book was going to press, Ford announced that it was taking a 50% stake in Mazda's US manufacturing subsidiary, Mazda Motor Manufacturing Corporation. Mazda Motor's Flat Rock, Michigan, plant produces the Mazda 626 and MX-6 models and the Ford Probe.

Kia Motors (Korea): Ford stake 10%

The Festiva is made by Kia to Ford's design.

Aston Martin Lagonda (Britain): Ford stake 75%

Jaguar Motors (Britain): Ford stake 100%

Autolatina (Brazil, Argentina): Ford stake 49%

Iveco Ford Truck (Britain): Ford stake 48%

2.   PARTS PRODUCTION

Cummins (engines): Ford stake 10.8%

Cummins is designing and building diesel engines for Ford medium-duty trucks.

Excel Industries (windows): Ford stake 40%

Decoma (Canada, body parts and wheels): Ford stake 49%

3.   OTHERS

Ford owns 49% of Hertz; it extends consumer credit through seven wholly owned financial companies; it belongs to eight consortia that carry out research into environmental issues, better engineering techniques, etc.

Table 8.1   Ford's strategic alliances

Ford is not untypical: Rover Group collaborates with Honda, Volvo has allied very closely with Renault, Bertone has designed and assembled a Daihatsu four-wheel drive with a BMW engine, to name just a few. Figure 8.1 shows the extent of the cross-alliances in the world motor industry.

Nissan has brought its approach to its network of subcontractors to the UK when making its investment in the north-east, but this has not been without pain as its UK component suppliers have realised the high quality and performance that would be required in order to become one of Nissan's partners. Suppliers have been asked to take on design responsibility and the greater investment that is increasingly necessary to produce the high quality,

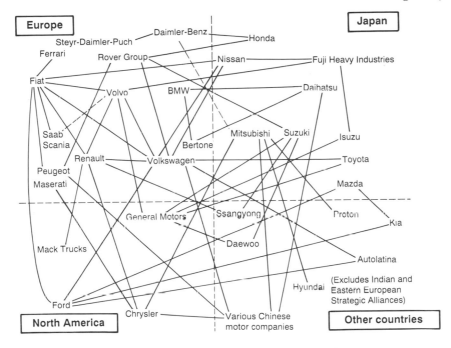

Figure 8.1 Strategic alliances within the motor vehicles industry
Source: *Finanzmeister*, Pitman Publishing 1991

reliable, environmentally friendly and cost-effective sub assemblies for Nissan's vehicles. A typical project demands two years' up-front spending followed by five to six years' profitable production. Under such a business profile, long-term stable relationships are vital.

WHAT ABOUT THE WORKERS?

Employee participation and development

Whether they allow them board representation or not, companies are coming under unremitting pressure to provide a quality service to their employees. We have already identified Glaxo's positive attitudes to governance in Chapter 3. We would also single it out as one of the leaders of what could be regarded as enlightened British best practice in employee relations. Glaxo was the third largest company in Europe by market capitalisation in 1990, and has been renowned for its profitable growth. In 1990 it employed some 43,400 staff world-wide, of whom around 12,400 were in the UK. Its employee policies cover the following:

  (i) Company newspapers and journals.
 (ii) An annual *Report to Staff* in booklet and video form in nine languages.
(iii) Share option scheme for employees and a savings-related share option scheme.
(iv) Non-discriminatory employee policies and practices.
 (v) Consideration for the employment of disabled persons.

Everything, one might say, but allowing the employees a share in corporate governance! Our view is that British companies will have to concede this latter, though the German Chamber of Commerce, commenting on the Maastricht accord of December 1991, wondered whether British industry would be able to afford to pay for the social issues in the same way as continental companies could. This was despite the fact that British labour wages were up to 50 per cent below German ones.

  Britain alone stood out against the EC Social Charter, but nonetheless we regard it as inevitable that Britain will eventually – must eventually – fall into line with Maastricht or its equivalent, despite the Danish referendum vote in June 1992. There are three critical clauses of this charter which are already implicitly accepted by the quality companies that seek to adopt best practice:

  (i) Right of access to life-long vocational training, without discrimination on the grounds of nationality.
 (ii) Right to information, consultation and participation for employees, particularly in conditions of technological change, restructuring, redundancies, and for trans-frontier workers.
(iii) Right to health, protection and safety at the workplace, including training, information, consultation and participation for employees.

Internationalism

British multinational companies, despite popular myths about their insularity, have always prided themselves on their international approach. The Anglo-Dutch Shell company inevitably leads the way with expatriate executives drawn from some 60 countries, but other companies too, such as ICI, Grand Metropolitan and BP, go out of their way to develop their non-British managers. The Dutch, Swiss and Swedes have always appreciated the importance of developing international executives, and now, finally, German and French companies are increasingly having to invest heavily in international staff development as they expand their horizons. Our survey of their 1990 accounts reveals that Rhône-Poulenc has over a third of its R&D staff outside France, and that Bayer and Hoechst are expanding their international R&D. The Swiss company Ciba-Geigy already has half its R & D staff outside its home country. Deutsche Bank has realised that the price for being an international bank is to build up an international staff cadre and by 1990 a quarter of its staff being trained for international business were non-Germans.

We have to say, however, that Italian and Spanish international companies have a long way to go. They are making substantial investments in training and employee development, but it is still heavily concentrated on parent company nationals.

We look forward to the day when European multinationals no longer think in terms of national staff. It will be enough to have the EC passport.

GLOBALISM AND PROVINCIALISM

Companies will have to adapt themselves in the 1990s to two apparently contradictory, trends: supranationalism and provincialism. How is it that a world where people describe themselves as good Europeans, where the EC Commission is becoming increasingly powerful and where European states are learning to act together, still has such powerful regional tendencies: where autonomy for Scotland, Catalonia, Corsica and the German *Länder*, and the Belgian hostility between French and Flemish speakers are so important? The answer is not difficult to find. The European Community is making the nation state seem less important than previously, and people therefore feel freer to indulge in their regional and provincial aspirations (and prejudices?) as they never previously could. The result could well be a Europe of provinces rather than of nation states. The tensions in Eastern Europe show how serious and dangerous these can be if carried to an extreme.

Companies will have to adapt themselves to these new circumstances: it will not be easy for a European multinational to be operating on a global scale, and yet at the same time to be sensitive to Walloon or southern Italian susceptibilities, but it will, nonetheless, have to cope with these pressures.

9 THE EUROPEAN COMPANY OF THE LATE 1990s

THE EMERGING TRANSNATIONAL

The determinants

The competitive environment of the last decade of the century is having a dramatic effect in reshaping companies. The focus on core competences is central to corporate thinking: woe betide a manager whose business is no longer regarded as core! What was core yesterday may no longer be core today. Companies are becoming change-based, to use the current management jargon, businesses are being sold, functions are being contracted out.

Companies are also thinking more in terms of alliances, and less in terms of being self-contained fortresses. The boundary-less company has to adopt a collaborative style. Companies have to beware of relying on alliances alone, however. Every company has to have its core competences at which it excels. A major criticism of Italy's Olivetti Corporation is that it appears to rely too much on strategic alliances, to the point where such a reliance on so many alliances can be regarded as a sign of weakness, not of strength.

The pressure on the sheer quality of management will be enormous. The emphasis will be on cultures and styles rather than on organisation trees and methodologies. Managements will (and are already) having to pay more attention to international processes through people, rather than through structures. Horizontal relationships through networking will be just as important as the classical head office–subsidiary pattern: after all, that is what activity-based costing teaches us, that costs are driven horizontally through relationships, even if they are reported vertically. Managing internationally means building corporate commitment and identification across borders, that is, the sharing of visions, values and styles. The leading companies are already there: the Shell culture, refined and developed over the best part of a century is a powerful binding force. Shell is a network as much as a company, that has an emotional pull even on those who have left it,

If we were to hazard a guess we would say that the five drivers for business in this last decade of the century would be in addition to profitability, of course:

(i) *The market share imperative.* Big business has to have market share (coupled with cost control) especially as it has retreated to its core competences. That was the rationale for Nestlé's take over of Rowntree-Mackintosh, at a high price, and we shall see the same trend in the shake-out that is already hitting the banking industry and will hit the European food industry by the mid-1990s.

(ii) *Let down the drawbridge.* Companies must emerge from their castles and form alliances and partnerships, horizontally and with suppliers and customers.

(iii) *Go green.* The environmental and ecological issue is one of the biggest challenges facing companies not only in the obvious sectors such as minerals, extraction, oil and chemicals. We have mentioned this issue so often in this book because we believe many companies, particularly the medium-sized and smaller ones, have still not realised the impact these issues will have on them and their businesses.

(iv) *Invest in people.* Successful companies will be expected to invest heavily in their staff and to communicate with them and consult them. Taking their staff genuinely into their confidence for real may come as a shock to some companies that have in the past only talked a lot about the subject, but now may actually have to do something about it.

(v) *A new Puritan age.* Here we are really going out on a limb to make a prediction, but we believe that in business, as in social and sexual behaviour, the last decade will see a retreat from the 'anything goes' mentality of the previous 30 years. Companies' freedom for manoeuvre will increasingly, we believe, be limited by rules and regulations, and by social pressures themselves. Anyone who doubts this may reflect on the social changes in business life that have occurred in the past decade: the virtual elimination of smoking in many places of work; the dramatic decline of that great British tradition, the liquid business lunch; the laws about sexual harassment and discrimination; the insider legislation, the need for compliance officers, and so on.

All these changes and trends impact on governance, the last one most of all, and in the rest of this chapter we explore how companies will be affected.

Towards a European company

One of the biggest drivers of change is the EC itself, and the idea of a common Europe. Gradually, imperceptibly and almost without realising it, we are witnessing the creation of a specific European model of transnational management with identifiable 'European' standards and corporate values.

Of course Europe is not and can never be, one single entity. There are various groupings as we have already seen:

(i) The Anglophone grouping: the US multinationals in Europe, the UK and perhaps The Netherlands.

(ii) The Nordic countries: Scandinavia and Finland, and, who knows, eventually Estonia, Latvia and Lithuania.

(iii) The Germanic world: Germany, Austria and Switzerland, and perhaps, again, Czechoslovakia.

(iv) The Latin world: Belgium, Italy and Spain, and perhaps Hungary though it is not a Latin country. France, on the other hand, is a Latin country but it has so many special characteristics that it is often in a category all of its own.

These countries and their companies have different cultures, but we foresee a convergence on certain 'European' business norms:

(i) Accepting the fact that there are various interest groups within and outside the company, that is the stakeholders, and taking account of them. The European transnational's legitimacy is derived from the support of these internal, local and national stakeholders. A small but revealing example: Electrolux controls the Italian Zanussi, but when it took the company over, Italy's Friuli Region also took a stake of some 10.4 per cent in the company.

(ii) A concentration on social issues, personnel development and training and a concern for the environment.

(iii) Development of an open management style with mobility across frontiers, which is easier in Europe than anywhere else, where it is possible to commute from The Netherlands to a job in Antwerp, from Germany to Luxembourg, and even from the Pas de Calais to London. Already financial institutions are targeting the executive with a trans-European career path.

(iv) Business unit decentralisation combined with the sharing of mission and strategies across borders. This is certainly nothing new: we could name dozens of European multinationals from Akzo and BP through to Solvay and Unilever, that practise this very successfully already. Executives will increasingly look to a European (if not a more international) career path.

(v) The building of co-ordinated networks through task forces, meetings and conferences to create a transnational culture, based in an increasing number of cases, on the English language.

There will be a convergence in governance too. Boards of directors of international companies are already becoming more international and will become increasingly more so, especially the supervisory element of the board, whatever it will be called. International directors (or advisory or supervisory directors) will bring international attitudes to their jobs and we foresee a certain consensus as to the norms of corporate behaviour and governance that will become established. Inevitably there will be a push from the EC Commission.

The Japanese multinationals certainly appreciate the need for a specific European identity. Toyota is determined to be and to think European and it has located a £20 million technical and training centre for its European operations at Zaventem by Brussels airport to back up its enormous £750 million investment in its Derbyshire site. Backing this is a network of local suppliers. We have no doubt, given the Japanese thoroughness and attention to detail, that by the end of the decade the Toyota operation in Europe will be managed and governed in a distinctive European way.

Mergers and acquisitions

The European perspective

Globalizing markets, instantaneous communications, travel at the speed of sound, political realignments, changing demographies, technological transformations in both products and production, corporate alliances, flattening organisations – all these and more are changing the structure of the corporation. The once very rigid and unbreachable boundaries are fading in the face of change. (Rosabeth Moss Kanter 'Transcending Business Boundaries: 12,000 World Managers View Change' *Harvard Business Review*, May–June 1991).

The trend towards a free market is inexorable. By the end of the 1980s exchange controls had all but vanished in the EC countries apart from Greece, Ireland and Portugal. Speaking at the Chartered Institute of Management Accountants' (CIMA) annual conference in September 1991, Sir John Harvey-Jones said that he expected to see half of Europe's companies disappear within the next five years. The focus will be on corporate restructuring. One has only to look at the USA, where a market leader has perhaps a fifth or a quarter of the market, and at Europe, where it will have a twentieth, to realise the scope for consolidation.

We have talked a lot about alliances in this book. There will be all types of business alliance, including some in Eastern Europe that will surely break new ground in corporate structure and governance. Already the creative new groupings such as GEC and Alsthom, ABB, Mitsubishi and Daimler-

Benz, and Renault and Volvo, to name just a few, demonstrate that the management theories developed in the last half of this century can no longer be appropriate to meet today's business challenges. There are still vast cultural differences in Europe – as CMB's problems have amply demonstrated – but integration has already begun with cross cultural links as between Germany's Siemens and Britain's GEC, GEC and France's Alcatel-Alsthom, Alcatel-Alsthom with the Italian Fiat, and between Guinness and LVMH, and Cap Gemini Sogeti and Hoskyns, to show that (even!) Anglo-French differences can be bridged. Of course, where there is an enormous disparity in strength between the two sides as with Honda and Rover, the alliance can surely only be a half-way house to an eventual merger.

Alliances have to be worked at. As the Renault–Volvo link shows, it is not just a question of two boards being in agreement: middle managers have to co-operate as well. Renault and Volvo are working on two contrasting principles: they are keeping their brands separate but they are determined to operate together as if they were one company. They exchange engines and parts, they are working together on commuter buses, they are beginning to manufacture each other's vehicles, they are merging their sales divisions, they are collaborating on research to the point of setting up a joint research centre, and they are co-ordinating their accounting. They are already beginning to exchange senior staff. Who knows where this will end up by the end of the century?

There are two types of European merger. The first will be a purely domestic merger such as a company linking up with its local competitors in order to gain operating size in the European market. The second is where a company allies itself with other companies from other nations so as to fill out its European (and, indeed, international) network. Asea Brown Boveri (ABB) is a much quoted example of this: It is moving towards 'centres of excellence', that is there is a home base for each product area, for example Sweden for transmission equipment. Nestlé has deliberately built on the confectionery skills of Rowntree-Mackintosh in Britain and on the pasta know-how of Buitoni in Italy, taking advantage of the product expertise in those companies.

We believe that companies will have to go more and more into this method of operating. Co-ordinating dispersed production, R & D and product development among equal subsidiaries in different countries, is next to impossible, despite the management theorists. This international product co-ordination that we have just described is different from the confederation of baronies which was the traditional way that European companies operated in the past.

There are interesting repercussions for governance. With this world of corporate equals it will not only be the composition of the top board that is important, but also the boards of those key subsidiaries that are the product champions in a multinational's stable.

United States companies have begun to form defensive groupings to face European alliances such as Airbus and the Japanese combines like Mitsubishi, and this trend, too, will increase. Apple and IBM already collaborate on research. 'It's hard to imagine what high-tech company will even try to get by in the 1990's without an alliance,' is the opinion of John Scully, CEO of Apple Computer Inc.

In the banking field, Manufacturers Hanover/Chemical Bank and Bank of America/Security Pacific have merged. Are we going back full circle to the days at the turn of the century when the trust busters had to break up Rockefeller's Standard Oil and Andrew Carnegie's US Steel?

The European construction industry

As an example of mergers and alliances in a specific industry we show, in Table 9.1, some examples from the situation of the European construction industry in 1991. The European single market has been a dynamic spur to the construction sector to create cross-border linkages, and as can be seen from the table, French and German firms have been particularly active. The examples of Dumez and Phillip Holzmann show that companies no longer go only for the 50 per cent+ control so beloved of the financial people. The route favoured by the German and French companies has been to acquire strategic stakes in other companies by taking cross-holdings in each other to strengthen trading relationships as well as being a defence against hostile takeover bids. Thus the shares of the five leading German contractors, Phillip Holzmann, Hochtief, Bilfinger, Strabag and Dywidag are tightly held by each other or by friendly banks. It is the same situation in France where there are large cross-shareholdings: Dumez controls GTM Entrepose, while Générale des Eaux owns a majority of SGE and has a substantial stake in Fougerolle.

Ford and Mazda

We have already mentioned the linkages in the automobile industry in the previous chapter. With the cost of developing a new car being anything up to £1.2 billion, it is not surprising that automobile manufacturers are allying with each other. There have been many disappointments: GM–Daewoo and GM–Isuzu, Chrysler–Mitsubishi and Fiat–Nissan. The list is very long. The surprise is the relative success of Ford's link up with Mazda, in which it has a 25 per cent stake. We have already commented on this in the previous chapter (see p. 186). The alliance was formed in 1979 and it has stood the test of time. Ford, of course, is four times the size of Mazda but both have benefited from the alliance.

Company	Stake in	Country	Stake
France			%
Bouygues	Losinger	Czechoslovakia	85
	Fercaber	Spain	70
	Dragados	Spain	5
SGE	Norwest Holst	UK	100
Dumez	CFE	Belgium	34
	McAlpine	UK	12
	Hans Brochier	Germany	25
	Dumez-Copisa	Spain	100
Fougerolle	Maurice Delens	Netherlands	40
Germany			
Bilfinger	Birse	UK	15
Holzmann	Ed Ast	Austria	40
	Hillen & Roosen	Netherlands	100
	Jotsa	Spain	50
	Nord France	France	100
	Tilbury Douglas	UK	20
Hochtief	Guaranti-Insaat	Italy	42
	Hugo Durst	Austria	100
	Ferrovial	Spain	100
Britain			
AMEC	Kittelberger	Germany	50
	Serete	France	20

Table 9.1   Cross-border holdings in the European construction industry

Source: Salomon Brothers

Ford is the best-selling foreign marque in Japan, selling its cars and trucks through the dealer network it owns jointly with Mazda. By 1991 they had jointly worked on 10 car models, generally with Ford doing the styling and Mazda concentrating on the engineering. In all, one in every four Ford cars sold in the USA in 1990 had some degree of Mazda involvement, and two of every four Mazdas sold had some Ford involvement.

It is Ford's intention to use the lessons learnt from its relationship with Mazda as an example of how to structure its alliances in other parts of the world, such as its growing relationship with Volkswagen and Nissan. The relationship has not been without strain, but so far it has worked.

Social pressures

Board members will be expected to adhere to increasingly high standards of conduct. Legislation is everywhere becoming more severe, not just in Britain, and it is being backed up by a willingness to prosecute. The turn of the decade saw horrendous business scandals not just in Britain, but also in Japan, and, to a lesser extent, in Germany. But the pressures will come from other directions as well. Shareholder activism will grow. It is becoming an established feature of the US business world, and as US investors buy overseas shares so they are exporting their ideas of shareholder democracy abroad. Britain will be, and already is, one of their first ports of call. A US firm already exists that offers services to investors to help them vote at annual general meetings, even those of different Japanese firms that all hold their annual meetings on the same day. This firm ensures that shareholders are well informed and helps them to ask the 'right' questions at AGMs. There is no doubt that an aspect of governance that will grow in importance will be that of communication with investors, and companies will have to spend more time (and invest more resources) in this. It was noticeable in our 100-company survey, how many companies now have investor relations departments.

Social policy is also impacting on employee relations. We expect that the European company's attitude to employee relations will be oriented to the German/north European approach. This goes beyond training and leads to communication and openness of discussion. Bayer is a leading example. The company philosophy is to regard personnel development as an integral part of its corporate strategy. Vocational training and continuing education are aspects of this. Bayer has had employee committees since the early 1970s: these have, however, been a statutory requirement in Germany only since 1990. The company's view is that EC pressures will gain in significance as the single market nears fruition. The Commission is already beginning to influence the way people are working. As Bayer reports, this is not confined to the more peripheral suggestions, such as the abolition of the ban on night-time working of female manual workers, but to more central matters such as participation and the extent of co-determination rights for employee representatives. Bayer, for one, has not allowed itself to be left to the mercy of events, and in 1991 had already had discussions on the subject at five of its European subsidiary companies.

THE GREEN ISSUE

Environmental pressures

Bob Reid, formerly of Shell, has said that no business has a secure future unless it is environmentally acceptable. An increasingly influential ethical movement is practising positive discrimination against companies engaged in environmentally unfriendly activities: there are now many more categories than the original ones of armaments, tobacco, drugs and alcohol. It is significant that the ethical movement is more and more associated with the powerful pension fund industry and with investors with the most funds to invest, that is in the 55–69 age group. Both TSB and Eagle Star have already established green unit trusts and the Commercial Union is offering green investment services to pension fund clients. The brokers James Capel even run a green index. The trend is for environmental performance to be gradually added to profit performance criteria when analysts are evaluating companies.

Environmental issues are one of the biggest worries for today's CEOs, because they know that there will be severe implications and substantial costs for their companies, but they do not know how severe, or how expensive. The pressures will come from the EC, from governments, and from environment pressure groups. Companies will have to review and perhaps change their practices under these pressures. For one thing they will have to set up systems to track the key changes that take place in legislation, markets, customers and suppliers with regard to environmental issues. It will not be very easy to achieve a balance between profitability, unit costs and the environmental impact.

Environmental advisory boards

Companies are beginning to regard the creation of environmental advisory boards or panels as an increasingly effective way of keeping in touch with environmental expertise as well, perhaps, as demonstrating to the outside world how seriously they take environmental issues. This is an obvious example of how environmental issues link into governance. As always, the USA takes the lead. Several US companies have such boards: Dow Chemicals, for example, set up an international environmental advisory council of 14 persons in 1991, which is intended to meet three or four times a year. Britain is not so far behind. In the UK, Shanks & McEwan, the waste management and incinerator operator, has been advised by an environmental board since 1989. Banks, too, have committees to screen environmentally exposed investments: the TSB's committee, for instance, is chaired by the botanist and TV celebrity David Bellamy.

Having boards is one thing, listening to them is another, and it is clear that such boards can only work effectively if the company sets up a management structure to make them work and has the courage to listen to independent and, sometimes, unpalatable advice. At the moment, in Britain, they appear to be less important as strategic policy-makers and are more used in order to keep abreast of developments in the environmental field and to give advice to the main board. It may even be that for some companies the existence of such a board or committee is a public relations (PR) exercise; to be seen by outsiders to be taking environmental issues seriously. These are early days, and we believe that what is important is that the principle of such an advisory agency has been established, and that these environmental advisory boards will grow in seriousness and importance. After all, once a major company has established such a board, even if only for PR reasons, it can hardly afford the publicity of resignations from it especially if the members say they have not been taken seriously by the company.

Environmental audits

There is increasing pressure for companies to carry out or be submitted to environmental audits. In essence these involve a systematic examination of the environmental effects of a company's operations, and they are a means whereby a company can set an appropriate environmental policy and monitor progress against related objectives. The International Chamber of Commerce defines the environmental audit as 'a management tool comprising a systematic, documented, periodic and objective evaluation of how well environmental organisation, management and equipment are performing, with the aim of helping to safeguard the environment': CIMA (Chartered Institute of Management Accountants) Research Study, 'The Costs to Industry of Adopting Environmental Friendly Practices', p. 43, 1990.

The EC is gradually, imperceptibly, moving to environmental audits. It appears that these will start by being voluntary, but that if companies do carry them out, it may well be that they will be required to consult their employees. It has been suggested that participating companies will be able to display an eco-audit symbol on their products. It is already agreed that a European environmental agency will be established.

We note again the two planks of EC policy, the environment and the involvement of the workforce, both revolving round a company's corporate philanthropy and its participation in community affairs. We regard this start as a typical example of the Community's 'salami-slicing tactics', and are convinced that environmental audits will become obligatory by the end of the century, either under national regulations or under EC Directives. Environmental protection will move to the top of management priorities. There will be a growing trend towards environmental audits (eco-audits in Community terminology).

Leading companies have already started on the process. For example, BP has been carrying out regular audits since 1974, and it takes the view that if a company has an environmental policy, it cannot manage it without having an audit to back it up. These audits are taken very seriously indeed, and one managing director of a BP business unit told us that part of his business objectives (and therefore his remuneration) was directly tied into a successful outcome of the audit. It is now BP's intention to split the environmental from the health and safety audit. However, BP is an exception, and it was estimated in 1991 that fewer than 200 UK companies carry out such audits.

Environmental audits involve the gathering and reporting of data, and this too will become a feature of corporate management, and will doubtless be yet another cross for the corporate controller to bear. There are still many questions that need to be answered such as who will actually carry out the environmental audit. The thought is that it will inevitably be an outside body. Consultancies are already anticipating this prospect with great interest.

The costs of going green

It is still too early to estimate how much environmental issues will cost companies. All we know is that the figure will be enormous, estimated to put several percentage points on to the operating costs of vulnerable industries such as chemicals. A research paper put out by the Chartered Institute of Management Accountants ('The Costs to Industry of Adopting Environmental Friendly Practices', 1990) suggests that environmental audits could cost major companies as much as £400,000. Sweden, inevitably, is in the vanguard of the environmental movement, and its government already raises heavy energy taxes on industry. A government commission reporting at the end of 1990 drew attention to the heavy burden of energy taxes on Swedish industry, estimating that the abolition of such taxes would increase industrial production especially in the basic industries to the tune of some £2 billion, and would create an extra 10,000 jobs. The same trend is evident in Britain.

It is difficult to say where the balance will finish up. The likelihood is that continuing relentless pressure by environmentalists will force companies to take account of the green issue. It is already difficult to conceal a lack of action or ineffective action. Inevitably the environment will become an issue of governance and the corporate directorate will become involved in ensuring that proper action is taken and that proper figures are produced and reports issued. We do not envy the finance directors who will have to work out how this will be financed, or their subordinates who will have to devise the appropriate reporting systems. Who knows, by the turn of the century the audit committee of the board may well be involved in overseeing the environmental figures and their audit.

TWO COMPANIES' SOLUTIONS

IBM

For many years IBM has been one of the world's most admired companies from a marketing and business organisation point of view. Our own researches looked at its structure of governance and in Chapter 3 we noted the praiseworthy way in which it had created a world-wide hierarchy of advisory boards (see p. 48). The company, however, has been under world wide competitive pressure to adopt a looser and more decentralised management style. In December 1991 it startled the business world, and, we would surmise, its employees, by announcing a sweeping reorganisation to create subsidiary companies and a restructure of its businesses. The talk is of a 'commonwealth' of semi-autonomous business units, which will be product oriented at one level, and sales and marketing focused at another. One company, for instance, would become responsible for all IBM's computer printer operations and another for all of its data storage products. The intention appears to be to transform its product groups into subsidiary companies and also even to spin off the administrative services into separate companies. Some business units could become joint ventures, whilst others could be spun off entirely with their own independent boards of directors. The end result could be eventually for each business unit to be publicly accountable for its own commercial performance and to publish its own accounts. Inevitably, the price of operational freedom will be accountability.

The reorganisation had barely been announced as this book was going to press. Announcing a reorganisation is one thing. Carrying the changes through to the 350,000 staff and carrying the staff with the changes is another. It is far too early to give any opinion. One thing is certain, however, and that is that IBM will have to change its hierarchy of corporate governance. It will be interesting to see the structure that the company eventually comes up with: the top board at the 'conglomerate' level, the different boards of the horizontal and vertical business units, and what the fate of the regional advisory boards will be. The company could learn a lesson from BP, where the culture change of the early 1990s has appeared to drift close to a cost reduction programme and nothing more in the minds of many of the employees.

Siemens

Siemens, too, like a great many other multinationals, has reorganised itself to produce a flatter and more decentralised structure. The result is the classic organisation structure that we would expect to be a feature of the 1990s:

(i)   A top board that concerns itself with strategic issues.
(ii) Groups and divisions (some 19 in all) that concentrate on business policy and synergies.
(iii) Sectors (business units) whose task it is to achieve competitive advantage.

Overlaying these, as we have seen, are country structures to ensure the co-ordination of the Siemens businesses on national bases.

The way Siemens has restructured itself is a classical example of how many companies are seeking to organise themselves. Profit responsibility is devolved to the business groups, and their definition is not by size but (as with IBM) by technological orientation or customer base. Group responsibility is international, and it is total, from planning to customer service.

There are obvious managerial advantages to such reorganisations, but they do pose a big question mark. What is the purpose and role of the corporate headquarters at the centre now that so much more autonomy has been given to the subsidiary units? Companies will need to address this question in the next decade as they reorganise and grant autonomy down the line, and they need to have thought through their answer.

For Siemens it is quite clear. Corporate headquarters has a strategic role, and the functions there are responsible for formulating corporate guidelines and ensuring standard procedures throughout the company in areas such as finance, personnel, R & D, production and logistics.

It is not only the operational management that has been changed, significantly, the leadership structure too has been reorganised.

The company has its supervisory council and managing board, of course, but it is in fact operationally managed by the corporate executive committee of the managing board, whose members, significantly enough, are approved by the supervisory council. The role of this committee is to:

(i) Assure the quality of company policies and strategies and supervise their implementation.
(ii) Evaluate strategic businesses and utilise synergies to strengthen the competitive position.
(iii) Sift through the company to prepare, promote and select a leadership team.

The committee's responsibility is at the strategic level, but it does not intervene in the operations of the groups. That is in the hands of the groups' managements themselves. This is the formula that has served Shell and many others so well and is rapidly becoming the standard for multinationals.

NEW TYPES OF STRUCTURES

Siemens and IBM are established companies and are reorganising themselves in a classical, establishment way that management theorists will recognise. There will be other structures too that such theorists will not recognise, some perhaps that will be entirely new. The effects of change have been far-reaching. We have already seen the hybrid structures as firms ally with each other, form joint ventures and loose networks. There will also be new structures as organisations are created in Eastern Europe, not quite state companies, not quite capitalist: perhaps capitalist without the capital, as the Hungarian joke has it! Already in Eastern Europe the denationalised companies and state agencies that have been commercialised have resulted in a new type of organisational culture if not a new type of organisation. This is also in evidence in France where there are many major companies, such as Elf Aquitaine, Total and so on, that are commercial organisations and yet strongly under state influence. There is a whole world of governance relating to these organisations.

REPORTING

We see the 1990s as an era of growing regulation and control, and this will be reflected in increasing pressures from outside on companies for information. Reporting requirements will become heavier. There will be four areas where EC, national and financial regulators will press hard on companies:

(i) Financial reporting: the regulatory pressures in Britain will be on companies to prevent them playing games with goodwill and funds flow statements with a particular focus on extraordinary items; the pressure on continental, international and quoted companies will be to force them to give more detailed figures relating to items such as cash flows and hidden reserves. The pressures will also be very heavy on continental companies that aspire to a pan-European dimension. They will have to adopt a more open style of reporting to satisfy increasingly critical authorities and international investors. Paris and Frankfurt are leading the way as they seek to build up their status as financial centres to rival London. Italy, too, is tightening the rules with investor protection laws to safeguard minority shareholders and with regulations providing for more business transparency. It has been noted how this has wrong-footed even the mighty Mediobanca. The pressures are no fewer in a Switzerland seeking to enter the EC, and companies have been forced to admit foreigners into their governance. In a world of global business a country like Switzerland cannot be a law unto itself. In the more open Europe of the last decade of the century, continental companies will have to be more frank than they have been in the past. Dare we say it, but they will have to aspire to Anglophone standards in published reporting.

(ii) Companies will be required to explain their strategies more openly: what their objectives are, how they measure themselves and how they perceive success, as well as to give some indications of their targets and forecasts. This is already half done in many companies' annual statements.

(iii) We would also expect pressure from the EC for companies – especially continental companies who are unused to this – to give more information on their ownership and control. The requirement could bear particularly heavily on companies building up European operations, because of the European Commission's fear of cartels and monopolies.

(iv) Social reporting: the European company will be forced to report on its social activities, especially the following:

    (a) its performance with regard to its workforce as against its objectives in this respect, covering such items as benefits, policies (such as equal opportunities), education levels, training programmes, training policies, and the amount spent on training and development. More details will also have to be given on the management of company pension funds (see below).

    (b) Safety, health and environment: accident rates, occupational health, environmental programmes and investments, policies and goals. Eventually we would expect the results of eco-audits to be shown so that companies will be able to report a clean eco-audit certificate just as they can show a clean financial audit certificate.

(c) The fall-out from the Maxwell companies' débâcle in 1991/2 will put pressure on the management of pension funds. This will certainly affect British companies and we would expect that eventually continental companies will be affected as well. We cannot believe that in the long run it will continue to be acceptable for pension fund liabilities to be carried in the balance sheet as currently happens in German companies.

These statements will become part of the annual report, and therefore the directors will have to put their names to them.

There will therefore be a change from the reporting of purely financial performance measures to include the more intangible things such as customer satisfaction, environmental achievements, safety, training and human development and market share. For example, BP has already introduced bottom-up appraisals whereby the staff appraise their managers. This is part of the link into a constituency that is wider than the purely financial one. The old rule is that what gets measured gets attention. There is nothing new under the sun, and there is nothing new even in this. As early as 1951 Ralph Cordiner, then chief executive of General Electric of the USA, set up a high level task force to identify key performance measures, and the ones selected were the timeless ones. In addition to the financial/profitability measures the team came up with market share, productivity, employee attitudes, public responsibility and the balance between short- and long-term goals.

THE COMPANY OF THE LATE 1990s

In any ranking of profitable companies today a striking feature is that German and Japanese companies do not come out well against British and US ones. The UK and USA have over half of the top 800 world companies, including the oil majors. There are two explanations for this. One is that we are talking of reported profits, not wealth created: British and US companies need to report high profits even if balance sheet engineering is involved to make this happen. Otherwise their market valuation might be hit. Continental companies prefer profit-smoothing techniques and very conservative accounting formulae. Another reason is that we are using the word profitability not in the sense of the wealth created generally by a company, but in the sense of the amount of it that is available to the shareholders. A company may well create wealth but choose to pass it on to its wider stakeholders, such as its employees and customers, instead. Germany is a high value, high wage country, while Japanese firms pass on value to the customer, accepting lower prices and lower returns so as to achieve market share and growth. Such a choice is less common in the Anglophone countries where firms have to worry about their institutional shareholders and the dividends they are paid.

Today's market share is apt to be tomorrow's profit and market dominance, and we would expect to see a greater weighting of German and Japanese companies in the top 800 by the turn of the century, as British companies are not only overtaken but as the shareholder value conglomerates and those companies dominated by one or two people break up. With a greater weight of non-Anglophone companies we would also expect a correspondingly greater weight being given to their national ideas of governance.

We should expect the top companies, in *The Times* 100 or the Fortune 500, to have a shelf life of perhaps no more than 40 to 50 years at most. There will be many casualties before the year 2000. Readers should steel themselves to see casualties among clearing banks, building societies and conglomerates. Whole sectors will change: the chemical sector, for instance, will have to contract under the impact of over-capacity, ageing plants and environmental pressures; there will be fewer plants and fewer companies.

We have already alluded to the all-pervasiveness of change and of surprising change. In this book we can only make a few informed guesses: perhaps the biggest surprises of all will be in areas we never thought of! In such a world a company needs all the friends it can get. A wider world of stakeholders, alliances and corporate networking is not a luxury, it is plain commonsense and a business necessity.

10 EXCELLENCE IN GOVERNANCE

THE NEED FOR BOARDROOM EFFECTIVENESS

The successful company seeks to be successful in all areas: marketing, operations, production, R & D and so on, and it has to tackle those areas that are not contributing. The boardroom is not exempt from this cold scrutiny. It has to be as effective as any other area, and the directorate, whether executive or not, has to add value.

A non-performing board can cripple a company just as surely as a non-performing business area or product range. In our experience there are 10 deadly sins of non-performing boards:

 (i) The board is wrongly structured: it could be too big, in which case it is just a talking shop, or there could be a wrong balance between directors with executive responsibilities and the others; there could be too many executive directors, or they could all be business area managers with their own turf to protect, and so on.

 (ii) Information, particularly financial information, is inadequate *and nothing is done about this.*

 (iii) Major decisions, such as 'bet your company' acquisitions or disposals, are taken without challenge or with inadequate debate, or by cabals of the board . . .

 (iv) . . . and then there are no post mortems to see if the decisions were correct or not.

 (v) The board does not push management hard on succession, investment (including training), R & D, product or market development.

 (vi) The company's financing arrangements are not kept under review: the wrong banks, too many banks, the wrong means of finance, the wrong structure of indebtedness, the wrong risk profile.

 (vii) It is a 'yes-man' board that will not take hard and unpleasant (but necessary) decisions . . .

 (viii) . . . and that is, in fact, under the domination of an all-powerful person or influence.

 (ix) The board meetings are social occasions, over a good lunch, with inadequate time for discussion, and a rubber-stamping of decisions.

(x) There is no evidence of any rigorous review, such as the non-existence of audit or emoluments committees, or, if these exist, they are not taken seriously.

What we are suggesting is that companies carry out – or cause to be carried out – a regular annual boardroom audit, to ensure that their board is effective and is adding value to the company. Much as they may hate it, the directors should not be spared from the requirement to justify themselves and their performance.

This chapter sets out the basis for such an audit, and is particularly relevant to the medium-sized and smaller company, whose board perhaps grew up like Topsy, and which now therefore needs to look especially hard at how it is governed. We would also emphasise that we are looking at the board as a whole, and are making no distinction between different types of director, be they executive, independent, non-executive or part time. They are all part of the governance audit.

We are, of course, looking at the situation as it is, not as we would like it to be. We have to accept the unitary board structure in today's public company, the current state of the law, the fact that in some companies the chairman and CEO are one and the same person. The focus is on practical ways of improvement. In any case many of these companies will not be public companies and would therefore be excluded, under our definition, from the eventual requirement to set up formal supervisory councils. They would, however, we are sure, want to include the supervisory concept in their governance.

THE CHAIRMAN

The chairman is the key, and though technically a chairman is only the chairman of the board, we are taking the role in the popular sense of the understanding to mean the chairman of the company.

There is no template, as it were, for the ideal chairman for all circumstances: the focus of the job depends on the times and the company's state of development. One thing is certain, however: chairmen must have a view of where they want to go, both for the company and for the role of the board within it.

In the long term our view is clear: the supervisory structure will automatically separate the job of the chairman from that of the CEO in public companies. Until the law is changed, however, some companies may well continue to combine the two for perfectly valid reasons. However, we would normally expect the two roles to be separated, and, what is most important of all, to be clearly defined. It is the chairman's job to ensure that the board (or boards) work effectively and add value to the company. It is his or her job to ensure that there is the right balance between executive directors and those without portfolio, that the latter fit into the board, and add to it, and that there is a proper induction programme to ensure that they understand the company, its products, people and culture, and are put in a position to add value. Where the directors do not contribute, they should not be directors, and ought not to be on the board. That evaluation is also part of the chairman's job.

The conduct of the meetings, too, is a critical factor. A passive chairman is ineffective. Board meetings take up valuable time and need to be used properly in order to be meaningful. It is up to the chairman to ensure that there is a correct balance (for the company in question) between diplomacy, to smooth things over, and creative tension, to get the best out of people under some stress. We put great emphasis on the need for everyone in every sphere of the company's operations and activities to make a contribution. No company can afford passengers, least of all if they are on the board of directors.

The chairman's role is therefore one of leadership and vision: chairmen have to have a vision for the company and how it should be governed. That being so there is no room for a 'non-executive' chairman: it may be a part-time role, but the responsibility is full-time and cannot be abdicated. Chairmen are on call every day of the year, 24 hours a day.

We have emphasised the chairman's role because this is an essential *sine qua non* for any boardroom audit. If a company has the wrong chairman or an inadequate one, then there is no point in seeing if the board adds value or is doing its job properly. If it did its job properly it would have thrown him or her out long ago!

THE BOARDROOM AUDIT

Why have a boardroom audit?

There are many good boards of directors, it is true, but there are also all too many bad ones, as the events of the last few years have shown, and there are even more mediocre ones. Both the bad and the mediocre are a detriment to the national economy at a time of increasing international competition. A country needs the highest standards of boardroom management. Standards are still recognised as being too low in too many public companies. A proper structure of governance is one classic way of improving standards, and the topic is very much under the spotlight today. It will not go away: it is being debated, commented on, written about and legislated for. Companies cannot but take notice, and the danger is that if they do not, they will be forced into it by regulation and law. There is widespread public concern about the standard of governance. Medium-sized and smaller companies cannot escape by reason of their size. While they cannot afford the investment in governance that the majors have made, they too will have to give some careful consideration to the topic. They will be under scrutiny and the quality and operation of their boards will be under review. There has been a tendency by some companies to regard governance as a matter of window-dressing, to please the outside world. Nothing could be further from real life, and we believe companies will make a great mistake if they do not take the subject seriously. The days of a bland board meeting over a gourmet lunch are rapidly disappearing for most public companies, just as the days of the business lunch itself have vanished in such companies.

We are not merely referring to social pressures, which are also becoming more insistent: legal obligations, too, are making it increasingly important for directors to be aware of the law and their position with regard to it. The penalties are getting more serious. Directors will need to be better trained for the job, and they will increasingly be expected to possess the requisite boardroom skills. The standards of the average will have to be raised.

So what is to be done? We in Britain tend to be somewhat impatient with organisation and structures, relying on the tradition of the brilliant amateur. But boards and their directors have to be professionals in this competitive world: they have to be properly selected, positioned and organised, in a well-thought-out framework, and they have to be trained and informed. In other words, companies must give the same careful thought to their boardroom structure as they give to any other organisational structure. To help them we set out an approach in this chapter in the form of a boardroom audit so that they can measure themselves against the best practice we have been discussing throughout this book. We would hope that the majors would have much of the structure in position: our message is to the smaller companies who are looking for excellence in governance.

The boardroom review

A boardroom review and its subsequent implementation cannot succeed unless it is carried out at the very highest level by the most experienced practitioners. This is too political a subject to be undertaken internally, from within the firm. It has to be carried out by outsiders working for the

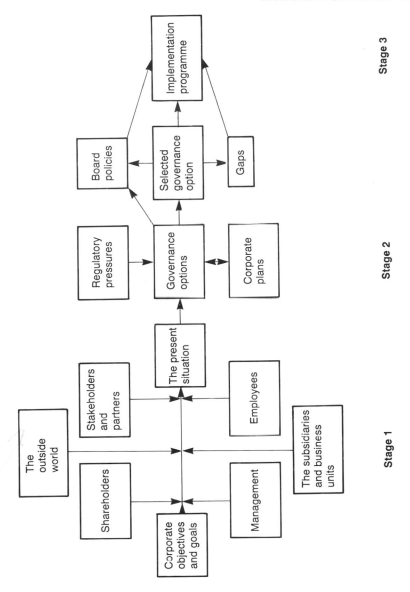

Figure 10.1 The boardroom review programme

chairman. Figure 10.1 sets out an overview of the boardroom review. The
boardroom review has the following goals:

(i) To measure the company's structure of governance against its business
objectives and to ensure that it has the right structure for its current

situation and circumstances; we emphasise that there is no one right structure: it depends on the time and the situation.

(ii) To ensure that the board(s) has (have) the right balance.

(iii) To ensure that the structure of governance conforms not only with the legal and regulatory requirements, but is also in accord with best practice.

(iv) To plan boardroom development in accordance with the foreseen development of laws and regulations.

(v) Above all to make sure that the whole structure of governance, present and planned, is in the best interests of the company and its stakeholders.

There are three important points to be made at the outset:

(i) It is no accident that the framework is similar to that of a classical strategic review: this is a strategic review, and its objective is to improve the company's performance.

(ii) The review covers the whole board with no distinction between directors with executive posts in the company and those with none.

(iii) There is no purpose in having a review unless the outcome is some action. A review by itself achieves nothing, and is only a means to an end.

There are three stages to such a boardroom review, or audit as it is sometimes called, the company position, the options and the implementation plan, which are all discussed below.

The company position

As in any strategic plan the first stage has to be an objective look at the company's position.

The starting point will be the company's objectives and goals, and in a sense the whole review is carried out in the shadow of these. There is no point in looking at the boardroom structure and governance if the company is drifting rudderless, without direction and without goals: the leadership and goals issue will have to be rectified before anything else can be done. The corporate objectives have certain specific implications for governance, as is shown in Figure 10.2.

The review would follow a logical progression: the mission and objectives would be the starting point, and these would lead to a consideration of the corporate culture, the fitness of the organisation structure, the staff profile (what training and skills?), the financing requirement and so on. The consideration of all these factors would begin to give pointers as to the outside

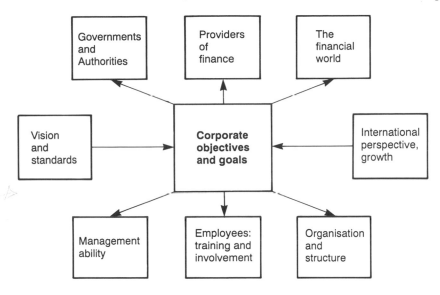

Figure 10.2 Corporate objectives and governance

expertise and advice required. These would then be projected forward in the light of the corporate plans: what structures and skills are required in future, what boardroom balance, what financing requirements, what geographical and operational coverage, and so on?

The analysis of requirements as brought out by the objectives and plans will result in a template, as it were, to measure the company's current boardroom structure against. It is helpful at this point, when considering the directorate, to think in terms of the three components: the executives, that is those with portfolios; the advisers, that is those who are there to fill knowledge or relationship gaps; and the stakeholders, that is those with a commercial interest in the success of the business. As in any strategic study, the current position is evaluated in terms of the inside and the outside world.

The first part is the internal review, details of which are shown in Figure 10.3. The internal review looks at the current board, its structure, its range of skills and contacts, its succession, and its impact on the company. Does it impact on the company's R & D (as a German supervisory council would)? What is the relationship with the management team? Does the board appear to have a grip on audit and controls (is there an audit committee and what does it do)? The review would look at the different committees and their actions; it would examine the workings of the board with regard to its impact on employees, and would map out the way the top board related to the different subsidiary boards. The focus on employees is particularly

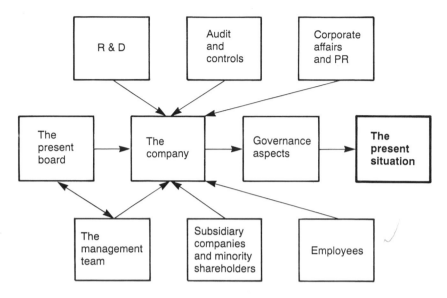

Figure 10.3   The internal review

significant in view of the likely trends of developments in EC Directives. Britain might have been a lone dissenting voice at the EC's Maastricht meeting at the end of 1991, but in the long run Britain, we are sure, has no other option but to be carried along by the tide of EC developments. Employee influence and employee participation in companies will grow.

Everything would need to be looked at, from the way the different relationships and spheres of influence were delineated (an important point) to the actual form of board meetings: what is discussed, is there enough time, is the documentation sufficient?

Such a review looks at very sensitive and delicate areas, some of which are often regarded as no-go areas by companies. We make no apologies for this: companies that are frightened to take a hard look at how they are run at the very top level do not deserve to succeed.

The outside view is just as important, and, in our experience, just as rarely looked at. We have illustrated this in Figure 10.4. Even if a company were not carrying out a boardroom review, the information gathered together in the outside review is important by itself because of the impact the different pressure points can have on the company.

Merely to review the stakeholders is an important exercise in its own right. Who are they, what is their interest, how does this interest manifest itself, how can it be harnessed to help the company? The definition of stakeholders should be as wide as possible, going so far as to include the company's

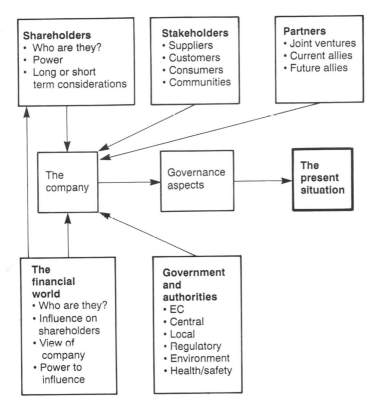

Figure 10.4 The outside review

pensioners. The financial world needs to be reviewed as well: some companies can afford to take a cavalier attitude to the financial world; most realise its influence on them and their progress. The financial world's impact makes itself felt in the areas of reporting and financial transparency, which leads back to audit and emoluments committees.

Partners and alliances also need to be reviewed and in the world of business networks a partnership review is an essential part of any strategic study. Many companies keep constantly updated files on partners and potential partners. The whole relationship with governments, the authorities and, increasingly, the EC, is a vital area the company has to understand, plan and organise itself for. There is an increasing trend to employ former EC senior bureaucrats as well as to try to entice former EC Commissioners on to the board.

The regulatory question has been a constant topic of comment by us.

Here, too, the pressures are growing and companies need to be aware of the need to forearm themselves against such pressures, whether locally or from the EC Commission. One chairman told us that his rule of thumb was to take cognizance of the Directives passed by the Commission, and then to factor them for each country in line with that country's historical rate of speed in implementing EC Directives.

The result of the internal and outside reviews will be a statement of the company's position on governance in the light of its objectives. This sets out the classical strengths, weaknesses, opportunities and threats (SWOT) matrix in the form of options, priorities and time scales for action. The focus is governance for competitive edge.

The options and action (stages 2 and 3)

Options are easier to deal with in the classical strategy review than in a boardroom audit. In the former case it is up to the top management to decide what to do in the light of its resources. In a governance review the options stage may face the chairman and chief executive with some unpalatable choices, particularly if it emerges that they have the wrong structure or an inadequate board. This cannot be fudged, however: whether the issue is a business one or a regulatory one, action has to be taken, and it is up to the chairman and the CEO to take it.

The action programme should be seen as one of the key aspects of corporate strategy and of the strategic plan. The responsibility is the chairman's, and will cover a range of topics:

(i)   The biggest gap is often that of the succession to the chairman himself/herself, and in companies as far apart as the French BSN and the British Lonhro, it is the area that the shareholders are often most concerned about. There are other aspects too: the present board may be excellent, but what about board renewal? Are new people being brought up to replace the present board in time? This is a question that concerns even the most major companies such as ICI, who have the potential board appointees available but would like to give them experience on plc boards to train them. The question is, how?

(ii) Recruitment and training have to be looked at. Directors of a public company need to be not just professional accountants, engineers or personnel managers, but also professional directors. Increasingly they will need specific training to enable them to fill the role of directors.

(iii) Boardroom committees must be considered. But this is not just a question of forming a committee and hoping for the best. Committees need terms of reference, and those committees in the spotlight such as the audit committees most particularly, must have their relationships with internal and external auditors and compliance officers clearly established. It goes without saying that there have to be demonstrably good financial controls to back up such a committee.

An action programme must be well thought through, and needs to deal with policies and roles, job descriptions and back-up, remuneration and ways in which the directorate will add value. If it is the job of the chairman to have a vision, the board structure will be the means for fulfilling that vision. We set out the key elements of an implementation programme in Figure 10.5.

Training

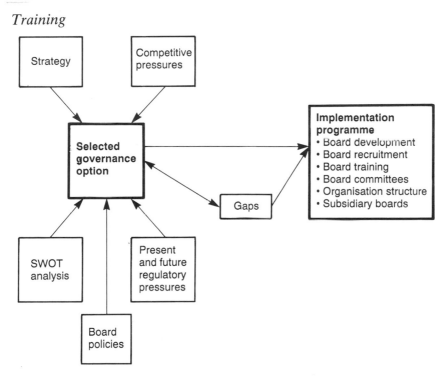

Figure 10.5   Stage 3 – implementation programme

Training for directors is a very fashionable topic nowadays, and there are already a large number of specialised courses available. It is not our role to comment on these in this book. We shall limit ourselves to a general discussion of directors' training needs. There are three elements to such training for directors.

The first is formal instruction in the technical aspects of the job of being a director. Directors need to understand what the job entails, what their legal position is, what their liability is and under which laws. In the UK this means they must understand the provisions of the relevant Companies Acts (which change and are amended with the passage of time) and the key points of case law, what they need to do with regard to the accounts, their responsibility for the directors' report in the annual accounts, the insider trading provisions, when they can trade in the company's shares, and so on. They need to know about the Insolvency Act 1986 and the Company Directors Disqualification Act 1986. They should be advised as to what indemnity insurance they need to take out.

Directors need also to be aware of the way directors' meetings should be conducted and what is expected of them at such meetings, the role of the memorandum and articles of association, and the information they have to give to the authorities and which authorities.

The above is general information which can be obtained from general courses. The second aspect of their training is specific to the company in question and it is up to companies to ensure that they give it and to the directors that they ask for and receive it. This information is basically a potted course in the company the director is joining and would cover:

  (i) Their job description (i.e. what is required of them and how they will be judged), which is absolutely essential, but alas not very common, in the case of outside directors.

 (ii) Information on the company background, the organisation, products, results, strategies, policies, culture, people. There is no quick way of doing this and it cannot be done by means of documentation alone. The directors in question, especially if they are outside directors, have to be exposed to the company, go round it and meet people (and not only the most senior people). There is thus a considerable amount of work to be done when a director is appointed, especially if appointed from outside.

(iii) Many companies use their regular board meetings as the occasion for a function or business unit to make a presentation so that the outside directors in particular can extend their knowledge of the company. Grand Metropolitan and BP are typical of organisations that also hold their board meetings in different locations – not all of them in the UK – for the same reason.

The third aspect of training is the personal responsibility of the director in question. Inside directors will be presumed to know and to understand their company in depth, but outsiders come in without such knowledge. They will need to establish very clearly what is expected of them, who they will report to and how their performance will be judged, as well, of course, as the basis of their remuneration.

Outside directors will have to carry out their own due diligence, as it were, and many of their checks will mirror the checks the company should be making about them! Their investigation of the company should cover its accounts, its standing in the community, how it is regarded in financial circles, the analysts' views, media comments, the shareholding. There are any number of databases available to make that investigation an easy one.

There are also technicalities to take account of, such as ensuring that the new director has provided a written consent to act as a director, which is now required under UK law, and to enquire whether any 'directors and officers' insurance has to be amended in the light of the new appointment.

On appointment, the director ought to review corporate plans and strategic statements, the regular management accounts, at least for the past year, and the comparison against the budget, and the auditors' management letter, as well as the board minutes. Most of all the newly appointed director needs to have a long discussion with the chairman to get a feel for the boardroom culture and requirements.

WHAT IS SO IMPORTANT ABOUT GOVERNANCE

Governance is now a matter of major concern in the UK. It has practically been politicised, and therefore it is not a topic that will easily go away. The institutions are reluctantly becoming involved as they realise the pressures on them to do so. They are locked in.

If we were to make a prediction about the future we would say that the UK is moving more to the continental position on governance, while continental countries and their companies are inching to a position nearer to that of UK companies on financial reporting. A convergence is therefore emerging in Europe. Companies need to understand the way the Community is moving and adapt themselves accordingly, and, indeed, stay ahead of the game. That is why we have set out this programme of action and why we consider it so important. We have not addressed management issues specifically, but it must be self-evident that the company that has put its boardroom structure and issues in order has a better chance of competitive success than the company that has not done so.

Companies and their owners need to ask themselves what sort of board they must have. Have they the board of directors and the structure that they deserve and must have to succeed? That is what corporate governance is all about. In the final analysis we are not talking about something abstract in this book, such as corporate governance for its own sake. We are talking about the profitable management of companies. Companies need to consider whether they have the right board structure to achieve that.

THE 10 KEY ISSUES

When looking at successful boards, there are 10 key issues in our experience:

    (i) The key role of the chairman and of the chief executive.

   (ii) A proper distinction between their roles, and if the two roles are combined in one person, the rationale for such an action.

  (iii) The need for checks and balances in any board structure.

  (iv) The importance of outsiders in the sense of directors who do not have an executive role in the company; theirs is a leadership rather than purely control role.

   (v) The need to harness wisdom and experience to direction.

  (vi) The importance of succession and board renewal: balancing experience with a fresh approach.

 (vii) Quality is vital: you cannot regulate for that. . . .

(viii) . . . but at the same time there has to be an acceptable and definable structure. Without a good structure there will be chaos.

  (ix) The committee structure needs to be carefully defined. In particular that of the audit committee has to be looked at to ensure that control does not degenerate into second-guessing and policing, and that the work of the committee does not duplicate that of the auditors or the internal accounting departments.

   (x) There has to be open and honest disclosure.

The successful board is the one that has achieved the right balance of direction whilst at the same time liberating entrepreneurial drive and stimulating it.

BIBLIOGRAPHY

Anderson, Charles A. and Robert N. Anthony, *The New Corporate Directors*, Wiley, 1986

Barnett, C., *The Audit of War*, Macmillan, 1986.

Burroughs, Bryan and John Helyar, *Barbarians at the Gate*, Jonathan Cape, 1990.

CEPR discussion paper no. 603, Centre for Economic Policy Research, 1991.

Cochran, Philip L. and Steven L. Wartick, *Corporate Governance: A review of the literature*, Morristown, NJ, Financial Executives Research Foundation, *c.* 1988.

'Corporate governance; the role of boards of directors in take-over bids and defenses; a round table discussion with John Wilcox and others, moderated by Harry de Angelo', *Continental Bank Journal of Applied Corporate Finance*, vol. 2, summer 1989, pp. 7–35.

Coulson-Thomas, Colin, 'Developing directors', *European Management Journal*, vol. 8, no. 4, December 1990.

Crystal, Graef S., *In Search of Excess*, Norton, 1991.

Demb, Ada and F-Friedrich Neubauer, 'Subsidiary company boards reconsidered', *European Management Journal*, vol. 8, no. 4, December 1990.

Ghoshal, Sumantra and Haspeslagh, Philippe, 'Electrolux acquires Zanussi – a case study', *European Management Journal*, vol. 8, no. 4, December 1990.

Goldenberg, S., *International Joint Ventures in Action*, Hutchinson, 1988.

Handy, C., *The Age of Unreason*, Hutchinson, 1990.

Institute of Chartered Accountants of Scotland, *Corporate Governance: Directors' responsibilities for financial statements*, 1992.

Kendall, Nigel and Thomas Sheridan, *Finanzmeister*, Pitman, 1991.

Midgley, Kenneth (ed.), *Management Accountability and Corporate Governance*, Macmillian, 1982.

Mitchell de Quillacq, Leslie, *Powerbrokers: An insider's guide to the French financial élite*, Lafferty Publications, 1992.

Monks, Robert and Nell Minow, *Power and Accountability*, Harper Business, 1991.

Peters, T., *Thriving on Chaos*, Macmillan, 1987.

Porter, M. E., *Competition in Global Industries*, HBS, 1986.

Sheard, 'The main bank systems and corporate monitoring and control in Japan', *Journal of Economic Behaviour and Organisation*, vol. 11, 1989, pp. 399–422.

Van Dijk, Jules J.J., 'Transnational management in an evolving European context', *European Management Journal*, vol. 8, no. 4, December 1990.

INDEX